Contents

Executive Summary 3

Task Force Recommendations 9

Chapter One: Ending the Epidemic of Children Exposed to Violence 25

Chapter Two: Identifying Children Exposed to Violence 63

Chapter Three: Treatment and Healing of Exposure to Violence 79

Chapter Four: Creating Safe and Nurturing Homes 105

Chapter Five: Communities Rising Up Out of Violence 139

Chapter Six: Rethinking Our Juvenile Justice System 169

Conclusion 203

Glossary of Key Terms 207

Activities of the Task Force and List of Witnesses 213

Individuals and Organizations That Submitted Written Testimony 223

Task Force Member Biographies 231

EXECUTIVE SUMMARY

The Attorney General's National Task Force on Children Exposed to Violence

Exposure to violence is a national crisis that affects *approximately two out of every three of our children.* Of the 76 million children currently residing in the United States, an estimated 46 million can expect to have their lives touched by violence, crime, abuse, and psychological trauma this year. In 1979, U.S. Surgeon General Julius B. Richmond declared violence a public health crisis of the highest priority, and yet 33 years later that crisis remains. Whether the violence occurs in children's homes, neighborhoods, schools, playgrounds or playing fields, locker rooms, places of worship, shelters, streets, or in juvenile detention centers, the exposure of children to violence is a uniquely traumatic experience that has the potential to profoundly derail the child's security, health, happiness, and ability to grow and learn — with effects lasting well into adulthood.

Exposure to violence in any form harms children, and different forms of violence have different negative impacts.

Sexual abuse places children at high risk for serious and chronic health problems, including posttraumatic stress disorder (PTSD), depression, suicidality, eating disorders, sleep disorders, substance abuse, and deviant sexual behavior. Sexually abused children often become hypervigilant about the possibility of future sexual violation, experience feelings of betrayal by the adults who failed to care for and protect them.

Physical abuse puts children at high risk for lifelong problems with medical illness, PTSD, suicidality, eating disorders, substance abuse, and deviant sexual behavior. Physically abused children are at heightened risk for cognitive and developmental impairments, which can lead to violent behavior as a form of self-protection and control. These children often feel powerless when faced with physical intimidation, threats, or conflict and may compensate by becoming isolated (through truancy or hiding) or aggressive (by bullying or joining gangs for protection). Physically abused children are at risk for significant impairment in memory processing and problem solving and for developing defensive behaviors that lead to consistent avoidance of intimacy.

Intimate partner violence within families puts children at high risk for severe and potentially lifelong problems with physical health, mental health, and school and peer relationships as well as for disruptive behavior. Witnessing or living with domestic or intimate partner violence often burdens children with a sense of loss or profound guilt and shame because of their mistaken assumption that they should have intervened or prevented the violence or, tragically, that they caused the violence. They frequently castigate themselves for having failed in what they assume to be their duty to protect a parent or sibling(s) from being harmed, for not having taken the place of their horribly injured or killed family member, or for having caused the offender to be violent. Children exposed to intimate partner violence often experience a sense of terror and dread that they will lose an essential caregiver through permanent injury or death. They also fear losing their relationship with the offending parent, who may be removed from the home, incarcerated, or even executed. Children will mistakenly blame themselves for having caused the batterer to be violent. If no one identifies these children and helps them heal and recover, they may bring this uncertainty, fear, grief, anger, shame, and sense of betrayal into all of their important relationships for the rest of their lives.

Community violence in neighborhoods can result in children witnessing assaults and even killings of family members, peers, trusted adults, innocent bystanders, and perpetrators of violence. Violence in the community can prevent children from feeling safe in their own schools and neighborhoods. Violence and ensuing psychological trauma can lead children to adopt an attitude of hypervigilance, to become experts at detecting threat or perceived threat — never able to let down their guard in order to be ready for the next outbreak of violence. They may come to believe that violence is "normal," that violence is "here to stay," and that relationships are too fragile to trust because one never knows when violence will take the life of a friend or loved one. They may turn to gangs or criminal activities to prevent others from viewing them as weak and to counteract feelings of despair and powerlessness, perpetuating the cycle of violence and increasing their risk of incarceration. They are also at risk for becoming victims of intimate partner violence in adolescence and in adulthood.

The picture becomes even more complex when children are "polyvictims" (exposed to multiple types of violence). As many as 1 in 10 children in this country are polyvictims, according to the Department of Justice and Centers for Disease Control and Prevention's groundbreaking National Survey of Children's Exposure to Violence (NatSCEV). The toxic combination of exposure to intimate partner violence, physical abuse, sexual abuse, and/or exposure to community violence increases the risk and severity of posttraumatic injuries and mental health disorders by at least twofold and up to as much as tenfold. Polyvictimized children are at very high risk for losing the fundamental capacities necessary for normal development, successful learning, and a productive adulthood.

The financial costs of children's exposure to violence are astronomical. The financial burden on other public systems, including child welfare, social services, law enforcement, juvenile justice, and, in particular, education, is staggering when combined with the loss of productivity over children's lifetimes.

It is time to ensure that our nation's past inadequate response to children's exposure to violence does not negatively affect children's lives any further. We must not allow violence to deny any children their right to physical and mental health services or to the pathways necessary for maturation into successful students, productive workers, responsible family members, and parents and citizens.

We can stem this epidemic if we commit to a strong national response. The long-term negative outcomes of exposure to violence can be prevented, and children exposed to violence can be helped to recover. Children exposed to violence can heal if we identify them early and give them specialized services, evidence-based treatment, and proper care and support. We have the power to end the damage to children from violence and abuse in our country; it does not need to be inevitable.

We, as a country, have the creativity, knowledge, leadership, economic resources, and talent to effectively intervene on behalf of children exposed to violence. We can provide these children with the opportunity to recover and, with hard work, to claim their birthright … life, liberty, and the pursuit of happiness. We invest in the future of our nation when we commit ourselves as citizens, service providers, and community members to helping our children recover from exposure to violence and ending all forms of violence in their lives.

To prepare this report, U.S. Attorney General Eric Holder commissioned a task force of diverse leaders dedicated to protecting children from exposure to violence and to healing those who were exposed. The report calls for action by the federal government, states, tribes, communities, and the private sector across the country to marshal the best available knowledge and all of the resources needed to defend all of our children against exposure to violence. The Attorney General's task force asks all readers of this report to imagine a safe country for our children's creative, healthy development and to join together in developing a national plan to foster that reality.

The findings and recommendations of the task force are organized into six chapters. The first chapter provides an overview of the problem and sets forth 10 foundational recommendations. The next two chapters offer a series of recommendations to ensure that we reliably identify, screen, and assess all children exposed to violence and thereafter give them support, treatment, and other services designed to address their needs. In the fourth and fifth chapters, the task force focuses on prevention and emphasizes the importance of effectively integrating prevention, intervention, and resilience across systems by nurturing children through warm, supportive, loving, and nonviolent relationships in our homes and communities. In the sixth and final chapter of this report, the task force calls for a new approach to juvenile justice, one that acknowledges that the vast majority of the children involved in that system have been exposed to violence, necessitating the prioritization of services that promote their healing.

The challenge of children's exposure to violence and ensuing psychological trauma is not one that government alone can solve. The problem requires a truly national response that draws on the strengths of all Americans. Our children's futures are at stake. Every child we are able to help recover from the impact of violence is an investment in our nation's future. Therefore, this report calls for a collective investment nationwide in defending our children from exposure to violence and psychological trauma, in healing families and communities, and in enabling all of our children to imagine and claim their safe and creative development and their productive futures. The time for action is now. Together, we must take this next step and build a nation whose communities are dedicated to ending children's exposure to violence and psychological trauma. To that end, the task force offers the following recommendations.

TASK FORCE
RECOMMENDATIONS

TASK FORCE RECOMMENDATIONS

1. Ending the Epidemic of Children Exposed to Violence

1.1 Charge leaders at the highest levels of the executive and legislative branches of the federal government with the coordination and implementation of the recommendations in this report.

The executive branch should designate leadership at the highest levels of government to implement the recommendations in this report. Working with the executive branch, Congress should take legislative action on the recommendations in this report, making these recommendations a bipartisan priority.

1.2 Appoint a federal task force or commission to examine the needs of American Indian/Alaska Native children exposed to violence.

A federal task force or commission should be developed to examine the specific needs of American Indian/Alaska Native (AIAN) children exposed to violence and recommend actions to protect AIAN children from abuse and neglect and reduce violence. The management of this task force or commission, and the selection of its members, should be carried out through an equal collaboration between the Attorney General and the Secretary of the Interior.

1.3 Engage youth as leaders and peer experts in all initiatives defending children against violence and its harmful effects.

Local, state, and regional child-serving initiatives and agencies should be directed to involve youth as leaders, planners, problem solvers, and communicators and be given the support they need to do this. Engagement with youth is essential in order to develop effective solutions to the complex problems leading to and resulting from children's exposure to violence.

1.4 Ensure universal public awareness of the crisis of children exposed to violence and change social norms to protect children from violence and its harmful effects.

Precedents exist for solving epidemic and seemingly intractable problems. Federal, state, and regional initiatives should be designed, developed, and implemented to launch a national public awareness campaign to create fundamental changes in perspective in every organization, community, and household in our country.

1.5 Incorporate evidence-based trauma-informed principles in all applicable federal agency grant requirements.

The federal government should lead the development of standards of care for identification, assessment, treatment, protection, and other crucial services for children exposed to violence and psychological trauma as well as the development of protocols for monitoring the quality of these services as measured against the national standards.

1.6 Launch a national initiative to promote professional education and training on the issue of children exposed to violence.

Standards and a curriculum must be developed to ensure that all students and professionals working with children and families are aware of the scope of the problem of children's exposure to violence as well as their responsibility to provide trauma-informed services and trauma-specific evidence-based treatment within the scope of their professional expertise.

1.7 Continue to support and sustain the national data collection infrastructure for the monitoring of trends in children exposed to violence.

Continued support for the National Survey of Children's Exposure to Violence (NatSCEV) is essential to ensure that the survey is conducted at frequent, regular intervals. The government must gather and examine additional data on a regular basis, in concert with the NatSCEV, to address related justice, education, health, and human services issues; to establish a clear picture of children's continuing exposure to violence; and to track and demonstrate the progress our country makes in ending this epidemic.

1.8 Create national centers of excellence on children's exposure to violence.

To ensure the success of this report's recommendations, national centers of excellence should be established and fully funded to support the implementation of a sustained public awareness campaign, reforms to maximize efficiencies in funding, standards for professional education and practices, and ongoing monitoring of trends and the translation of data; and to bring together the scientific, clinical, technical, and policy expertise necessary to systematically ensure the success of each of the foregoing goals.

1.9 Develop and implement public policy initiatives in state, tribal, and local governments to reduce and address the impact of childhood exposure to violence.

Every community's governing institutions and leaders should be provided with guidance from national centers of excellence to enable them to create local public policy initiatives, regulations, and services that ensure that children are protected against the harmful effects of exposure to violence and psychological trauma to the fullest extent possible.

1.10 Finance change by adjusting existing allocations and leveraging new funding.

The federal government should provide financial incentives to states and communities to redirect funds to approaches with an established record of success in defending children against exposure to violence and enabling victimized children to heal and recover.

2. Identifying Children Exposed to Violence

Every year, millions of children in this country are exposed to violence, and yet very few of these children ever receive help in recovering from the psychological damage caused by this experience. The first crucial step in protecting our children is to *identify and provide timely and effective help to those who already are being victimized by violence.* The recommendations below are offered to address identification, assessment, and screening:

2.1 Galvanize the public to identify and respond to children exposed to violence.

Sustained public information and advocacy initiatives should be implemented in every community in order to create an informed citizenry that can advocate for higher levels of services and support from policymakers for both prevention and early intervention for children exposed to violence. These initiatives are crucial to challenge the misplaced pessimism that makes violence seem like an inevitable part of life.

2.2 Ensure that all children exposed to violence are identified, screened, and assessed.

Every professional and paraprofessional who comes into contact with pregnant women and children must routinely identify children exposed to (or at risk for) violence, provide them with trauma-informed care or services, and assist them and their families in accessing evidence-based trauma-specific treatment.

2.3 Include curricula in all university undergraduate and graduate programs to ensure that every child- and family-serving professional receives training in multiple evidence-based methods for identifying and screening children for exposure to violence.

It is imperative to equip all professionals who serve children and families with the knowledge and skills they need to recognize and address the impact of violence and psychological trauma on children.

2.4 Develop and disseminate standards in professional societies and associations for conducting comprehensive specialized assessments of children exposed to violence.

Professional societies and associations of educators, law enforcement personnel, public health workers, providers of faith-based services, athletic coaches, physicians, psychologists, psychiatrists, social workers, counselors, and marriage and family therapists — and those representing specialists in child abuse and domestic violence prevention and treatment — should develop, update, and disseminate standards for training and practice in the specialized assessment of children exposed to violence.

3. Treatment and Healing of Exposure to Violence

The majority of children in our country who are identified as having been exposed to violence never receive services or treatment that effectively help them to stabilize themselves, regain their normal developmental trajectory, restore their safety, and heal their social and emotional wounds. But help isn't optional or a luxury when a child's life is at stake; it's a necessity. Even after the violence has ended, these child survivors suffer from severe problems with anxiety, depression, anger, grief, and posttraumatic stress that can mar their relationships and family life and limit their success in school or work, not only in childhood but throughout their adult lives. Without services or treatment, even children who appear resilient and seem to recover from exposure to violence still bear emotional scars that may lead them to experience these same health and psychological problems years or decades later.

3.1 Provide all children exposed to violence access to trauma-informed services and evidence-based trauma-specific treatment.

Service and treatment providers who help children and their families exposed to violence and psychological trauma *must* provide trauma-informed care, trauma-specific treatment, or trauma-focused services.

3.2 Adapt evidence-based treatments for children exposed to violence and psychological trauma to the cultural beliefs and practices of the recipients and their communities.

Federal, regional, and state funding should be dedicated to the development, testing, and distribution of evidence-based, trauma-specific treatments that have been carefully adapted to recipients' cultural beliefs and practices in order to reach the millions of children currently in need in diverse communities throughout the country.

3.3 Develop and provide trauma-informed care in all hospital-based trauma centers and emergency departments for all children exposed to violence.

Hospital-based counseling and prevention programs should be established in all hospital emergency departments — especially those that provide services to victims of violence — including victims of gang violence. Professionals and other staff in emergency medical services should be trained to identify and engage children who have been exposed to violence or to prolonged, extreme psychological trauma.

3.4 Share information and implement coordinated and adaptive approaches to improve the quality of trauma-specific treatments and trauma-focused services and their delivery by organizations and professionals across settings and disciplines to children exposed to violence.

To be effective, trauma-specific treatments and trauma-focused services must be provided in a consistent manner across the many systems, programs, and professions dedicated to helping children exposed to violence.

3.5 Provide trauma-specific treatments in all agencies and organizations serving children and families exposed to violence and psychological trauma that are suitable to their clinicians' and staff members' professional and paraprofessional roles and responsibilities.

Agencies and organizations serving children and families should have access to training on and assistance in sustained, effective implementation of widely available trauma-specific treatments that have been shown scientifically to be effective with young children, school-age children, and adolescents.

3.6 Ensure that every professional and advocate serving children exposed to violence and psychological trauma learns and provides trauma-informed care and trauma-focused services.

Treatment providers should be made available in every setting in which children spend their days — schools, youth centers, even the family's home — as well as where children receive care — clinics, hospitals, counseling centers, the offices of child protective services, homeless shelters, domestic violence programs — and where they encounter the legal system — on the street with police officers, in the courts, in probation and detention centers — to help children recover from violence and psychological trauma by providing trauma-informed care and trauma-focused services.

3.7 Grow and sustain an adequate workforce of trauma-informed service providers, with particular attention paid to the recruitment, training, and retention of culturally diverse providers.

Trauma-informed care and trauma-focused services should be taught as a required part of the curriculum for all graduate and undergraduate students enrolled in professional education programs in colleges, universities, and medical and law schools where these students are preparing for careers in the healthcare, human services, public health, child welfare, or juvenile justice fields. The same recommendation applies to technical and vocational schools in which the students are preparing to work in similar fields.

3.8 Ensure that professional societies develop, adopt, disseminate, and implement principles, practices, and standards for comprehensive evidence-based treatment of children exposed to violence or psychological trauma.

Every professional society in the United States that represents children and families should develop and formally adopt principles, practices, guidelines, and standards for evidence-based trauma-informed care, trauma-specific treatments, and trauma-focused services for violence-exposed children and their families.

3.9 Provide research funding to continue the clinical and scientific development of increasingly effective evidence-based treatments for children exposed to violence.

Research and funding infrastructures that encourage the creation and testing of innovative practices and programs that allow for the evolution of increasingly effective evidence-based treatments for children exposed to violence must be expanded or newly developed.

3.10 Provide individuals who conduct services and treatment for children exposed to violence with workforce protection to prepare them for the personal impact of this work and to assist them in maintaining a safe and healthy workplace.

All providers should receive training and resources in their workplace that enable them to maintain their own emotional and physical health and professional and personal support systems.

3.11 Incentivize healthcare providers and insurance providers to reimburse trauma-focused services and trauma-specific treatment.

Even evidence-based treatments will fail if they are poorly implemented. Treatment providers must be incentivized in their practices to routinely monitor and report on the quality, reach, and outcomes of the evidence-based or evidence-informed services they provide using established methods for doing so.

4. Creating Safe and Nurturing Homes

Each year, millions of children in this country are exposed to violence and abuse in their homes or, less often, outside the home. Violence in the home can take many forms, including, but not limited to, physical and sexual abuse of children; intimate partner violence; and violence among family members, including siblings, grandparents, or extended family. In some cases, family members may even lose their lives because of criminal violence.

Recognizing that the best place for children and adolescents to not only survive but also to thrive is in families that keep them safe and nurture their development, the task force offers 11 recommendations that are described below.

4.1   Expand access to home visiting services for families with children who are exposed to violence, focusing on safety and referral to services.

Home visitation programs should be expanded to address the dynamics of child abuse and domestic violence; to provide evidence-based safety planning for parents, including pregnant mothers who are victims of domestic violence and sexual assault; and to strengthen the connections between children and their non-offending and protective parent(s), recognizing that every violence-exposed child's well-being is inextricably linked to the safety of that child's home and the well-being of her/his parents and caregivers.

4.2 Increase collaborative responses by police, mental health providers, domestic violence advocates, child protective service workers, and court personnel for women and children who are victimized by intimate partner violence.

We need to enhance coordination between law enforcement and service providers to identify children who are traumatized by domestic violence in order to assess immediate and subsequent threats and to follow up with visits to evaluate safety and other concerns of victims.

Coordinated responses must be developed to address safety issues, basic needs, trauma-focused assessment, and identification of children needing treatment, to support children's recovery from the impact of exposure to intimate partner violence.

Models for integrated planning and intervention following initial police responses to domestic disturbances to law enforcement, mental health, child protective services, and domestic violence services agencies and courts should be disseminated nationwide.

4.3 Ensure that parents who are victims of domestic violence have access to services and counseling that help them protect and care for their children.

Parents who have experienced intimate partner violence should be provided with trauma-informed services and treatment themselves in order to assist them in providing their children with emotional security and support for healthy development.

4.4 When domestic violence and child sexual or physical abuse co-occur, ensure that the dependency and family courts, the child protection system, and domestic violence programs work together to create protocols and policies that protect children and adult victims.

When domestic violence and child abuse co-occur in a family, all victims need protection. Adult caregivers who are victimized, and their children involved in custody and dependency cases, should be provided with coordinated trauma-informed services and trauma-specific treatment appropriate to their circumstances and developmental stage. Every reasonable effort should be made to keep the violence-exposed child and non-offending parent(s) or other family caregiver(s) together.

4.5 Create multidisciplinary councils or coalitions to assure systemwide collaboration and coordinated community responses to children exposed to family violence.

Every city, county, or tribe should be directed and supported to establish and sustain a multidisciplinary network or council that includes every provider and agency that touches the lives of children exposed to violence, including key decision makers who affect policy, programs, and case management.

Coordinated multidisciplinary teams that screen, assess, and respond to victims of family violence involved in the child protection and juvenile justice systems, and standards and procedures to prevent families and children who are exposed to violence in the home from becoming unnecessarily involved in those systems, are needed in every community.

4.6   Provide families affected by sexual abuse, physical abuse, and domestic violence with education and services to prevent further abuse, to respond to the adverse effects on the family, and to enable the children to recover.

Programs should be supported and developed to engage parents to help protect and support children, ideally working to stop child sexual or physical abuse before it occurs — and also enabling parents to assist their children in recovery if sexual or physical abuse does occur. Prevention programs that equip parents and other family members with the skills needed to establish healthy, supportive, proactive relationships with children should be available to all families in every community.

4.7   Ensure that parenting programs in child- and family-serving agencies, including fatherhood programs and other programs specifically for men, integrate strategies for preventing domestic violence and sexual assault and include reparation strategies when violence has already occurred.

All agencies, programs, and providers working with fathers who have been violent toward their children, partners, or other family members must provide in-depth assessment, diagnosis, treatment planning, and educational services that are linked to the specific problems of each offender. Fathers who use violence also must be held accountable and monitored, as change does not always come easily or quickly.

4.8   Provide support and counseling to address the unique consequences for children exposed to lethal violence, both in the home as a result of domestic violence homicides and suicides, and in the community.

Evidence-based treatments that have been developed specifically to help children recover and heal from the traumatic grief of a violent death in their family should be available to all children who experience a loss due to violence, in every community in this country.

4.9 Develop interventions in all child- and family-serving agencies that build on the assets and values of each family's culture of origin and incorporate the linguistic and acculturation challenges of immigrant children and parents.

Evidence-based interventions should be created specifically for immigrant children and their families who have been exposed to violence, providing them with a network of services and supports that are grounded in the beliefs and values of their culture and language of origin rather than forcing them to renounce or relinquish those crucial ties and foundations.

4.10 Ensure compliance with the letter and spirit of the Indian Child Welfare Act (ICWA).

Thirty-five years after its passage, full implementation of the ICWA remains elusive. Because the ICWA is a federal statute, successful implementation will be best ensured through strong, coordinated support from the Department of the Interior, Bureau of Indian Affairs; Department of Health and Social Services, Administration for Children and Families; and the Department of Justice, Office of Juvenile Justice and Delinquency Prevention.

4.11 Initiate a nationally sponsored program similar to the Department of Defense's community and family support programs that provides military families with specialized services focused on building strengths and resilience, new parent support, youth programs, and forging partnerships with communities.

The unique challenges of military families are widely recognized, but military families are too frequently underserved. Family support programs developed in concert with the President's "Strengthening Our Military Families" initiative should be expanded to fully provide for the safety and well-being of the children of military families and veterans living in civilian communities.

5. Communities Rising Up Out of Violence

Every year, community violence affects tens of millions of children in this country. This violence can occur in episodic incidents such as shootings in schools or other public places that cause children and families to feel terror in their own neighborhoods and schools and leave them to recover from the traumatic grief of losing friends or peers who are killed or who never fully recover. In addition, countless children are victimized when violence becomes part of the fabric of American communities as a result of gangs, or when bullying or corporal punishment is tolerated or sanctioned in schools or youth activities.

To reduce the extent of this pandemic of children's exposure to community violence, on behalf of children not yet exposed to community violence, and to help children who have been victims recover and heal from the trauma and grief caused by violence in their neighborhoods and schools, the task force proposes the following recommendations:

5.1   Organize local coalitions in every community representing professionals from multiple disciplines and the full range of service systems (including law enforcement, the courts, health care, schools, family services, child protection, domestic violence programs, rape crisis centers, and child advocacy centers) as well as families and other community members, to assess local challenges and resources, develop strategies, and carry out coordinated responses to reduce violence and the number of children exposed to violence.

Nationwide, local coalitions should be formed to increase children's safety and well-being through public awareness, wraparound support services, and immediate access to services that are tailored to meet the individual needs of children and families exposed to violence in their schools, neighborhoods, or homes.

5.2   Recognize and support the critical role of law enforcement's participation in collaborative responses to violence.

Child-serving professionals from all disciplines and law enforcement professionals should partner to provide protection and help in recovery and healing for children exposed to violence.

5.3   Involve men and boys as critical partners in preventing violence.

Initiatives must be supported and expanded to involve men and boys in using nonviolence to build healthy communities and to develop a network of men and boys across the country who are committed to creating widespread change that will help break the cycle of violence in our homes, schools, and communities.

5.4   Foster, promote, and model healthy relationships for children and youth.

Community- and school-based programs should be developed and supported to prevent violence within adolescent relationships, to promote healthy relationships, and to change social norms that tolerate and condone abuse.

5.5 Develop and implement policies to improve the reporting of suspected child sexual abuse in every institution entrusted with the care and nurturing of children.

To break the silence and secrecy that shrouds child sexual abuse, every institution entrusted with the care and safety of children must improve its policies on mandatory reporting, implement them fully, educate its employees about them, and ensure full compliance.

5.6 Train and require child care providers to meet professional and legal standards for identifying young children exposed to violence and reducing their exposure to it.

Child care providers must be trained and provided with ongoing supervision and continuing education so as to be able to recognize children in their care who have been exposed to violence and to be able to help their families to access the services and treatment that these children need in order to recover.

5.7 Provide schools with the resources they need to create and sustain safe places where children exposed to violence can get help.

Every school in our country should have trauma-informed staff and consultants providing school-based trauma-specific treatment. In addition, these professionals should help children who have severe chronic problems to access evidence-based treatment at home or in clinics.

5.8 Provide children, parents, schools, and communities with the tools they need to identify and stop bullying and to help children who have been bullied — including the bullies themselves — to recover from social, emotional, and school problems.

Trauma-informed services and support should be provided to all children who are bullies or victims of bullying in order to stop the spread of emotional and physical violence in our schools and communities.

5.9 Put programs to identify and protect children exposed to community violence who struggle with suicidality in place in every community.

Every community in the nation should have immediate access to evidence-based, trauma-informed, trauma-specific, community-adaptive suicide prevention and treatment programs for children and youth at high risk because of their severe suicidality.

5.10 Support community programs that provide youth with mentoring as an intervention and as a prevention strategy, to reduce victimization by and involvement in violence and to promote healthy development by youths.

All children's mentoring programs should provide ongoing trauma-informed training and supervision to their adult mentors to ensure the children's safety and maximize the benefits of the mentoring relationship.

5.11 Help communities learn and share what works by investing in research.

A coordinated national initiative should be created to develop public-private partnerships and funding to ensure that scientific research on the causes of children's exposure to community violence, ways to prevent such exposure, and methods of treating its adverse effects is translated into effective and efficient interventions that are available to, and used successfully in, every community in our country.

6. Rethinking Our Juvenile Justice System

The vast majority of children involved in the juvenile justice system have survived exposure to violence and are living with the trauma of those experiences. A trauma-informed approach to juvenile justice does not require wholesale abandonment of existing programs, but instead it can be used to make many existing programs more effective and cost-efficient. By correctly assessing the needs of youth in the justice system, including youth exposed to violence, and matching services directly to those needs, the system can help children recover from the effects of exposure to violence and become whole.

As a guide to addressing the needs of the vast majority of at-risk and justice-involved youth who have been exposed to violence, the task force offers the recommendations listed below.

6.1 Make trauma-informed screening, assessment, and care the standard in juvenile justice services.

All children who enter the juvenile justice system should be screened for exposure to violence. The initial screening should take place upon the child's first contact with the juvenile justice system and should include youth who meet the criteria for diversion from the system. Where feasible, juvenile justice stakeholders should develop trauma-informed care and treatment for children diverted to prevention, mental health, or dependency programs.

6.2 Abandon juvenile justice correctional practices that traumatize children and further reduce their opportunities to become productive members of society.

Juvenile justice officials should rely on detention or incarceration as a last resort and only for youth who pose a safety risk or who cannot receive effective treatment in the community. Facilities must eliminate practices that traumatize and damage the youth in their care.

6.3 Provide juvenile justice services appropriate to children's ethnocultural background that are based on an assessment of each violence-exposed child's individual needs.

Culturally sensitive role models, practices, and programs aimed at healing traumatized youth and preventing youth from being further exposed to violence in the juvenile justice system should be expanded nationwide and incorporated into statewide juvenile justice systems.

6.4 Provide care and services to address the special circumstances and needs of girls in the juvenile justice system.

Programs that provide gender-responsive services for girls healing from violence and other traumatic events, including sexual and physical abuse, should be supported and developed.

6.5 Provide care and services to address the special circumstances and needs of LGBTQ (lesbian-gay-bisexual-transgender-questioning) youth in the juvenile justice system.

Every individual who works in the juvenile justice system should be trained and provided with ongoing supervision in order to be able to deliver trauma-informed care while demonstrating respect and support for the sexual orientation of every youth.

6.6 Develop and implement policies in every school system across the country that aim to keep children in school rather than relying on policies that lead to suspension and expulsion and ultimately drive children into the juvenile justice system.

Successful school-based programs that help students develop better ways of handling emotional distress, peer pressures, and problems in family and peer relationships and that integrate recovery from trauma should be expanded and then embedded into existing school curricula and activities to increase students' abilities to have positive experiences with education, recreation, peer relationships, and the larger community.

6.7 Guarantee that all violence-exposed children accused of a crime have legal representation.

We should ensure that all children have meaningful access to legal counsel in delinquency proceedings. Screen all children who enter the juvenile and adult justice systems for exposure to violence and provide access to trauma-informed services and treatment. Train defense attorneys who represent children to identify and obtain services for clients who have been exposed to violence and to help identify and prevent abuses of children in juvenile detention and placement programs.

6.8 Help, do not punish, child victims of sex trafficking.

Child victims of commercial sex trafficking should not be treated as delinquents or criminals. New laws, approaches to law enforcement, and judicial procedures must be developed that apply existing victim protection laws to protect the rights of these child victims.

6.9 Whenever possible, prosecute young offenders in the juvenile justice system instead of transferring their cases to adult courts.

No juvenile offender should be viewed or treated as an adult. Laws and regulations prosecuting them as adults in adult courts, incarcerating them as adults, and sentencing them to harsh punishments that ignore and diminish their capacity to grow must be replaced or abandoned.

CHAPTER ONE:

Ending the Epidemic of Children Exposed to Violence

CHAPTER ONE:
Ending the Epidemic of Children Exposed to Violence

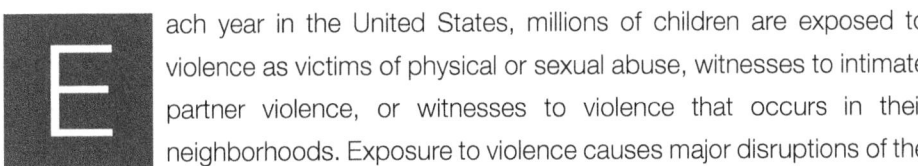ach year in the United States, millions of children are exposed to violence as victims of physical or sexual abuse, witnesses to intimate partner violence, or witnesses to violence that occurs in their neighborhoods. Exposure to violence causes major disruptions of the basic cognitive, emotional, and brain functioning that are essential for optimal development and leaves children traumatized. When their trauma goes unrecognized and untreated, these children are at significantly greater risk than their peers for aggressive, disruptive behaviors; school failure; posttraumatic stress disorder (PTSD); anxiety and depressive disorders; alcohol and drug abuse; risky sexual behavior; delinquency; and repeated victimization. When left unaddressed, these consequences of violence exposure and the impact of psychological trauma can persist well beyond childhood, affecting adult health and productivity. They also significantly increase the risk that, as adults, these children will engage in violence themselves. Exposure to violence constitutes a major threat to the health and well-being of our nation's children, ages 0 to 21 years. As a nation, we must protect children from the traumatization that results from exposure to violence.

For far too many children, exposure to violence is a matter of life and death. Eighty percent of child fatalities due to abuse or neglect occur within the first 3 years of life and almost always at the hands of adults responsible for their care. Every day, we lose five children in this country to violent deaths caused by abuse or neglect.[1,2]

Homicide is the second leading cause of death for children, youth, and young adults between the ages of 10 and 24, and suicide is a close third. Among very young children (ages 1 to 4), homicide is the third leading cause of death and accounted for 9 percent of deaths in the United States in 2008, an increase of 7 percentage points since 1970. Among children ages 5 to 14, homicide is the fourth leading cause of death, causing 2 percent of child deaths in 1970 and 6 percent in 2008. Suicide is close behind, the fifth leading cause of death in the United States in 2008 among school-age and pre-adolescent children.[3]

In the United States, we lose an average of more than 9 children and youths ages 5 to 18 to homicide or suicide per day — a total of 3,000 children each year.[4]

In addition to the human costs of unaddressed consequences of children's exposure to violence, the financial costs are astronomical. The predicted incremental cost of violence and abuse on the healthcare system alone ranges from $333 billion to $750 billion annually, or up to 37½ cents of every dollar spent on health care.[5] The financial burden on other public systems — child welfare, social services, law enforcement and justice, and education, in particular — combined with the loss of productivity over lifetimes is incalculable.

Exposure to violence is a national crisis that affects almost two in every three of our children. According to the National Survey of Children's Exposure to Violence (NatSCEV), an estimated 46 million of the 76 million children currently residing in the United States are exposed to violence, crime, and abuse each year.[6] In 1979, U.S. Surgeon General Julius B. Richmond declared that violence was a public health crisis of the highest priority. Although the past 30 years have seen dramatic reductions in the prevalence of violent crime, as measured in certain sectors such as violent crimes in households with children, children's exposure to violence and ensuing psychological trauma remains a national epidemic. As a nation, we must face the horrors of violence and resulting psychological trauma, resist the temptation to turn away, and make sure that children are not left to fend for themselves when they have been unable to escape their up-close and personal experiences of that horror.

We do not need to remain helpless, and our children do not need to remain alone with the consequences of their exposure to violence. With greater awareness of the enormous strides that have been made in developing effective ways of interrupting and responding to the consequences of violence exposure, our country is poised to confront the reality of violence in children's lives and initiate effective and long-lasting changes. It is time, as a nation, to commit to the protection of our children and to ensuring that they receive the assistance they need to recover when violence enters their lives.

It is time to use effective, coordinated approaches that address the needs of children traumatized by

"When placed in the most devastating context — the loss of innocence and the loss of innocent lives — the impact of this proliferation of violence against children is overwhelming. Faced with such a reality, it may be easy to become overwhelmed to the point of inaction. But doing nothing can never be considered a viable option. We must meet these overwhelming circumstances with deliberate and intentional action."

— Dr. William Bell, President and CEO, Casey Family Programs

violence — and their families and communities. It is time to ensure that interrupting the cycle of costly life-altering consequences of children's violence exposure becomes a national priority.

To prepare this report, U.S. Attorney General Eric Holder commissioned a diverse group of leaders who are dedicated to protecting children from violence and helping them to heal in the wake of violence. The task force is issuing this report as a call to action for the federal government, states, tribes, communities, the private sector, and people from all walks of life across the country to marshal the best available knowledge and the resources needed to defend our children against exposure to violence.

The Traumatic Impact of Exposure to Violence

When children are exposed to violence, the convergence between real life events and their worst fears — about physical injury and loss of life, loved ones, and control of their actions and feelings — is an "experience of overwhelming and often unanticipated danger [that] triggers a traumatic disruption of biological, cognitive, social and emotional regulation that has different behavioral manifestations depending on the child's developmental stage."[7] These traumatic disruptions of brain functioning, healthy development, relationships, and subjective experience often lead to symptoms of distress, including difficulties with sleeping and eating, irritability, attention and concentration problems, aggression, depressed mood and withdrawal, relationship problems, anxiety and intrusive thoughts, and impulsivity (such as dangerous risk-taking, alcohol and drug abuse, delinquency, or promiscuous sexual behavior).

These symptoms result from abrupt changes in brain activity and altered perceptions of self, others, and the environment, leaving the child "stuck" or "frozen" without a way to escape the state of fear (and also often shock, anger, grief, betrayal, and guilt or shame) from the original violent experience.[8] Children traumatized by exposure to violence cannot move forward in their lives. When parents, caregivers, and others identify the impact of the violence exposure and provide adequate support and treatment, affected children are able to heal and recover.[9–11] However, when violence is chronic or sources of support are inadequate, the result can be a severe and lasting impact on every aspect of the child's development.[12]

In these situations, exposure to violence may "substantially alter a child's biological makeup through long-lasting changes in brain anatomy and physiology."[7,13–17] These children are at high risk of suffering chronic and severe symptoms of traumatic stress, including long-term psychiatric problems and lifelong limitations on health, well-being, relationships, and personal success.[18] These risks are especially high when exposure to violence involves a fundamental loss of trust and security, which happens when children are exposed to sexual and physical abuse, witness intimate partner violence, or are severely victimized or witness extreme violence outside the home.[7]

Too many children endure cruel physical and sexual abuse and exploitation — most often by adults they know and trust and upon whom they rely, but also by strangers who prey upon them on the Internet or in their communities. Also, too many children see one of their parents, usually their mother, threatened or beaten by another adult in the home. Others see friends or loved ones assaulted in dangerous neighborhoods where violence is part of the fabric of everyday life. Others are left feeling helpless and overwhelmed when they are bullied or when they become trapped in abusive dating relationships. Their fear, anxiety, grief, anger, guilt, shame, and hopelessness are further compounded by isolation and a sense of betrayal when no one takes notice or offers protection, justice, support, or help.

When children's recovery from these posttraumatic symptoms is delayed or fails, the children adopt the attitude of "survivors" who can rely only upon themselves for safety and to cope with feelings of despair and helplessness. We know from recent advances in neuroscience that such survival coping comes at a high price to developmental achievement and success. Children's emotions, thinking, and behavior become organized around learning how to anticipate, cope with, and — for the sake of preparedness — never forget the danger and pain. The violence-exposed brain becomes expert at threat detection and survival, but the areas of the brain that engender and support capacities for problem solving, trust, confidence, happiness, social interaction, and overall self-esteem and self-control become delayed and compromised and may not develop to full capacity.[19–21] Survival-oriented biological changes are necessary for the traumatized child's immediate coping and self-protection during the actual violence exposure, but when they persist after the danger has subsided, brain and psychological development are significantly compromised.[22–27] These children's brains are not faulty or broken; they are stuck in a perpetual state of readiness to react without thinking to even the smallest threat. The children live in a near-constant state of high alert, a survival mode in which they never trust anyone — even people who really are trustworthy — can never relax, and never stop bracing for the next assault or betrayal.

Many of these children meet the criteria for PTSD. However, PTSD is only one of several emotional and behavioral disorders that can result from exposure to violence in childhood. Children exposed to violence and psychological trauma also are at high risk for developing anxiety and depressive disorders; becoming socially isolated, depressed, and suicidal; and engaging in harmful behaviors — drug and alcohol abuse, self-injury, promiscuous sexual activity, and delinquency and crime, in particular — that also increase their risk of being victimized or becoming violent themselves.[18]

Additionally, research shows that exposure to violence in the first years of childhood deprives children of as much as 10 percent of their potential intelligence (IQ), leaving them vulnerable to serious emotional, learning, and behavior problems by the time they reach school age.[28] In adolescence, these children continue to be seriously disadvantaged, often underachieving or failing in school; being ostracized or bullied by peers (or turning the tables and victimizing other children); and developing serious problems such as addictions, impulsive or reckless behavior, depression and suicidality, or delinquency.[29] Too often, they are labeled as "bad," "delinquent," "troublemakers," or "lacking character and positive motivation." Few adults will stop and, instead of asking "What's wrong with you?" ask the question that is essential to their recovery from violence: *"What happened to you?"*

It is important to realize that, although exposure to violence in any form harms children, exposure to different forms of violence can have different effects. **Sexual abuse** places children at high risk for serious and often chronic problems with health,[30–32] PTSD and other mental health disorders,[33–37] suicidality,[36,38] eating disorders,[34,37,39–41] sleep disorders,[42,43] substance abuse,[44–47] and sexuality and sexual behavior.[44,48–50] Sexually abused children often become hypervigilant about future sexual violation[51] and experience a sense of betrayal that breaks down the innate trust they feel for adults who should care for and protect them.[52] Sexual abuse also creates a sense of profound confusion and doubt about the child's own body and self that can develop into severe problems with shame and even self-hatred.[53] In the extreme, this can lead a child to detach physically and psychologically, leading to symptoms of psychological dissociation,[54] such as "blanking or spacing out," or acting on "automatic pilot" without conscious thought, as a way of escaping overwhelmingly intense feelings of fear, horror, rage, and shame.[52,55] Children exposed to sexual abuse also are at high risk for becoming phobic of any kind of physical closeness or touch or, alternately, promiscuously seeking intimacy or sexual activity.[56,57] As a result, sexually abused girls are likely to develop secondary sex characteristics and become sexually active earlier than their peers,[58] to more often and earlier become involved in intimate partnerships involving cohabitation, and to be at risk for intimate partner violence and lower investment and satisfaction in intimate relationships.[59] They also are vulnerable to predators and exploitive adults or older peers who re-victimize them, and they have difficulty caring for and protecting their own children.[60–62]

Children exposed to **physical abuse** also are at high risk for severe and often lifelong problems with physical health,[63–65] PTSD and other mental health disorders,[66–69] suicidality,[38,70–72] eating disorders,[73,74] substance abuse,[75,76] and sexuality and sexual behavior.[57,77,78] In addition, physically abused children are particularly likely to develop a sense of powerlessness when faced with physical intimidation or threats and to attempt to compensate either by hiding from people (for example, by skipping school or becoming socially isolated) or by using anger or aggression to protect themselves[79,80] or seeking relationships with peers or adults who do so (including becoming bullies or joining gangs). They are at risk for impairment in memory and thinking[81–83] and for developing beliefs that lead either to adopting violence as a form of self-protection and control of other people — reactive aggression — or to developing a phobia of even the slightest degree of conflict or anger that can result in avoidance of intimacy. Both of these defensive reactions to having been physically abused tend to result in isolation or rejection from family and peers, as well as both aggressive behavior and victimization in adolescent and adult intimate relationships,[84–86] which can result in a lifetime of violent or broken relationships[87] or no relationships at all. Scientific studies have shown that abused children are at risk of engaging in criminal behavior beginning early in life and continuing into adulthood.[88]

Children who have been exposed to **intimate partner violence** in their families also are at high risk for severe and potentially lifelong problems with physical health,[89–91] mental health,[92–97] school and peer relationships,[98–101] and disruptive behavior.[102–104] Children who witness or live with intimate partner violence are often burdened by a sense of loss[105,106] or by profound guilt[107] because they believe that they should have somehow intervened or prevented the violence — or, tragically, that they actually caused the violence. They frequently castigate themselves for having failed in what they assume to be their duty to protect their parents or siblings from being harmed,[107] including wishing that they could take the place of their victimized family member even if that means being horribly injured or killed themselves. Children exposed to intimate partner violence also often feel a sense of terror that they will lose an essential caregiver, such as a battered parent who is severely injured and could be killed.[94,108–110] To complicate things even further, they also often fear losing their relationship with a battering parent who may be taken away and incarcerated or even executed,[111] and they sometimes mistakenly blame themselves for having caused the batterer to be violent.[112] These children bring a deep sense of uncertainty and fear, as well as grief, anger, and shame, into all of their important relationships for the rest of their lives if not helped to heal and recover.[113,114]

The harm caused by childhood exposure to domestic or intimate partner violence can put future generations of children at risk of family conflict, abuse, neglect, or other exposure to violence and psychological trauma, potentially creating an inter-generational cycle of violence: Men who witnessed domestic violence in their families growing up are at risk for perpetrating domestic violence.[115] When, as adolescents or adults, they have children of their own, childhood victims of domestic violence often have difficulty being stable and nurturing parents, caregivers, and role models despite their best intentions.[116] The cycle of domestic violence exposure in childhood leading to re-victimization as an adult in intimate partner relationships is a serious problem,[117,118] but it is important to recognize that witnessing intimate partner violence in childhood does not necessarily lead to becoming a victim of domestic violence.[119]

Children who are exposed to **community violence** in their neighborhoods or schools often see family members, peers, trusted adults, or strangers (both innocent bystanders and active participants in violent activities) being injured or even murdered.[6] Violence can prevent children from ever feeling safe in their own schools and neighborhoods, leading them to adopt an attitude of hypervigilance — never letting their guard down so they will be ready for the next outbreak of violence.[120–124] They may come to believe that violence is "normal" and that relationships are too fragile to trust because one never knows when violence will take the life of a friend or loved one. They may feel compelled to resort to violence to avoid being viewed as weak and being targeted by bullies or other violent community members.[121,124] They may turn to gangs or criminal activities due to despair and powerlessness, perpetuating a cycle of violence by inflicting violence on others and becoming targets for further violence or incarceration. They are at risk for becoming victims of intimate partner violence as adolescents and adults.[125] When children exposed to community violence can turn to a loving, protective parent in their home[126,127] or a supportive mentoring adult or peers in their neighborhood or at school[127,129] — and, for boys, have a family in which conflict is handled effectively[128] — they can be highly resilient in the face of community violence, and in many cases they are able to recover and continue to develop successfully. However, parenting, family security, and mentoring cannot completely compensate for the harmful effects of exposure to community violence on children's adjustment.[130]

"Being hurt and hurting people was part of everyday life for us growing up.... There was no day or place where the threat of violence wasn't ever-present and entirely possible. From my perspective, that has not changed in the lives of the young men I serve today."

— **Roy Martin, Sr., Program Manager, Partnership Advancing Communities Together, Boston Health Commission**

The picture becomes even more complex when children are exposed to **multiple types of violence**; these children are called "polyvictims." The Department of Justice and Centers for Disease Control and Prevention's groundbreaking National Survey of Children's Exposure to Violence demonstrates that as many as 1 in 10 children in this country are polyvictims. The toxic combination of exposure to family violence, child physical and sexual abuse, and exposure to community violence increases the risk and severity of posttraumatic injuries and health and mental health disorders for exposed children by at least twofold and up to tenfold.[131–136] Polyvictimized children are at high risk for losing the fundamental capacities they need to develop normally and to become successful learners and productive adults.

"The ACE Study reveals how…adverse life experience[s] in childhood are lost in time, and then protected by shame, secrecy, and social taboos against exploring certain areas of human experience, ultimately costing us heavily in health, humanity, and dollars."

— Dr. Vincent Felitti, Co-Principal Investigator of the ACE Study; President and CEO, California Institutes of Preventive Medicine; Clinical Professor of Medicine, University of California, San Diego; and Fellow, American College of Physicians

The Adverse Childhood Experiences (ACEs) Study has greatly enriched our knowledge of the long-term effects of exposure to violence and trauma in childhood.[137–141] This study of more than 17,000 adults explored the relationship between significantly negative childhood experiences and adult health and well-being. Nearly two-thirds of people studied reported having at least one adverse experience in childhood (most of which involved some form of violence or threat of violence). One in five people reported at least three of the eight types of adversity. Moreover, the number of ACEs reported was strongly associated with severe health and social problems, including early initiation of smoking and sexual activity; multiple sexual partners and teen pregnancy; intimate partner violence; alcoholism and alcohol abuse; depression and suicide attempts; liver, heart, and lung diseases; and other problems related to poor health and diminished quality of life.

Poverty Increases Both Risk and Adverse Impact of Exposure to Violence

Although no community is untouched, the epidemic of children's exposure to violence does not play out evenly across the country. *Children living in poverty are far more likely to be exposed to violence and psychological trauma, both at home and in the surrounding community.*[142–144]

Compounding the problem, economically impoverished families and communities typically lack the resources needed to protect children. Poverty and scarcity of resources do not occur only in urban areas. Child welfare agencies in 39 states are unable to fully serve rural communities, most often in states that have the fewest public and private economic resources to devote to all of their members' needs.[145]

Poverty is a greater problem for minority ethnocultural groups that have historically been subjected to political and cultural trauma in this country and in their families' countries of origin. Roughly three times as many African-American, Hispanic, and American Indian/Alaska Native children live in poverty compared to White and Asian-American children.[146]

Asian-American children and their families who are immigrants from impoverished and violence-torn countries are more vulnerable to violence as a result of racism and the scars of historical trauma. Although they are spared the toxic violence of racism in some cases, White children whose communities and families have been isolated geographically and culturally — those from "the wrong side of the tracks" — often experience the burden of stigma, discrimination, and economic poverty.

Children, families, and communities living with deprivation and marginalization include not only the urban and rural poor and isolated tribal communities but also other groups that are at risk for exposure to violence in childhood: lesbian, gay, bisexual, transgender, and questioning sexual orientation (LGBTQ) youth and adults[48,147,148]; children and parents with physical disabilities[149] or mental illness and addictions[150,151]; and homeless individuals and families.[152,153]

In many poor communities, particularly those that are isolated and the victims of historical trauma and racism as well as poverty, violence has become the norm for children growing up.[143] On the Pine Ridge Indian Reservation in South Dakota, for example, 70 percent of adults are unemployed, and substance abuse, homelessness, rape, violence, and child abuse are everyday occurrences — nearly all of the children on this reservation will experience or witness violence.[154,155] Yet until a few years ago, the reservation had just eight police officers to respond to the needs of its 16,986 residents despite having a homicide rate more than five times the national average.[156]

> "For us in Rosebud, our reservation, the question is not who has been exposed to violence, it's who hasn't been exposed to violence?"
>
> — **Mato Standing High, Attorney General of the Rosebud Sioux Tribe**

Although economically impoverished or marginalized communities include many safe homes and protective and nurturing caregivers, just as there are violent homes in "mainstream" communities, neighborhoods where poverty or discrimination is concentrated often are not safe for the children and families who live in them. Those communities also include legions of individuals and organizations committed to ending violence and protecting all children. These advocates and concerned citizens and the families and children who are at highest risk of exposure to violence can help break the toxic cycle of violence if they can break out of the trap of isolation that can condemn them to endless poverty and violence. *They are not poor in spirit, resilience, or courage, but they cannot address the problems associated with exposure to violence alone. We need to recognize that these are our children as well, and we all must solve this problem or no child will be safe.*

Toward a Coordinated National Response

Children's exposure to violence represents a national crisis and a threat to the health and well-being of our nation's children and of our country. We cannot afford to be passive in the face of this threat. But we can succeed if we commit to a strong national response. We can prevent the long-term negative outcomes of exposure to violence, and we can help children exposed to violence recover. When these children are identified early and receive specialized services, evidence-based treatment, and proper care and support, they can heal.

It is time to ensure that violence exposure no longer goes unanswered and that the lives of children affected by such exposure are not further impacted by our failure to act. We must not allow violence to deny any child the physical and mental health; learning, skills, and knowledge; and pathways to development that all children need to become successful students, productive workers, and responsible family members, parents, and citizens.

"Fortunately, there is strong and growing evidence that violence is preventable…. The next step for the field requires expanding the overarching dialogue, moving from a focus on the individual and after-the-fact efforts to an approach that can prevent children and youth from being exposed to violence in the first place."

— Larry Cohen, Founder and Executive Director, Prevention Institute

We, as a country, have the creativity, knowledge, leadership, economic resources, and talent to effectively intervene on behalf of children exposed to violence. We can provide these children with the opportunity to recover and to claim their birthright and that of our nation: life, liberty, and the pursuit of happiness. When our children no longer have to bear the traumatic burden of violence exposure but are supported by an informed and committed citizenry and well-trained and trauma-informed providers and community members, they will have the opportunity to contribute to the social capital, productivity, strength, and security of our country, which is still looked upon by other nations to lead the world. Every child we help recover from exposure to violence is an investment in our nation's future.

This report therefore calls for a collective investment nationwide in defending our children from exposure to violence and psychological trauma, healing families and communities, and enabling all of our children to imagine their safe and creative development and productive futures. *The Attorney General's Defending Childhood Initiative asks the readers of this report, including the leaders of this country and the citizenry at large, to join together in developing a national plan that will allow our country to move steadily toward providing all children with the hope and security they deserve — resulting in a country in which every family and community is safe for children.*

What Readers Will Find in This Report

The findings and recommendations of the task force are organized into six chapters, each addressing a crucial issue in resolving the crisis of children exposed to violence.

In the second and third chapters, we offer a series of recommendations to ensure that all children exposed to violence are reliably identified, screened, and assessed and then receive support, treatment, and other services designed to address the traumatic impact of exposure to violence. The first step in defending children against violence is to find the millions of children who are exposed to violence and need help in recovering. The second step is to work toward stopping the exposure itself — making children safe in the future and helping them recover from the violence that was not prevented.

In the fourth and fifth chapters, we focus on prevention, recommending ways to create safe and nurturing homes and ways for communities to rise up out of violence. In the sixth and final chapter, we call for a new approach to juvenile justice, one that reflects the fact that the vast majority of children in the system have been exposed to violence and that prioritizes services that promote healing from the trauma of violence.

The challenge of children's exposure to violence cannot be solved by government alone. It requires a truly national response that draws on the strengths of all Americans. Children's futures are at stake. The time for action is now. Together, we must build a nation whose communities are dedicated to ending children's exposure to violence and psychological trauma. To that end, the task force proposes the following foundational recommendations.

1.1 Charge leaders at the highest levels of the executive and legislative branches of the federal government with the coordination and implementation of the recommendations in this report.

The executive branch should designate leaders at the highest levels of government to implement the recommendations in this report. Working with the executive branch, Congress should take legislative action on the recommendations in this report, making these recommendations a bipartisan priority. The task force recognizes that implementation of its recommendations will require the assistance of multiple Cabinet offices and federal departments to shape and sustain a truly national response to this epidemic. It also recommends that a consortium of leaders from all levels of state, local, and tribal government and the private sector who are committed to advancing the legislative, regulatory, and programmatic reforms work together to implement the recommendations in this report.

1.2 Appoint a federal task force or commission to examine the needs of American Indian/Alaska Native children exposed to violence.

American Indian/Alaska Native (AIAN) children have an exceptional degree of unmet need for services and support to prevent and respond to the extreme levels of violence they experience. The federal government has a unique legal responsibility for the welfare of AIAN children. It also has a special relationship with Indian tribes based, at least in part, on its trust responsibility. In fact, in much of Indian country, the U.S. Attorneys act as the primary prosecutors of violent crime. Sadly, federal partners working in Indian country are all too familiar with the societal impacts of children exposed to violence. The National Task Force on Children Exposed to Violence heard compelling testimony that underscored this reality. Although this task force could not adequately address the complexity of the issues, it recognizes the urgent need for further attention. To that end, a federal task force or commission should be developed to examine the specific needs of AIAN children exposed to violence and recommend actions to reduce crime and violence and protect AIAN children from abuse and neglect. The task force or commission should explore the additional burdens confronting AIAN communities in meeting the needs of children exposed to violence and propose policies and courses of action for addressing the current gaps in services.

Priorities for this task force or commission should include improving the identification and appropriate treatment of AIAN children who have been exposed to violence, helping AIAN communities and tribes rise out of violence, and involving AIAN youth in solutions. This task force or commission also must examine and address the needs of AIAN children living outside of reservations, in urban or rural settings off of AIAN lands. The task force should be developed through a consultation process consistent with the government-to-government relationship between the federal government and tribal governments. The appointment and management of the task force or commission and the selection of its members should be carried out through an equal collaboration between the Attorney General and the Secretary of the Interior. Special attention should be paid to the incarceration of AIAN children who are convicted and sentenced in the federal judicial system.

1.3 Engage youth as leaders and peer experts in all initiatives defending children against violence and its harmful effects.

The National Advisory Committee on Violence Against Women put the case clearly: "Youth engagement is critical to preventing violence. Youth are well-positioned to inform efforts that prevent teen dating and sexual violence and abuse; creating opportunities for them to do so offers lasting benefits and is consistent with the literature on positive youth development."

As stated in that report and confirmed by numerous scientific studies,[157–159] youth are the most credible and motivating spokespersons for children their own age and younger. This is increasingly the case with the widespread multimedia Internet and social media communication channels that enable children to interact with and influence each other almost constantly and instantaneously. Youth's own experiences also can be powerful sources of new and motivating information for adults. Seeing the challenges and dilemmas facing young people through their own eyes can produce immediate change in the attitudes and behavior of people of all ages.[158,160–164] Although trusted adults can serve as credible and influential sources of information and guidance concerning children's safety and well-being, there is no substitute for the personal experience and youthful creativity that children can provide.

Involving youth as planners and problem solvers, as well as communicators, is essential to develop effective solutions to the complex problems leading to and resulting from children's exposure to violence. When the voices and minds of young people are included in formulating an understanding of these problems and potential solutions, these and other youth are motivated to become "advocates in shaping anti-violence and pro-healthy-relationship initiatives — turn[ing] youth into dedicated activists who have an enduring commitment to this work [and] creating a cadre of positive 'up-standers.'"[165] This *positive youth development* model has been proven to build on and enhance the strengths that youth bring to their families, peer groups, schools, and communities, particularly their ability to form and sustain healthy relationships, a positive work ethic, and leadership skills, which can serve as a foundation for future generations for years to come in this country.

1.4 Ensure universal public awareness of the crisis of children exposed to violence and change social norms to protect children from violence and its harmful effects.

The general public has a limited understanding of the extent of children's exposure to violence and its adverse impact on health, social-emotional development, and academic and economic achievement. Moreover, the public has even less awareness that solutions to this crisis are within our grasp. The destructive consequences of children's exposure to violence need not be inevitable, and healing for children is possible in the aftermath of violence, if children who are at risk and those who actually are exposed to violence are identified in a timely manner. An informed citizenry can advocate for higher levels of services and support from policymakers for prevention and early intervention for children exposed to violence. It can challenge the misplaced pessimism that makes violence seem like an inevitable part of growing up for some children. It can be the engine to advance good public policy that embraces an alternative positive norm that no child's life and future should be scarred by the fear, mistrust, and sense of failure that violence causes. In addition, it can teach children and adults to reject violence as a tool or solution and instead to find strength and success through knowledge, responsibility, and kindness.

A national public awareness campaign would open the door to a fundamental change for the better in which every organization, community, and household in our country expects that every child should grow up safe and achieve his or her unique individual potential, and everyone takes responsibility for making this a reality. We all want our children to be safe and successful in their families, neighborhoods, schools, and future careers and to be good and productive citizens. We do not want to see them punished for making the mistakes that result from not yet having a fully formed brain or the maturity and life experience of an adult — yet we also do not want them to harm or endanger their peers, families, schools, or communities by acting irresponsibly or violently. When children are exposed to violence, they need protection, care, and help in healing that restores their trust, so that they do not go astray by resigning themselves to a life of violence, either as a victim or as a perpetrator. We can provide that help only if we find those children as soon as possible and let none of them fall between the cracks into a life of despair and more violence. On the national, state, and local community levels, this will require leadership from the federal and state governments, as described in the first recommendation, and also from the national and local media; child and family advocacy and services organizations; civic and business leaders and organizations; all ethnocultural groups; and opinion leaders from entertainment, sports, popular culture, education, politics, and the family and child welfare, healthcare, and justice systems.

"All of the work that we need to do is a shared responsibility. From a public health standpoint, this is our opportunity to redefine the unacceptable in our communities. It begins with us learning our cultural way of life. It begins with respect, courage, and tolerance. It begins by us being the change we wish to see."

— Coloradas Mangas, Mescalero Apache Tribe and Youth Board Member for the Center for Native American Youth

There are precedents for solving epidemic and apparently intractable problems. Just a few decades ago, smoking was more the norm than the exception. But as mounting research on the health impact of firsthand and secondhand smoke became impossible to ignore, the executive and legislative branches of the federal government acted on the recommendations of the Surgeon General to protect the entire nation. Whereas smoking was formerly seen as an individual choice affecting only the smoker, it is now understood to be an act with adverse consequences for everyone — not only the smoker and those within breathing distance, but every citizen as a result of escalating healthcare and insurance costs, losses in economic productivity, and the burden of caring for and grieving the loss of others with smoking-related illnesses. Through research, education, and the leadership of the federal government, coordinated efforts in the public and private sectors at the local, state, and national levels have changed the trajectory of that epidemic 180 degrees toward a rejection of the myth that smoking is a harmless vice and a massive reduction in smoking, all within the timespan of a single generation.

Violence toward children requires a similar national effort with all hands on deck. Stopgap solutions, no matter how well intended and carried out, cannot turn this tide. Federal leadership combined with sustained involvement by every state and all local communities is needed to prevent violence from marring the lives and undermining the well-being of all of our children. Action is needed on many fronts to identify children who are victims of violence or at risk, to provide them with help in recovery, and to make them safer and help them heal in their families, their communities, and the legal or child welfare systems. The rest of this report describes how social norms that tolerate or encourage violence can be changed if we take action now.

"We need an infrastructure to support developing evidence-based practices; a variety of them that are out there — that are great — don't have the evidence behind them to test out and then translate what we find to the field, and there is very little support for that at this point."

— **Dr. Jeffrey Edelson, Director of Research, School of Social Work, University of Minnesota, and Founding Director, Minnesota Center Against Violence and Abuse**

1.5 Incorporate evidence-based trauma-informed principles in all applicable federal agency grant requirements.

The federal government should lead the development of standards of care for identification, assessment, treatment, protection, and other crucial services for children exposed to violence, as well as protocols for monitoring the quality of these services as measured against the standards. The Administration for Children and Families' blueprint for embedding trauma-informed services and trauma-specific evidence-based treatment into all federally funded child welfare and children's health program requirements should be extended to all comparable funding programs involving services to children exposed to violence and their families.

1.6 Launch a national initiative to promote professional education and training on the issue of children exposed to violence.

Federal, state, and local government agencies overseeing post-secondary and professional education in colleges, universities, and professional schools should work with the leadership of these educational systems and the leadership of their professions. They should establish standards and a curriculum ensuring that every pre-professional student and all practicing professionals who provide services to children and families are aware of the scope of the problem of children's exposure to violence. The curriculum should also ensure that these professionals understand their responsibility to provide trauma-informed services and trauma-specific evidence-based treatment within the scope of their professional expertise.

1.7 Continue to support and sustain the national data collection infrastructure for the monitoring of trends in children exposed to violence.

The groundbreaking National Survey of Children's Exposure to Violence has established beyond doubt the scope and prevalence of exposure to violence in childhood. The survey has conducted second and third waves of interviews to monitor trends that warrant rapid intervention when there is evidence of increasing violence or a failure to reduce the prevalence of and harm caused by children's exposure to violence. Continued support is essential to ensure that this survey is conducted at regular frequent intervals.

"The Department of Justice, through the National Institute of Justice and the Office of Juvenile Justice and Delinquency Prevention, has helped to create and publicize an outstanding body of research about what works in preventing juvenile delinquency and offending.... We need that same highly evolved body of research about how to prevent and intervene in juvenile victimization, abuse, and exposure to violence."

— Dr. David Finkelhor, Director, Crimes Against Children Research Center; Co-Director, Family Research Laboratory, and Professor of Sociology, University of New Hampshire

Surveys of violence conducted using governmental data from the justice system (such as the Bureau of Justice Statistics National Crime Victimization Survey), education (such as Department of Education monitoring of the Race to the Top program), and health and human services (such as the National Survey of Adolescents and the Centers for Disease Control and Prevention's Adverse Behavioral Risk Factor Surveillance program to monitor ACEs) must be examined in concert with the NatSCEV on a regular basis to establish a clear picture of children's continuing exposure to violence.

1.8 Create national centers of excellence on children's exposure to violence.

The scientific, clinical, and technical expertise necessary to coordinate the implementation of a sustained public awareness campaign, reforms to maximize outcomes and efficiencies in funding requirements, standards for professional education and practices, and ongoing monitoring of trends and translation of the findings into continued progress in all these initiatives exist throughout the country. However, they need to be consolidated in centers of excellence to systematically ensure the success of these crucial goals. The National Child Traumatic Stress Network Treatment and Services Adaptation Centers provide a model for the development of a full complement of the needed centers of excellence.

1.9 Develop and implement public policy initiatives in state, tribal, and local governments to reduce and address the impact of childhood exposure to violence.

The ultimate success of the national initiatives outlined in previous recommendations depends upon adoption and implementation at the state, local, and tribal level in every community. Every community's governing institutions and leaders should receive guidance from the national centers of excellence to enable them to create local public policy initiatives, regulations, and services that ensure that children are protected against exposure to violence to the fullest extent possible.

1.10 Finance change by adjusting existing allocations and leveraging new funding.

The federal government should redirect funds to proven approaches for defending children against exposure to violence by providing financial incentives and encouragement to the states and, through them, to communities. Significant budget cuts are a reality at all levels of government, but they cannot be an excuse for failing to protect and heal our nation's children. We must use our resources more wisely by seizing opportunities for new funding, like those provided in the Affordable Health Care for America Act (AHA); shifting resources to produce better outcomes, like spending more to support struggling families than to place children in foster care; exploring how best to use federal formula and block grants to stimulate change; and pooling resources across government agencies to support common goals. Public-private partnerships also are essential. The following examples are illustrative but by no means a complete or final path toward enhanced funding.

In the child welfare system, in 1974, the landmark Child Abuse Prevention and Treatment Act (CAPTA) was enacted to fund grants to states for child abuse and neglect investigation, prosecution, prevention, and treatment programs. It also funded states, Indian tribes or tribal organizations, and public or private agencies and organizations to establish demonstration and workforce development initiatives. Additional funding has been allocated through the enactment of the Family Preservation and Support Services Program Act (1993) and the Adoption and Safe Families Act (1997), as well as a number of specialized child protection, family services, foster care, and adoptions legislative initiatives since 2002. Over these decades, funding for children's mental health through block grants to states has underwritten a parallel network of therapeutic programs, such as child guidance clinics. In 2001, the Child Traumatic Stress Initiative Act established funding through the Department of Health and Human Services (DHHS) to create a national network of specialized treatment programs and technical assistance centers for traumatized children. Coordinating all programs and initiatives funded by these legislative mandates to reduce redundancy could provide the resources needed to expand therapeutic services for children exposed to violence to all communities in this country.

In the field of family and domestic violence, the 1984 Family Violence Prevention and Services Act (FVPSA) was enacted to fund formula grants to states and tribal organizations for shelter and supportive services and state- and territory-wide domestic violence coalitions, as well as a national hotline for victims. Also in 1984, the Victims of Crime Act (VOCA) was enacted to fund state and local programs for crisis intervention, counseling, and support services for crime victims. VOCA has continued without lapsing, and FVPSA was reauthorized in 2010 (after expiring in 2008) as a part of the CAPTA reauthorization. In 1994, the Violence Against Women Act (VAWA) was enacted to fund "community-coordinated responses" to domestic violence, sexual assault, and dating violence and stalking, including Centers for Disease Control and Prevention demonstration projects in several states to end rape (EMPOWER) and prevent intimate partner violence (DELTA). Some VAWA programs focusing on prevention and early intervention with children and youth have yet to be fully funded. The statutes and funding provided by FVPSA, VOCA, and VAWA should serve as a basis for a national infrastructure to address the needs of children exposed to violence, aiding interruption of and recovery from violence.

Although some movement has been made toward integration of programs and funding across systems, initiatives and programs tend to be primarily focused on specific subsets of problems for which children's exposure to violence remains a largely unstated common core issue. At the local community level, families and providers often break through the silos with innovative initiatives that cut across multiple systems, as described by many testimonials provided to the task force. Those efforts must be capitalized upon as templates for a coordinated national effort that uses their lessons learned and systematically encourages and funds the dissemination of these models (always adapted by each local community based on its unique circumstances and resources).

With the implementation of healthcare reform through AHA, states will have more resources and increased pressure to focus on prevention and early intervention services as a way to improve health. Funding directed toward evidence-based treatment by AHA should be designated specifically to address the psychological and behavioral problems that result from children's exposure to violence. Funding also should go to prevention programs designed to enhance children's and families' wellness and to reduce healthcare costs associated with inadequate or delayed treatment of the effects of children's exposure to violence.

VOCA funds can be better allocated to help children exposed to violence. These funds are collected from criminal penalties that are designed to serve victims of the crimes committed against them. Congress has placed a limit, or "cap," on the amount of funds that are distributed to each state under the mandate of this legislation. If those caps were removed, the states could receive more money to provide trauma-informed services and trauma-specific treatment for children exposed to violence without any new government outlays.

Funding formulas in the child protection system can be shifted to allow states to increase support services for struggling families and children before the option of foster care. Currently, $7 billion annually pays for out-of-home placements for children who have been taken from their homes. Of this, only slightly more than 10 percent ($900 million annually) goes to prevention and protection services for families instead of funding child welfare agencies.

Congress can require states that receive formula and block grant funds to develop intervention programs that treat children exposed to violence and to develop multidisciplinary training for all professionals who work or come into contact with children.[166]

Funds available to states through Social Security Act Title 4E waivers can be used to invest in national dissemination of innovative community-designed models for sexual assault services for victims of child sexual abuse and sexual exploitation, such as those currently funded as limited pilot or demonstration projects under the Family Violence Prevention and Services Program at DHHS. Tax incentives can be provided to public and private organizations that provide services to prevent children's exposure to violence and treat children who have been victimized.

These are important potential sources of funding to accomplish the goals the task force has set forth to protect children from exposure to violence and its harmful effects – *but they are by no means the only possible sources of funding for these crucial initiatives.* Leadership in all levels of government and the private sector, as well as advocates working on the national and local levels, must come together to find or create the funding needed in order to defend our nation's children from exposure to violence.

References

1. U.S. Department of Health and Human Services Administration for Children and Families Children's Bureau (2011). *Child Maltreatment 2010.*

2. U.S. Government Accountability Office (2011). *Child maltreatment: strengthening national data on child fatalities could aid in prevention (GAO-11-599).*

3. U.S. Health Resources and Services Administration (2011). *Child Health 2011.*

4. U.S. Bureau of Justice Statistics (2011). *Indicators of school crime and safety 2010.*

5. Dolezal, T., McCollum, D., & Callahan, M. (2009). *Hidden costs in healthcare: The economic impact of violence and abuse.* Eden Prairie, MN: Academy on Violence and Abuse.

6. Finkelhor, D., et al. (2010). Trends in childhood violence and abuse exposure: evidence from 2 national surveys. *Archives of Pediatric and Adolescent Medicine, 164*(3), 238–42.

7. Harris, W. W., Lieberman, A. F., & Marans, S. (2007). In the best interests of society. *Journal of Child Psychology and Psychiatry and Allied Disciplines, 48*(3–4), 392–411.

8. Ford, J. D. (2009). Neurobiological and developmental research: clinical implications. In C. A. Courtois & J. D. Ford (Eds.), *Treating complex traumatic stress disorders: an evidence-based guide,* (pp. 31–58). New York, NY: Guilford Press.

9. Berkowitz, S. J., Stover, C. S., & Marans, S. R. (2011). The Child and Family Traumatic Stress Intervention: secondary prevention for youth at risk of developing PTSD. *Journal of Child Psychology and Psychiatry, 52*(6), 676–85.

10. Ghosh Ippen, C., et al. (2011). Traumatic and stressful events in early childhood: can treatment help those at highest risk? *Child Abuse & Neglect, 35*(7), 504–13.

11. Ford, J. D., et al. (2012). Randomized trial comparison of emotion regulation and relational psychotherapies for PTSD with girls involved in delinquency. *Journal of Clinical Child & Adolescent Psychology, 41*(1), 27–37.

12. D'Andrea, W., et al. (2012). Understanding interpersonal trauma in children: why we need a developmentally appropriate trauma diagnosis. *American Journal of Orthopsychiatry, 82*(2), 187–200.

13. Carrion, V. G., et al. (2009). Converging evidence for abnormalities of the prefrontal cortex and evaluation of midsagittal structures in pediatric posttraumatic stress disorder: an MRI study. *Psychiatry Research, 172*(3), 226–34.

14. McCrory, E. J., et al. (2011). Heightened neural reactivity to threat in child victims of family violence. *Current Biology, 21*(23), R947–8.

15. Tomoda, A., et al. (2009). Childhood sexual abuse is associated with reduced gray matter volume in visual cortex of young women. *Biological Psychiatry, 66*(7), 642–8.

16. De Bellis, M. D., & L. A. Thomas (2003). Biologic findings of post-traumatic stress disorder and child maltreatment. *Current Psychiatry Reports, 5*(2), 108–17.

17. Dannlowski, U., et al. (2012). Limbic scars: long-term consequences of childhood maltreatment revealed by functional and structural magnetic resonance imaging. *Biological Psychiatry, 71*(4), 286–93.

18. Ford, J. D. (2010). Complex adult sequelae of early life exposure to psychological trauma. In R. A. Lanius, E. Vermetten, & C. Pain (Eds.), *The hidden epidemic: The impact of early life trauma on health and disease,* (pp. 69–76). New York, NY: Cambridge University Press.

19. Andersen, S. L., & Teicher, M. H. (2009). Desperately driven and no brakes: developmental stress exposure and subsequent risk for substance abuse. *Neuroscience and Biobehavioral Review, 33*(4), 516–24.

20. Andersen, S. L., et al. (2008). Preliminary evidence for sensitive periods in the effect of childhood sexual abuse on regional brain development. *Journal of Neuropsychiatry and Clinical Neurosciences, 20*(3), 292–301.

21. De Bellis, M. D., et al. (2009). Demographic, maltreatment, and neurobiological correlates of PTSD symptoms in children and adolescents. *Journal of Pediatric Psychology.*

22. Thayer, J. F., et al., (2009). Heart rate variability, prefrontal neural function, and cognitive performance: the neurovisceral integration perspective on self-regulation, adaptation, and health. *Annals of Behavioral Medicine, 37*(2), 141–53.

23. Miller, G. E., Chen, E., & Parker, K. J. (2011). Psychological stress in childhood and susceptibility to the chronic diseases of aging: Moving toward a model of behavioral and biological mechanisms. *Psychological Bulletin, 137*(6), 959–97.

24. Althoff, R. R., et al. (2010). Adult outcomes of childhood dysregulation: a 14-year follow-up study. *Journal of the American Academy of Child & Adolescent Psychiatry, 49*(11), 1105–16.

25. Olson, S. L., et al. (2009) Self-regulatory processes in the development of disruptive behavior problems: The preschool-to-school transition. In S. L. Olson & A.J. Sameroff (Eds.), *Biopsychosocial regulatory processes in the development of childhood behavioral problems,* (pp. 144–185). New York, NY: Cambridge University Press.

26. Gestsdottir, S., & Lerner, R. M., (2007). Intentional self-regulation and positive youth development in early adolescence: Findings from the 4-h study of positive youth development. *Developmental Psychology, 43*(2), 508–521.

27. Koenen, K. C., (2006). Developmental epidemiology of PTSD: self-regulation as a central mechanism. *Annals of the New York Academy of Sciences, 1071,* 255–66.

28. Koenen, K. C., et al. (2003). Domestic violence is associated with environmental suppression of IQ in young children. *Development and Psychopathology, 15*(2), 297–311.

29. Ford, J. D., et al. (2006). Pathway from traumatic child victimization to delinquency: Implications for juvenile and permanency court proceedings and decisions. *Juvenile and Family Court Journal, 57*(1), 13–26.

30. Hager, A. D., & Runtz, M. G. (2012). Physical and psychological maltreatment in childhood and later health problems in women: An exploratory investigation of the roles of perceived stress and coping strategies. *Child Abuse & Neglect, 36,* 393–403.

31. Paras, M. L., et al. (2009). Sexual abuse and lifetime diagnosis of somatic disorders: a systematic review and meta-analysis. *Journal of the American Medical Association, 302*(5), 550–61.

32. Maniglio, R. (2009). The impact of child sexual abuse on health: a systematic review of reviews. *Clinical Psychology Review, 29*(7), 647–57.

33. Bedi, S., et al. (2011). Risk for suicidal thoughts and behavior after childhood sexual abuse in women and men. *Suicide and Life-Threatening Behavior, 41*(4), 406–15.

34. Chen, L. P., et al. (2010). Sexual abuse and lifetime diagnosis of psychiatric disorders: systematic review and meta-analysis. *Mayo Clinic Proceedings, 85*(7), 618–29.

35. Balsam, K. F., et al. (2010). Childhood abuse and mental health indicators among ethnically diverse lesbian, gay, and bisexual adults. *Journal of Consulting and Clinical Psychology, 78*(4), 459–68.

36. Afifi, T. O., et al. (2008). Population attributable fractions of psychiatric disorders and suicide ideation and attempts associated with adverse childhood experiences. *American Journal of Public Health, 98*(5), 946–52.

37. Jonas, S., et al. (2011). Sexual abuse and psychiatric disorder in England: results from the 2007 Adult Psychiatric Morbidity Survey. *Psychological Medicine, 41*(4), 709–19.

38. Ystgaard, M., et al. (2004). Is there a specific relationship between childhood sexual and physical abuse and repeated suicidal behavior? *Child Abuse & Neglect, 28*(8), 863–75.

39. Rohde, P., et al. (2008). Associations of child sexual and physical abuse with obesity and depression in middle-aged women. *Child Abuse & Neglect, 32*(9), 878–87.

40. Sanci, L., et al. (2008). Childhood sexual abuse and eating disorders in females: findings from the Victorian Adolescent Health Cohort Study. *Archives of Pediatric and Adolescent Medicine, 162*(3), 261–7.

41. Carter, J. C., et al. (2006). The impact of childhood sexual abuse in anorexia nervosa. *Child Abuse & Neglect, 30*(3), 257–69.

42. Noll, J., et al. (2006). Sleep disturbances and childhood sexual abuse. *Journal of Pediatric Psychology, 31*(5), 469–480.

43. Trickett, P. K., Kurtz, D. A., & Noll, J. G. (2005). The consequences of child sexual abuse for female development. In D. Bell, S. L. Foster, & E. J. Mash (Eds.), *Handbook of behavioral and emotional problems in girls,* (pp. 357–379). New York, NY: Kluwer Academic/Plenum Publishers.

44. Jones, D. J., et al. (2012). Linking childhood sexual abuse and early adolescent risk behavior: the intervening role of internalizing and externalizing problems. *Journal of Abnormal Child Psychology.*

45. Meade, C. S., et al. (2012). Methamphetamine use is associated with childhood sexual abuse and HIV sexual risk behaviors among patrons of alcohol-serving venues in Cape Town, South Africa. *Drug and Alcohol Dependence, 126*(1–2), 232–9.

46. Maniglio, R. (2011). The role of child sexual abuse in the etiology of substance-related disorders. *Journal of Addictive Disorders, 30*(3), 216–28.

47. Asgeirsdottir, B. B., et al. (2011). Associations between sexual abuse and family conflict/violence, self-injurious behavior, and substance use: the mediating role of depressed mood and anger. *Child Abuse & Neglect, 35*(3), 210–9.

48. Friedman, M. S., et al. (2011). A meta-analysis of disparities in childhood sexual abuse, parental physical abuse, and peer victimization among sexual minority and sexual nonminority individuals. *American Journal of Public Health, 101*(8), 1481–94.

49. Wilson, H. W., & Widom, C. S. (2011). Pathways from childhood abuse and neglect to HIV-risk sexual behavior in middle adulthood. *Journal of Consulting and Clinical Psychology, 79*(2), 236–46.

50. Lacelle, C., et al. (2012). Sexual health in women reporting a history of child sexual abuse. *Child Abuse & Neglect, 36(*3), 247–59.

51. Staples, J., Rellini, A. H., & Roberts, S. P. (2012). Avoiding experiences: sexual dysfunction in women with a history of sexual abuse in childhood and adolescence. *Archives of Sexual Behavior, 41*(2), 341–50.

52. Barnes, J. E., et al. (2009). Sexual and physical revictimization among victims of severe childhood sexual abuse. *Child Abuse & Neglect, 33*(7), 412–20.

53. Feiring, C., Cleland, C. M., & Simon, V. A. (2010). Abuse-specific self-schemas and self-functioning: a prospective study of sexually abused youth. *Journal of Clinical Child & Adolescent Psychology, 39*(1), 35–50.

54. Hulette, A. C., Freyd, J. J., & Fisher, P. A. (2011). Dissociation in middle childhood among foster children with early maltreatment experiences. *Child Abuse & Neglect, 35*(2), 123–6.

55. Marysko, M., et al. (2010). History of childhood abuse is accompanied by increased dissociation in young mothers five months postnatally. *Psychopathology, 43*(2), 104–9.

56. Messman-Moore, T. L., Walsh, K. L., & Dilillo, D. (2010). Emotion dysregulation and risky sexual behavior in revictimization. *Child Abuse & Neglect, 34*(12), 967–976.

57. Wilson, H. W., & Widom, C. S. (2010). The role of youth problem behaviors in the path from child abuse and neglect to prostitution: A prospective examination. *Journal of Research in Adolescence, 20*(1), 210–236.

58. Shenk, C. E., et al. (2010). A prospective examination of the role of childhood sexual abuse and physiological asymmetry in the development of psychopathology. *Child Abuse & Neglect, 34*(10), 752–61.

59. Friesen, M. D., et al. (2009). Childhood exposure to sexual abuse and partnership outcomes at age 30. *Psychological Medicine,* 1–10.

60. Noll, J. G., et al. (2009). The cumulative burden borne by offspring whose mothers were sexually abused as children: descriptive results from a multigenerational study. *Journal of Interpersonal Violence, 24*(3), 424–49.

61. Bailey, H. N., et al. (2012). The impact of childhood maltreatment history on parenting: a comparison of maltreatment types and assessment methods. *Child Abuse & Neglect, 36*(3), 236–46.

62. Kim, K., Trickett, P. K., & Putnam, F. W. (2010). Childhood experiences of sexual abuse and later parenting practices among non-offending mothers of sexually abused and comparison girls. *Child Abuse & Neglect, 34*(8), 610–22.

63. Boynton-Jarrett, R., et al. (2012). Child and adolescent abuse in relation to obesity in adulthood: the Black Women's Health Study. *Pediatrics, 130*(2), 245–53.

64. Hager, A. D., & Runtz, M. G. (2012). Physical and psychological maltreatment in childhood and later health problems in women: an exploratory investigation of the roles of perceived stress and coping strategies. *Child Abuse & Neglect, 36*(5), 393–403.

65. Slopen, N., et al. (2012). Childhood adversity and cell-mediated immunity in young adulthood: Does type and timing matter? *Brain, Behavior, and Immunity.*

66. Hovens, J. G., et al. (2012). Impact of childhood life events and trauma on the course of depressive and anxiety disorders. *Acta Psychiatrica Scandinavica, 126*(3), 198–207.

67. Larsson, S., et al. (2012). High prevalence of childhood trauma in patients with schizophrenia spectrum and affective disorder. *Comprehensive Psychiatry.*

68. Plaza, A., et al. (2012). Childhood physical abuse as a common risk factor for depression and thyroid dysfunction in the earlier postpartum. *Psychiatry Research.*

69. Sugaya, L., et al. (2012). Child physical abuse and adult mental health: a national study. *Journal of Traumatic Stress, 25*(4), 384–92.

70. Hadland, S. E., et al. (2012). Suicide and history of childhood trauma among street youth. *Journal of Affective Disorders, 136*(3), 377–80.

71. Huang, M. C., et al. (2012). Impact of multiple types of childhood trauma exposure on risk of psychiatric comorbidity among alcoholic inpatients. *Alcoholism, Clinical and Experimental Research, 36*(6), 1099–107.

72. Wanner, B., et al. (2012). Childhood trajectories of anxiousness and disruptiveness explain the association between early-life adversity and attempted suicide. *Psychological Medicine,* 1–10.

73. Jaite, C., et al. (2012). Etiological role of childhood emotional trauma and neglect in adolescent anorexia nervosa: a cross-sectional questionnaire analysis. *Psychopathology, 45*(1), 61–6.

74. Shin, S. H., & Miller, D. P. (2012). A longitudinal examination of childhood maltreatment and adolescent obesity: results from the National Longitudinal Study of Adolescent Health (AddHealth) Study. *Child Abuse & Neglect, 36*(2), 84–94.

75. Shin, S. H., Miller, D. P., & Teicher, M. H. (2012). Exposure to childhood neglect and physical abuse and developmental trajectories of heavy episodic drinking from early adolescence into young adulthood. *Drug and Alcohol Dependence.*

76. Huang, S., et al. (2011). The long-term effects of childhood maltreatment experiences on subsequent illicit drug use and drug-related problems in young adulthood. *Addictive Behaviors. 36*(1–2), 95–102.

77. Roberts, A. L., Glymour, M. M., & Koenen, K. C. (2012). Does maltreatment in childhood affect sexual orientation in adulthood? *Archives of Sexual Behavior.*

78. Tenkorang, E. Y., & Obeng Gyimah, S. (2012). Physical abuse in early childhood and transition to first sexual intercourse among youth in Cape Town, South Africa. *Journal of Sex Research. 49*(5), 508–17.

79. de Boer, S.B., et al. (2012). Childhood characteristics of adolescent inpatients with early-onset and adolescent-onset disruptive behavior. *Journal of Psychopathology and Behavioral Assessment, 34*(3), 415–422.

80. Bevilacqua, L., et al. (2012). Interaction between FKBP5 and childhood trauma and risk of aggressive behavior. *Archives of General Psychiatry, 69*(1), 62–70.

81. Bosquet Enlow, M., et al. (2012). Interpersonal trauma exposure and cognitive development in children to age 8 years: a longitudinal study. *Journal of Epidemiology and Community Health, 66*(11), 1005–10.

82. Chen, P., et al. (2012). Moderating effects of childhood maltreatment on associations between social information processing and adult aggression. *Psychological Medicine, 42*(6), 1293–304.

83. Spann, M. N., et al. (2012). Childhood abuse and neglect and cognitive flexibility in adolescents. *Child Neuropsychology, 18*(2), 182–9.

84. Boivin, S., et al. (2012). Past victimizations and dating violence perpetration in adolescence: the mediating role of emotional distress and hostility. *Journal of Interpersonal Violence, 27*(4), 662–84.

85. Maneta, E., et al. (2012). Links between childhood physical abuse and intimate partner aggression: the mediating role of anger expression. *Violence and Victims, 27*(3), 315–28.

86. Renner, L. M., & Whitney, S. D. (2012). Risk factors for unidirectional and bidirectional intimate partner violence among young adults. *Child Abuse & Neglect, 36*(1), 40–52.

87. Cavanaugh, C. E., et al. (2012). Patterns of violence against women: A latent class analysis. *Psychological Trauma, 4*(2), 169–176.

88. DeGue, S., & Spatz Widom, C. (2009). Does out-of-home placement mediate the relationship between child maltreatment and adult criminality? *Child Maltreatment, 14*(4), 344–55.

89. Jun, H. J., et al. (2012). Growing up in a domestic violence environment: relationship with developmental trajectories of body mass index during adolescence into young adulthood. *Journal of Epidemiology and Community Health, 66*(7), 629–35.

90. Hart-Johnson, T., & Green, C. R. (2012). The impact of sexual or physical abuse history on pain-related outcomes among blacks and whites with chronic pain: gender influence. *Pain Medicine, 13*(2), 229–42.

91. Greenfield, E. A., & Marks, N. F. (2009). Profiles of physical and psychological violence in childhood as a risk factor for poorer adult health: evidence from the 1995–2005 National Survey of Midlife in the United States. *Journal of Aging and Health, 21*(7), 943–66.

92. Margolin, G., et al. (2009) Youth exposed to violence: stability, co-occurrence, and context. *Clinical Child and Family Psychology Review, 12*(1), 39–54.

93. Luthra, R., et al. (2009). Relationship between type of trauma exposure and posttraumatic stress disorder among urban children and adolescents. *Journal of Interpersonal Violence, 24*(11), 1919–27.

94. Schechter, D. S., et al. (2008). Distorted maternal mental representations and atypical behavior in a clinical sample of violence-exposed mothers and their toddlers. *Journal of Trauma and Dissociation, 9*(2), 123–47.

95. El-Sheikh, M., et al. (2008). Marital psychological and physical aggression and children's mental and physical health: direct, mediated, and moderated effects. *Journal of Consulting and Clinical Psychology, 76*(1), 138–48.

96. Kilpatrick, K. L., & Williams, L. M. (1998). Potential mediators of post-traumatic stress disorder in child witnesses to domestic violence. *Child Abuse & Neglect, 22*(4), 319–30.

97. Kilpatrick, K. L., & Williams, L. M. (1997). Post-traumatic stress disorder in child witnesses to domestic violence. *American Journal of Orthopsychiatry, 67*(4), 639–44.

98. Holt, S., Buckley, H., & Whelan, S. (2008). The impact of exposure to domestic violence on children and young people: a review of the literature. *Child Abuse & Neglect, 32*(8), 797–810.

99. El-Sheikh, M., et al. (2007). Child emotional insecurity and academic achievement: the role of sleep disruptions. *Journal of Family Psychology, 21*(1), 29–38.

100. Kouros, C. D., Cummings, E. M., & Davies, P. T. (2010). Early trajectories of interparental conflict and externalizing problems as predictors of social competence in preadolescence. *Development and Psychopathology, 22*(3), 527–37.

101. McCoy, K., Cummings, E. M., & Davies, P. T. (2009). Constructive and destructive marital conflict, emotional security and children's prosocial behavior. *Journal of Child Psychology and Psychiatry, 50*(3), 270–9.

102. Kouros, C. D., & Cummings, E. M. (2011). Transactional relations between marital functioning and depressive symptoms. *American Journal of Orthopsychiatry, 81*(1), 128–38.

103. El-Sheikh, M., et al. (2009). Marital conflict and children's externalizing behavior: interactions between parasympathetic and sympathetic nervous system activity. *Monographs of the Society for Research in Child Development, 74*(1), vii, 1–79.

104. Spilsbury, J. C., et al. (2008). Profiles of behavioral problems in children who witness domestic violence. *Violence and Victims, 23*(1), 3–17.

105. Gaensbauer, T., et al. (1995). Traumatic loss in a one-year-old girl. *Journal of the American Academy of Child & Adolescent Psychiatry, 34*(4), 520–8.

106. Botsis, A. J., et al. (1995). Parental loss and family violence as correlates of suicide and violence risk. *Suicide and Life-Threatening Behavior, 25*(2), 253–60.

107. Fortin, A., Doucet, M., & Damant, D. (2011). Children's appraisals as mediators of the relationship between domestic violence and child adjustment. *Violence and Victimology, 26*(3), 377–92.

108. Cummings, E. M., et al. (2006). Interparental discord and child adjustment: prospective investigations of emotional security as an explanatory mechanism. *Child Development, 77*(1), 132–52.

109. Schermerhorn, A. C., Cummings, E. M., & Davies, P. T. (2008). Children's representations of multiple family relationships: organizational structure and development in early childhood. *Journal of Family Psychology, 22*(1), 89–101.

110. Davies, P. T., et al. (2002). Child emotional security and interparental conflict. *Monographs of the Society for Research in Child Development, 67*(3), i–v, vii–viii, 1–115.

111. Beck, E., & Jones, S. J. (2007). Children of the condemned: grieving the loss of a father to death row. *Omega (Westport), 56*(2), 191–215.

112. Davies, P. T., Cummings, E. M., & Winter, M. A. (2004). Pathways between profiles of family functioning, child security in the interparental subsystem, and child psychological problems. *Development and Psychopathology, 16*(3), 525–50.

113. Cummings, E. M., et al. (2009). Children and violence: the role of children's regulation in the marital aggression-child adjustment link. *Clinical Child and Family Psychology Review, 12*(1), 3–15.

114. Perkins, S. C., et al. (2012). The mediating role of self-regulation between intrafamilial violence and mental health adjustment in incarcerated male adolescents. *Journal of Interpersonal Violence, 27*(7), 1199–224.

115. O'Leary, K. D., Smith Slep, A. M., & O'Leary, S. G. (2007). Multivariate models of men's and women's partner aggression. *Journal of Consulting and Clinical Psychology, 75*(5), 752–64.

116. Davies, P. T., et al. (2009). A process analysis of the transmission of distress from interparental conflict to parenting: adult relationship security as an explanatory mechanism. *Developmental Psychology, 45*(6), 1761–73.

117. Fargo, J. D. (2009), Pathways to adult sexual revictimization: direct and indirect behavioral risk factors across the lifespan. *Journal of Interpersonal Violence, 24*(11), 1771–91.

118. Renner, L. M., & Slack, K. S. (2006). Intimate partner violence and child maltreatment: understanding intra- and intergenerational connections. *Child Abuse & Neglect, 30*(6), 599–617.

119. Ernst, A. A., et al. (2007). Witnessing intimate partner violence as a child does not increase the likelihood of becoming an adult intimate partner violence victim. *Academy of Emergency Medicine, 14*(5), 411–8.

120. Fowler, P. J., et al. (2009). Community violence: a meta-analysis on the effect of exposure and mental health outcomes of children and adolescents. *Development & Psychopathology, 21*(1), 227–59.

121. Shields, N., Nadasen, K., & Pierce, L. (2008). The effects of community violence on children in Cape Town, South Africa. *Child Abuse & Neglect, 32*(5), 589–601.

122. Malik, N. M. (2008). Exposure to domestic and community violence in a nonrisk sample: associations with child functioning. *Journal of Interpersonal Violence, 23*(4), 490–504.

123. Kliewer, W., & Sullivan, T. N. (2008). Community violence exposure, threat appraisal, and adjustment in adolescents. *Journal of Clinical Child & Adolescent Psychology, 37*(4), 860–73.

124. Janosz, M., et al. (2008). Are there detrimental effects of witnessing school violence in early adolescence? *Journal of Adolescent Health, 43*(6), 600–8.

125. Taylor, C. A., et al. (2008). Cumulative experiences of violence among high-risk urban youth. *Journal of Interpersonal Violence, 23*(11), 1618–35.

126. Bailey, B. N., et al. (2006). The role of maternal acceptance in the relation between community violence exposure and child functioning. *Journal of Abnormal Child Psychology, 34*(1), 57–70.

127. Rosario, M., et al. (2008). Intervening processes between youths' exposure to community violence and internalizing symptoms over time: the roles of social support and coping. *American Journal of Community Psychology, 41*(1–2), 43–62.

128. McKelvey, L. M., et al. (2010). Growing up in violent communities: Do family conflict and gender moderate impacts on adolescents' psychosocial development? *Journal of Abnormal Child Psychology.*

129. Aisenberg, E., & Herrenkohl, T. (2008). Community violence in context: risk and resilience in children and families. *Journal of Interpersonal Violence, 23*(3), 296–315.

130. Spano, R., Vazsonyi, A. T., & Bolland, J. (2009). Does parenting mediate the effects of exposure to violence on violent behavior? An ecological-transactional model of community violence. *Journal of Adolescence, 32*(5), 1321–41.

131. Turner, H. A., et al. (2012). Family context, victimization, and child trauma symptoms: variations in safe, stable, and nurturing relationships during early and middle childhood. *American Journal of Orthopsychiatry, 82*(2), 209–19.

132. Sareen, J., et al. (2012). Adverse childhood experiences in relation to mood and anxiety disorders in a population-based sample of active military personnel. *Psychological Medicine,* 1–12.

133. Liu, Y., et al. (2012). Relationship between adverse childhood experiences and unemployment among adults from five US states. *Social Psychiatry and Psychiatric Epidemiology.*

134. Turner, H. A., Finkelhor, D., & Ormrod, R. (2010). Poly-victimization in a national sample of children and youth. *American Journal of Preventive Medicine, 38*(3), 323–30.

135. Dube, S. R., et al. (2009). Cumulative childhood stress and autoimmune diseases in adults. *Psychosomatic Medicine, 71*(2), 243–50.

136. Brown, D. W., et al. (2009). Adverse childhood experiences and the risk of premature mortality. *American Journal of Preventive Medicine, 37*(5), 389–96.

137. Anda, R. F., et al. (2010). Building a framework for global surveillance of the public health implications of adverse childhood experiences. *American Journal of Preventive Medicine, 39*(1), 93–8.

138. Anda, R. F., et al. (2006). The enduring effects of abuse and related adverse experiences in childhood: A convergence of evidence from neurobiology and epidemiology. *European Archives of Psychiatry and Clinical Neuroscience, 256*(3), 174–86.

139. Dube, S. R., et al. (2003). The impact of adverse childhood experiences on health problems: evidence from four birth cohorts dating back to 1900. *Preventive Medicine, 37*(3), 268–77.

140. Edwards, V. J., et al. (2003). Relationship between multiple forms of childhood maltreatment and adult mental health in community respondents: Results from the Adverse Childhood Experiences Study. *American Journal of Psychiatry, 160*(8), 1453–1460.

141. Felitti, V. J., et al. (1998). Relationship of childhood abuse and household dysfunction to many of the leading causes of death in adults. The Adverse Childhood Experiences (ACE) Study. *American Journal of Preventive Medicine, 14*(4), 245–58.

142. Cunradi, C. B., et al. (2000). Neighborhood poverty as a predictor of intimate partner violence among White, Black, and Hispanic couples in the United States: a multilevel analysis. *Annals of Epidemiology, 10*(5), 297–308.

143. Goodman, L. A., et al. (2009). When crises collide: how intimate partner violence and poverty intersect to shape women's mental health and coping, *Trauma Violence Abuse, 10*(4), 306–29.

144. Corzine, L., & Corzine, J. (1991). Deadly connections: Culture, poverty, and the direction of lethal violence. *Social Forces, 69*(3), 55–72.

145. Belanger, K. (2008). The welfare of rural children: A summary of challenges. Available from http://www.cwla.org/programs/culturalcompetence/welfareofruralchildren.pdf.

146. The Annie E. Casey Foundation. (2011). *2011 KIDS Count data book,* (p. 58). Baltimore, MD.

147. McLaughlin, K. A., et al. (2012). Disproportionate exposure to early-life adversity and sexual orientation disparities in psychiatric morbidity. *Child Abuse & Neglect, 36*(9), 645–55.

148. Roberts, A. L., et al. (2012). Childhood gender nonconformity: a risk indicator for childhood abuse and posttraumatic stress in youth. *Pediatrics, 129*(3), 410–7.

149. Turner, H. A., et al. (2011). Disability and victimization in a national sample of children and youth. *Child Maltreatment, 16*(4), 275–86.

150. Elbogen, E. B., & Johnson, S. C. (2009). The intricate link between violence and mental disorder: results from the National Epidemiologic Survey on Alcohol and Related Conditions. *Archives of General Psychiatry, 66*(2), 152–61.

151. Lu, W., et al. (2008). Correlates of adverse childhood experiences among adults with severe mood disorders. *Psychiatric Services, 59*(9), 1018–26.

152. Thrane, L. E., et al. (2006). Impact of family abuse on running away, deviance, and street victimization among homeless rural and urban youth. *Child Abuse & Neglect, 30*(10), 1117–28.

153. Miller, P., et al. (2004). Experiences of being homeless or at risk of being homeless among Canadian youths. *Adolescence, 39*(156), 735–55.

154. Kristof, N. (2012, May 9). Poverty's poster child. *New York Times.*

155. Eckholm, E. (2009, December 13). Gang violence grows on an Indian reservation. *New York Times.*

156. Williams, T. (2012 February 2). Brutal crimes grip an Indian reservation. *New York Times.*

157. Geldhof, G. J., Bowers, E. P., & Lerner, R. M. (2012). Special Section Introduction: Thriving in Context: Findings from the 4-H Study of Positive Youth Development. *Journal of Youth and Adolescence.*

158. McCammon, S. L. (2012). Systems of care as asset-building communities: implementing strengths-based planning and positive youth development. *American Journal of Community Psychology, 49*(3–4), 556–65.

159. Bird, J. M., & Markle, R. S. (2012). Subjective well-being in school environments: promoting positive youth development through evidence-based assessment and intervention. *American Journal of Orthopsychiatry, 82*(1), 61–6.

160. Cargo, M., et al. (2003). Empowerment as fostering positive youth development and citizenship. *American Journal of Health Behavior, 27 Suppl 1,* S66–79.

161. Catalano, R. F., et al. (2002). Prevention science and positive youth development: competitive or cooperative frameworks? *Journal of Adolescent Health, 31*(6 Suppl), 230–9.

162. Durlak, J. A., et al. (2007). Effects of positive youth development programs on school, family, and community systems. *American Journal of Community Psychology, 39*(3–4), 269–86.

163. Gestsdottir, S., et al. (2010). Intentional self regulation in middle adolescence: the emerging role of loss-based selection in positive youth development. *Journal of Youth and Adolescence, 39*(7), 764–82.

164. Mallon, G. P., (1997). Basic premises, guiding principles, and competent practices for a positive youth development approach to working with gay, lesbian, and bisexual youths in out-of home care. *Child Welfare, 76*(5), 591–609.

165. National Advisory Committee on Violence Against Women, *Draft report of the National Advisory Committee on Violence Against Women.* Unpublished, p. 25.

166. Samuels, B. (2012). *Promoting Social and Emotional Well-Being for Children and Youth Receiving Child Welfare Services.*

CHAPTER TWO:

Identifying Children Exposed to Violence

CHAPTER TWO:
Identifying Children Exposed to Violence

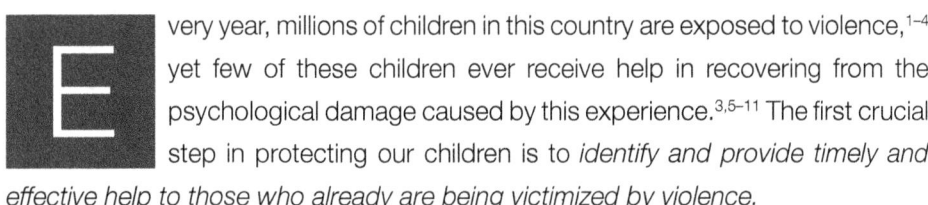

Every year, millions of children in this country are exposed to violence,[1–4] yet few of these children ever receive help in recovering from the psychological damage caused by this experience.[3,5–11] The first crucial step in protecting our children is to *identify and provide timely and effective help to those who already are being victimized by violence.*

We all know that children face many kinds of violence in their homes, schools, and communities, so why isn't every child who is victimized by violence identified and helped? The main reason is that we — as individuals, as families, and as a society — have not fully committed ourselves to identifying and eradicating violence and the deep harm it causes in the lives of American children. We have not prepared ourselves to take on the challenge of letting no instance of violence in any child's life go unrecognized.

We *can* make and achieve that commitment. We can and we must identify every child who is exposed to violence in every community in our country. We can and we must make sure that our children are protected from further violence.

The first step in making the commitment to protect children from violence is to make sure that each of us — in every community in this country — knows how to recognize the signs of children who have been exposed to violence. This can be difficult because most of us have become accustomed to seeing and hearing about violence every day. Too often, violence directed at or witnessed by children is ignored or left unquestioned because we make the mistake of assuming that it does not cause lasting harm or that it is just a "normal" part of life that all children are resilient enough to cope with. We may believe that these "ordinary" acts of violence actually help children by "building character" or inoculating them against serious assaults they may face as they grow older, but in fact, psychological science has thoroughly debunked the myths that violence in any form does not hurt our children and that violence in any form can be good for our children.[12–18]

Instead, science has shown that what appear to be "minor" forms of exposure to violence (such as witnessing violence without being physically touched) can cause substantial harm (see the Glossary for definitions of violence). Violence in many forms can cause psychological wounds that lead to severe anxiety, depression, anger, aggression, guilt, shame, school and employment failure, substance addiction, and criminal behavior.[17–27]

Early identification of violence exposure is essential for preventing and addressing these problems. If these wounds go unnoticed and the violence is allowed to occur repeatedly, the resulting psychological injures can compromise a child's entire future by creating a lifelong pattern of anger; aggression; self-destructive behaviors; academic and employment failures; and rejection, conflict, and isolation in every key relationship.[26,28,29]

In addition, early identification can save children exposed to violence — and their families and communities — from becoming trapped in a tragic revolving door of violence and damaging psychological trauma. Once a child has been exposed to violence, she or he is more likely than other children to be exposed to further violence.[27,30–34] This can happen when a bully or predator recognizes a child who is vulnerable or unprotected as an easy target for further victimization.[35,36] It also happens when children live in families and communities or go to schools in which violence has become so pervasive that further exposure is inevitable and may even be a daily phenomenon.[37–39] Finally, it can happen when a family, school, or community becomes resigned to tolerating violence and everyone who is exposed becomes paralyzed by a sense of unrelenting fear, helplessness, and hopelessness.[40]

To break the cycles of children's repeated exposure to violence, we must watch out for, identify, and help every victimized child. That may not eliminate the violence or its root causes, but it can build a new sense of watchfulness or gatekeeping, hope, and empowerment that is essential for families (see Chapter 3) and communities (see Chapter 4) to rise up out of violence.

Identification of children exposed to violence begins with teaching everyone in all of our communities to be more aware of and better able to recognize any instance and every form of violence to which children are exposed, from the "smallest" acts of emotional or physical assault or cruelty to the kinds of violence that maim and kill.

This means educating not only children but also their caregivers and all adults in every community in this country; so that everyone invests in and sustains a commitment to be watchful and never overlook or ignore any incident in which a child is exposed to violence.

For many adults, this will be a welcome reminder and encouragement to continue to be concerned and watchful on behalf of the children in their family and community. For others, this may be an initially unsettling wake-up call, challenging their belief that violence is not really such a big problem for children generally or for the children they know and care about. If the message is communicated respectfully, consistently, and without criticism or blame, the skeptics (or those who simply have not been informed) can become the strongest advocates for this cause.

> "We must acknowledge that we are all related. When one child is hurt, we all hurt. And the opposite is true as well: When one child is protected and loved, put in a place of honor, we all benefit."
>
> **— Elsie Boudreau, LMSW, Alaska Native Justice Center**

All adults in our country need to come together to advocate for the safety of our nation's children. In doing so, we will be advocating for our nation's social capital — our future workforce, educators, innovators, and caretakers. Our ability to protect and support positive development of our social capital is critical to our success as a nation and as a world leader.

If we all get on board and personally commit ourselves to proactively protecting children from exposure to violence and psychological trauma, we will achieve a massive shift and positive evolution in our country's fundamental social norms and in the very fabric of our society. Recognizing and protecting children from exposure to violence is a way to stand up for a universal value that is a foundation for our country: Every human being deserves freedom, safety, and security. Every human being deserves to live free from violence.

This also means formally preparing professionals and childcare workers who work with and watch children and families daily to systematically look for any sign that a child has been exposed to violence or sustained psychological trauma.[41] Many of the national organizations that represent professionals who care for, educate, or are legally responsible for children have made the identification of children exposed to some forms of violence — notably physical and sexual abuse and domestic violence — a high priority; many professions have taken

> "We need routine screening and assessment to identify individuals and communities who are suffering from exposure to violence. Not every child needs intensive therapy or case management, but our healthcare system, educational institutions, and child- and youth-serving institutions and organizations need to be able to identify the children who are being hurt and are in need of help."
>
> **— Esta Soler, President of Futures Without Violence**

the additional step of making the identification of children and families exposed to violence a fundamental legal requirement and ethical duty.[42] This needs to happen in *every* profession for *every* professional or paraprofessional whose work involves children and families.

A second crucial step is to learn how to recognize when a child is exposed to violence and psychological trauma. Experts have developed thorough descriptions of the precise ways in which children are exposed to violence[1] as well as the precise ways in which they express psychological trauma after violence exposure, including behavioral, medical, and educational and learning problems.[18,43,44] These descriptions and surveys are available in non-technical terms to the general public (see, for example, https://www.ncjrs.gov/pdffiles1/ojjdp/227744.pdf) and can serve as the basis for national and local public information campaigns. They also have been converted into practical tools that professionals can use in screening and assessment to identify children who need help recovering from violence (see, for example, fact sheets from www.nctsnet.org, www.istss.org, and www.ncptsd.va.gov).

Specialized assessments have been developed and scientifically proven effective in identifying the needs of children who have been exposed to different forms of violence, such as neglect, witnessing domestic violence, being assaulted during domestic violence, sexual abuse, assault and physical abuse, trafficking, dating violence, witnessing homicide and suicide, and community violence in neighborhoods and schools and by violent gangs.[45] Professionals working with children and families must be prepared to use these tools with every child they encounter. There is no single one-size-fits-all approach to assessing and designing treatment for children exposed to violence, so professional assessors must have specialized expertise in working with the unique problems caused by different forms of sexual violence, domestic violence, and community violence. The problems experienced by children exposed to multiple types of violence, also known as "polyvictimization," raise further, correspondingly complex issues for assessment and treatment service planning.[46,47]

A third essential step is to prepare ourselves to know how to help when we see or learn about a child who is exposed to violence. Most of us know we should do something, but we do not know exactly what, nor to whom we should turn. We also do not want to make things worse by pointing out a problem and

"Since all children are required to attend school, specially trained counselors should be available to work with children to help them process what is occurring in their lives. The goal…would be to identify stress and trauma symptoms in students; identify unsafe or potentially harmful situations in the home, school, or community that are creating trauma; and broker [appropriate] community services."

— Vicki Spriggs, CEO of Texas Court Appointed Special Advocates then failing to help the victimized children become safe and recover. Every adult should know how to contact the appropriate agencies and professionals who are charged with protecting children — child protective services, law enforcement, Child Advocacy Centers, courts and attorneys, pediatric providers, community- and school-based clinics, hospitals, and school administrators — when they see or learn about a child who may need help. Creating practical pathways to help is essential to ensuring that children who are identified get the right help in a timely manner. In the next chapter, we will discuss what kinds of help are appropriate and effective, but before that can happen, we need to know how to get children help that guarantees recovery and future health. Toward that end, the task force offers the following recommendations to ensure that no child exposed to violence goes without help.

2.1 Galvanize the public to identify and respond to children exposed to violence.

The general public has a limited understanding of the extent of children's exposure to violence and its adverse impact on health, social-emotional development, and academic and economic achievement. The public has even less awareness that solutions to this crisis are within our grasp. Violence against children is not inevitable,

and healing for children is possible in the aftermath of violence if they are identified in a timely manner. An informed citizenry can advocate for higher levels of services and support from policymakers for prevention and early intervention for children exposed to violence. They can challenge the misplaced pessimism that makes violence seem like an inevitable part of growing up for some children. An informed citizenry can be the engine to advance good public policy that embraces an alternative positive norm that no child's life and future should be scarred by the fear, mistrust, and sense of failure caused by violence. Research, skills, curricula, and tool kits are available today to help an informed citizenry teach children and adults to reject violence as a tool or solution and instead to find strength and success through knowledge, responsibility, and compassion. This opens the door to a fundamental change for the better in which every organization, community, and household in our country expects that every child should grow up safe and everyone takes responsibility for making this a reality.

"We need public awareness and prevention education…. The number of…children who will be abused over the next 18 years dwarfs anything else that we're doing, and [violence and abuse become] the root causes for all the other ailments that we're throwing money at right now, bullying and childhood obesity and truancy in school."

— **Adam Rosenberg, Executive Director, Baltimore Child Abuse Center**

The White House should take the lead in developing and implementing a national public awareness campaign on the impact of children's exposure to violence, the costs of failing to intervene, and effective approaches to trauma-informed services and trauma-specific treatment for these children. Such a campaign would be suitably launched with a White House conference on children exposed to violence. Regional, state, and local community campaigns to promote, advance, and sustain public awareness of the epidemic of children exposed to violence also must be mobilized and sustained with leadership from the federal and state governments. These public awareness campaigns also require leadership from the national and local media; child and family advocacy and service organizations; faith-based organizations; grassroots community organizations; civic and business leaders and organizations; and opinion leaders in sports, entertainment, popular culture, education, politics, and the justice system.

2.2 Ensure that all children exposed to violence are identified, screened, and assessed.

Professionals and paraprofessionals working with children and families recognize the vital role they play in identifying children exposed to violence. However, most view this as an optional rather than core part of providing care and services.[48,49] *Every professional and paraprofessional who comes into contact with pregnant women and children must routinely identify children exposed to (or at risk for) violence, provide them with trauma-informed care or services, and assist them and their families in accessing evidence-based trauma-specific treatment. This includes physicians; nurses; emergency medical technicians; therapists; police officers; family and juvenile court judges and attorneys; domestic violence and sexual assault advocates; child welfare workers; sexual abuse evaluation specialists; home visitors; childcare providers; teachers; school counselors; summer camp staff; faith-based organizations; local, regional, and national youth group organizations; and the paraprofessional staff working in all of these fields.*

"Child-serving agencies should be trauma-informed, understanding the impact of trauma exposure and trauma-related problems on children and adolescents. Children and adolescents engaged in either inpatient or outpatient treatment services should be routinely screened for trauma exposure and trauma-related problems utilizing evidence-based assessment approaches."

— **Dr. Michael de Arellano, National Crime Victims Research and Treatment Center, Department of Psychiatry and Behavioral Sciences, Medical University of South Carolina**

To support and sustain this trauma-informed change, screening to identify children exposed to violence should be established as required standard by professional organizations and government licensure or certification. All child- and family-serving practice groups, agencies, and institutions should be required to train their staff to identify, screen, and assess children for exposure to violence using tools that are suitable to their professional roles and responsibilities and consistent with the standards of the service systems in which they work.

Evidence-based screening tools for identifying children exposed to traumatic events, adverse childhood experiences, and victimization are readily available from those who developed them and from technical assistance centers (see, for example, www.nctsnet.org, www.istss.org, and www.ncptsd.va.gov). However, most professionals do not know how to efficiently screen for children exposed to violence, and they are unaware of the existence of or need for using these tools.[50] Scientifically proven tools available to professionals include screening instruments for the rapid identification of children exposed to violence — such as the Juvenile Victimization Questionnaire Screening Version[51,52] and the Traumatic Events Screening Instrument for Children and Parents[53,54] — as well as screening instruments for rapid identification of each child's specific needs for trauma-informed care and trauma-specific treatment, such as the UCLA PTSD Reaction Index[55] and the Trauma Symptom Checklist for Children.[56]

2.3 Include curricula in all university undergraduate and graduate programs to ensure that every child- and family-serving professional receives training in multiple evidence-based methods for identifying and screening children for exposure to violence.

Most undergraduate education programs and pre-professional graduate-level education programs provided by universities, professional schools, colleges, and technical schools include at most one or two class sessions or seminars — and often none at all — on children exposed to violence or the impact of violence or psychological trauma on development and physical health.[57] As a result, graduates from these programs lack knowledge about the pervasiveness and the impact of exposure to violence among children from birth through adolescence.

All professionals serving children and families must be equipped with the knowledge and skills they need to recognize and address the impact of violence and psychological trauma on children. National, regional, and local professional and educational organizations, institutions, experts, and other concerned youth and adults must work with government and private-sector leaders and agencies to organize a coordinated program of pre-professional and professional education and technical assistance centers. The centers must prepare all child- and family-serving professionals to understand the scope and seriousness of the epidemic of children exposed to violence and psychological trauma and to effectively screen every child and family they serve to identify children exposed to violence.

2.4 Develop and disseminate standards in professional societies and associations for conducting comprehensive specialized assessments of children exposed to violence.

Professional societies (such as national associations of educators; law enforcement, public health, and faith-based professionals; athletic coaches; physicians; psychologists; psychiatrists; social workers; counselors; marriage and family therapists; and specialists in child abuse and domestic violence prevention and treatment) should develop, update, and disseminate standards for training and practice in specialized assessments of children exposed to violence and psychological trauma.

"The first step, if anything is going to be done usefully on a large scale, is professional recognition of the problem, whether that be in a prison, whether it be in a medical office, whether it be in the foster care system…"

— **Dr. Vincent Felitti, Co-Principal Investigator of the ACE Study; President and CEO, California Institutes of Preventive Medicine; Clinical Professor of Medicine at the University of California, San Diego; and Fellow of the American College of Physicians**

Special consideration should be given to input from and adaptation by and for special populations, including children and families of color; AIAN children and families; LGBTQ youth; and children with emotional, cognitive, and physical disabilities. Licensing boards for professionals serving children and families should adopt continuing education requirements that include children's exposure to violence and approaches to identifying these children among the topics that professionals must complete at least once in the process of renewing their licenses.

References

1. Finkelhor, D., et al. (2010). Trends in childhood violence and abuse exposure: evidence from 2 national surveys. *Archives of Pediatric and Adolescent Medicine, 164*(3), 238–42.

2. Truman, J., & Smith, E. (2012). Prevalence of violent crime among households with children, 1993–2010. *Department of Justice Bureau of Justice Statistics Special Report* 238799.

3. U.S. Department of Health and Human Services Administration for Children and Families Children's Bureau. (2011). *Child Maltreatment 2010.*

4. U.S. Bureau of Justice Statistics. (2011). *Indicators of school crime and safety 2010.*

5. U.S. Health Resources and Services Administration. (2011). *Child Health 2011.*

6. Ghosh Ippen, C., et al. (2011). Traumatic and stressful events in early childhood: can treatment help those at highest risk? *Child Abuse & Neglect, 35*(7), 504–13.

7. Cohen, J. A., Mannarino, A. P., & Iyengar, S. (2011). Community treatment of posttraumatic stress disorder for children exposed to intimate partner violence: a randomized controlled trial. *Archives of Pediatric and Adolescent Medicine, 165*(1), 16–21.

8. Wells, R., et al. (2009). Health service access across racial/ethnic groups of children in the child welfare system. *Child Abuse & Neglect, 33*(5), 282–92.

9. Kolko, D. J., et al. (2009). Community treatment of child sexual abuse: a survey of practitioners in the National Child Traumatic Stress Network. *Administration and Policy in Mental Health, 36*(1), 37–49.

10. Fairbank, J. A., & Fairbank, D. W. (2009). Epidemiology of child traumatic stress. *Current Psychiatry Reports, 11*(4), 289–95.

11. Yanos, P. T., Czaja, S. J., & Widom, C. S. (2010). A prospective examination of service use by abused and neglected children followed up into adulthood. *Psychiatric Services, 61*(8), 796–802.

12. Turner, H. A., et al. (2012). Recent victimization exposure and suicidal ideation in adolescents. *Archives of Pediatrics & Adolescent Medicine,* 1–6.

13. Finkelhor, D., & Jones, L. (2012). Trends in child maltreatment. *Lancet, 379*(9831), 2048–9; author reply 2049.

14. Finkelhor, D., Turner, H. A., & Hamby, S. (2012). Let's prevent peer victimization, not just bullying. *Child Abuse & Neglect, 36*(4), 271–4.

15. Zinzow, H. M., et al. (2009). Prevalence and mental health correlates of witnessed parental and community violence in a national sample of adolescents. *Journal of Child Psychololgy and Psychiatry, 50*(4), 441–50.

16. McCart, M. R., et al. (2007). Do urban adolescents become desensitized to community violence? Data from a national survey. *American Journal of Orthopsychiatry, 77*(3), 434–42.

17. Harpaz-Rotem, I., et al. (2007). Clinical epidemiology of urban violence: responding to children exposed to violence in ten communities. *Journal of Interpersonal Violence, 22*(11), 1479–90.

18. Harris, W. W., Lieberman, A. F., & Marans, S. (2007). In the best interests of society. *Journal of Child Psychology and Psychiatry and Allied Disciplines, 48*(3–4), 392–411.

19. Chauhan, P., & Widom, C. S. (2012). Childhood maltreatment and illicit drug use in middle adulthood: the role of neighborhood characteristics. *Development and Psychopathology, 24*(3), 723–38.

20. Widom, C. S., et al. (2012). A prospective investigation of physical health outcomes in abused and neglected children: new findings from a 30-year follow-up. *American Journal of Public Health, 102*(6), 1135–44.

21. Wilson, H. W., & Widom, C. S. (2011). Pathways from childhood abuse and neglect to HIV-risk sexual behavior in middle adulthood. *Journal of Consulting and Clinical Psychology, 79*(2), 236–46.

22. Nikulina, V., Widom, C. S., & Czaja, S. (2011). The role of childhood neglect and childhood poverty in predicting mental health, academic achievement and crime in adulthood. *American Journal of Community Psychology, 48*(3–4), 309–21.

23. Currie, J., & Widom, C. S. (2010). Long-term consequences of child abuse and neglect on adult economic well-being. *Child Maltreatment, 15*(2), 111–20.

24. Bentley, T., & Widom, C. S. (2009) A 30-year follow-up of the effects of child abuse and neglect on obesity in adulthood. *Obesity (Silver Spring), 17*(10), 1900–5.

25. Wilson, H. W., & Widom, C. S. (2010). Does physical abuse, sexual abuse, or neglect in childhood increase the likelihood of same-sex sexual relationships and cohabitation? A prospective 30-year follow-up. *Archives of Sexual Behavior, 39*(1), 63–74.

26. Gilbert, R., et al. (2009). Burden and consequences of child maltreatment in high-income countries. *Lancet, 373*(9657), 68–81.

27. Widom, C. S., Czaja, S. J., & Dutton, M. A. (2008). Childhood victimization and lifetime revictimization. *Child Abuse & Neglect, 32*(8), 785–96.

28. Melchior, M., et al. (2007). Why do children from socioeconomically disadvantaged families suffer from poor health when they reach adulthood? A life-course study. *American Journal of Epidemiology, 166*(8), 966–74.

29. Jaffee, S. R., et al. (2007). Individual, family, and neighborhood factors distinguish resilient from non-resilient maltreated children: a cumulative stressors model. *Child Abuse & Neglect, 31*(3), 231–53.

30. Loeb, T. B., et al. (2011). Associations between child sexual abuse and negative sexual experiences and revictimization among women: Does measuring severity matter? *Child Abuse & Neglect.*

31. Ullman, S. E., Najdowski, C. J., & Filipas, H. H. (2009). Child sexual abuse, post-traumatic stress disorder, and substance use: predictors of revictimization in adult sexual assault survivors. *Journal of Child Sexual Abuse, 18*(4), 367–85.

32. Lindhorst, T., et al. (2009). Mediating pathways explaining psychosocial functioning and revictimization as sequelae of parental violence among adolescent mothers. *American Journal of Orthopsychiatry, 79*(2), 181–90.

33. Fargo, J. D. (2009). Pathways to adult sexual revictimization: direct and indirect behavioral risk factors across the lifespan. *Journal of Interpersonal Violence, 24*(11), 1771–91.

34. Barnes, J. E., et al. (2009). Sexual and physical revictimization among victims of severe childhood sexual abuse. *Child Abuse & Neglect, 33*(7), 412–20.

35. Finkelhor, D., Ormrod, R. K., & Turner, H. A. (2009). The developmental epidemiology of childhood victimization. *Journal of Interpersonal Violence, 24*(5), 711–31.

36. Barker, E. D., et al. (2008). Joint development of bullying and victimization in adolescence: relations to delinquency and self-harm. *Journal of the American Academy of Child & Adolescent Psychiatry, 47*(9), 1030–8.

37. Voisin, D. R., Neilands, T. B., & Hunnicutt, S. (2011). Mechanisms linking violence exposure and school engagement among african american adolescents: examining the roles of psychological problem behaviors and gender. *American Journal of Orthopsychiatry, 81*(1), 61–71.

38. Turner, H. A., et al. (2011). Specifying type and location of peer victimization in a national sample of children and youth. *Journal of Youth and Adolescence, 40*(8), 1052–67.

39. Finkelhor, D., et al. (2011). School, police, and medical authority involvement with children who have experienced victimization. *Archives of Pediatric and Adolescent Medicine, 165*(1), 9–15.

40. Fowler, P. J., et al. (2009). Community violence: a meta-analysis on the effect of exposure and mental health outcomes of children and adolescents. *Development & Psychopathology, 21*(1), 227–59.

41. Ko, S. J., et al. (2008). Creating trauma-informed systems: Child welfare, education, first responders, health care, juvenile justice. *Professional Psychology: Research and Practice, 39*(4), 396–404.

42. Ford, J. D., & Cloitre, M. (2009). Best practices in psychotherapy for children and adolescents. In C.A. Courtois & J.D. Ford (Eds.), *Treating complex traumatic stress disorders: an evidence-based guide* (pp. 59–81). New York, NY: Guilford.

43. Cook, A., et al. (2005). Complex trauma in children and adolescents. *Psychiatric Annals, 35*(5), 390–398.

44. D'Andrea, W., et al. (2012). Understanding interpersonal trauma in children: why we need a developmentally appropriate trauma diagnosis. *American Journal of Orthopsychiatry, 82*(2), 187–200.

45. Frueh, B. C., et al. (2012). *Assessment and treatment planning for PTSD,* Hoboken, NJ: John Wiley & Sons.

46. Ford, J. D. (2011). Assessing child and adolescent complex traumatic stress reactions. *Journal of Child & Adolescent Trauma, 4*(3), 217–232.

47. Briere, J., & Spinazzola, J. (2009). *Assessment of complex posttraumatic reactions.* In C.A. Courtois & J.D. Ford (Eds.), *Treating complex traumatic stress disorders: an evidence-based guide* (pp 104–121). New York, NY: Guilford.

48. Courtois, C. A. (2008). Complex trauma, complex reactions: Assessment and treatment. *Psychological Trauma: Theory, Research, Practice, and Policy, 1*(1), 86–100.

49. Courtois, C. A., & Ford, J. D. (2012). *Treating complex trauma: A sequenced relationship-based approach.* New York, NY: Guilford.

50. Courtois, C. A., & Gold, S. (2009). The need for inclusion of psychological trauma in the professional curriculum. *Psychological Trauma, 1*(1), 3–23.

51. Finkelhor, D., et al. (2005). The Juvenile Victimization Questionnaire: reliability, validity, and national norms. *Child Abuse & Neglect, 29*(4), 383–412.

52. Finkelhor, D., et al. (2005). Measuring poly-victimization using the Juvenile Victimization Questionnaire. *Child Abuse & Neglect, 29*(11), 1297–312.

53. Daviss, W. B., et al. (2000). Predicting posttraumatic stress after hospitalization for pediatric injury. *Journal of the American Academy of Child & Adolescent Psychiatry, 39*(5), 576–583.

54. Ford, J. D., et al. (2000). Child maltreatment, other trauma exposure, and posttraumatic symptomatology among children with oppositional defiant and attention deficit hyperactivity disorders. *Child Maltreatment, 5*(3), 205–17.

55. Steinberg, A. M., et al. (2004). The University of California at Los Angeles Post-traumatic Stress Disorder Reaction Index. *Current Psychiatry Reports, 6*(2), 96–100.

56. Lanktree, C. B., et al. (2008). Multi-informant assessment of maltreated children: convergent and discriminant validity of the TSCC and TSCYC. *Child Abuse & Neglect, 32*(6), 621–5.

57. Courtois, C. A., & Gold, S. N. (2009). The need for inclusion of psychological trauma in the professional curriculum: A call to action. *Psychological Trauma: Theory, Research, Practice, and Policy, 1*(1), 3–23.

CHAPTER THREE:
Treatment and Healing of Exposure to Violence

CHAPTER THREE:
Treatment and Healing of Exposure to Violence

T he majority of children in our country who are identified as having been exposed to violence never receive services or treatments that effectively help them to stabilize themselves, regain their normal developmental trajectory, restore their safety, and heal their social and emotional wounds.[1–5] But help isn't optional or a luxury when a child's life is at stake; it's a necessity. Even when our professionals and community members are able to put in place identification and assessment protocols for children exposed to violence, if effective services and treatment are not provided, children exposed to violence and psychological trauma become locked into a struggle to survive, constantly defending themselves against both real and perceived dangers or against further abuse and neglect.[6–8] For many victimized children, living in survival mode (constantly reacting in the flight-or-fight response, even when danger is not imminent) may fundamentally alter the rest of their lives, derailing their psychological, physical, and social-emotional development. Even after the violence has ended, these child survivors suffer from severe problems with anxiety, depression, anger, grief, and posttraumatic stress that can mar their relationships and family life and limit their success in school or work, not only in childhood but throughout their adult lives. Without services or treatment, even children who appear resilient and seem to recover from exposure to violence still bear emotional scars that may lead them to experience these same problems years or decades later (see http://acestudy.org).[9–16]

Fortunately, appropriately selected *evidence-based treatments*[17–20] and services[21–23] provided in a timely manner[24] can reverse the adverse effects of violence and psychological trauma and put children back on a healthy developmental course that allows them to once again resume normal academic and social engagements and achieve a healthy and fulfilling life.[19,25–29] This chapter describes the essential features of successful treatments and services for children exposed to violence and psychological trauma, and it makes specific recommendations for how such treatments and services can be made more reliably accessible for these children.

Treatments and services for children exposed to violence actually begin before these children ever meet a therapist or counselor. Every professional who comes into contact with pregnant women and children can make a vital contribution to the recovery, healing, and safety of children exposed to (or at risk for) violence by providing them and their families with *trauma-informed care* and *trauma-specific treatments* (see Glossary for complete definitions). These professionals include tens of thousands of physicians, nurses, emergency medical technicians, therapists, police officers, family and juvenile court judges and attorneys, domestic violence and sexual assault advocates, child welfare workers, sexual abuse evaluation specialists, home visitors, child care providers, teachers, school counselors, and the paraprofessional staff working in all of these fields in every community.

"What you've seen around trauma interventions… is that we have evidence-based strategies that cut across all age groups and have the capacity to work with adoptive families, foster care families, and biological families to really change the trajectory of outcomes for young people…. The gap is that those evidence-based strategies are rarely in use across systems."

— Bryan Samuels, Commissioner, Administration on Children, Youth and Families, U.S. Department of Health and Human Services

These providers offer trauma-informed care, trauma-specific treatments, and *trauma-focused services* to children and families when, according to an expert consensus panel of providers and parents convened by the National Center for Trauma-Informed Care, their work with children "incorporate[s] a thorough understanding of the prevalence and impact of trauma, the role that violence and trauma play, and the complex paths to healing and recovery." This means providing services that avoid "re-traumatizing those who seek assistance," focus on "safety first," are based on a commitment to "do no harm, … facilitate the participation of trauma survivors in planning the environments in which they live and the services they receive, and … correspondingly ensure the safety, well-being, and meaningful involvement in systemic decisions of the providers of services and supports."

Roger Fallot and Maxine Harris, who have led the initiative for trauma-informed services in this country for more than two decades, summarize the foundation of this approach in 10 values or principles that should guide every provider of services for children and their families: preserving safety, promoting choice, building resilience, including everyone, empowering with knowledge and skills, fostering collaboration, sharing information transparently, moving beyond stereotypes, developing a support network for each client, and, of special relevance here, promoting nonviolence.[23]

When these trauma-informed care principles are applied rigorously in every encounter with children and families, providers are able to demonstrate to the children and families they work with that it is possible — and actually can change life for the better — to work together on healing the social-emotional wounds and damage to relationships caused by violence. This can inspire the child and the family to utilize the services to their fullest instead of viewing providers as uncaring or insensitive adversaries. And it can fundamentally change the entire program or organization, making it a "sanctuary" in which healing can safely occur because the safety and well-being of everyone involved — including the providers — is valued and ensured (see http://www.sanctuaryweb.com/institute.php). Trauma-informed services can transform entire provider organizations and systems as well as the lives of the countless children they serve who have been exposed to violence.

As of 2012, however, the majority of professionals and paraprofessionals who provide services to children and families have never received any preparation on how to provide trauma-informed care, trauma-specific treatments, or trauma-focused services.[30] This means that despite the best of intentions, they often will not be aware that even the youngest child or the child who appears invulnerable and resilient may have been profoundly affected by exposure to violence and ensuing psychological trauma. Professionals and paraprofessionals who provide services to children and families normally don't see the connection between a child's presentation, behaviors, and symptoms and the exposure of that child to violence.[6,8] As a result, serious misdiagnoses and service and treatment mistakes are made that not only reduce the effectiveness of the service or treatment but also may increase the possibility of further psychological trauma and a resulting increase in the risk of future exposure to violence.[19]

When these misdiagnoses and mistakes are made — even with the best of intentions — the willingness of the child and family to work collaboratively with providers often disappears. Without approaches that use trauma-informed care, providers and parents may overlook the violence and exposures to trauma and thus feel powerless to change a child's serious social-emotional problems, as they assume that these are the immutable results of "bad" genes, "bad" choices, or "bad" family and peer influences. They may fall back on providing generic advice that rarely helps and can cause further alienation or stigma, such as simply diagnosing the child with a psychiatric, behavioral, or learning problem, or telling the child that she/he should simply stop worrying and misbehaving because "the violence wasn't so bad or is over now."

Frustrated and demoralized with obtaining poor outcomes, providers may see no point in helping the child and family who were exposed to violence to access effective treatment. This is a tragic mistake that not only violates the provider's ethical duty to the child and family but also costs that child and family the opportunity to heal and recover from violence, and it ultimately costs our states and our country hundreds of millions of dollars in ineffective, unsuccessful treatments, lost educational opportunities, and inappropriate use and overutilization of medical, public health, and law enforcement services.[22]

Moving every provider and all programs and organizations that work with children and families in the direction of becoming "trauma informed" is essential to preventing children who have been exposed to violence from suffering further when they should be — and are absolutely capable of — healing the wounds of exposure to violence and psychological trauma. And, importantly, expert consensus groups in trauma-informed care have the trauma-informed care technology developed and ready for dissemination and implementation now: this includes research evidence, tool kits, training curricula, and evidence-based trauma-informed service models and trauma-specific treatments[29] (see, for example, www.nrepp.samhsa.gov, www.crimesolutions.gov, www.ojjdp.gov/mpg/, http://www.colorado.edu/cspv/blueprints).

For many children exposed to violence, obtaining trauma-focused services is just the first step in healing. These are children who need timely and evidence-based trauma-specific treatment in order to stop suffering from the symptoms that result when violence interrupts development and traps a child in survival mode. A new generation of treatments has emerged and been proven highly effective in helping children recover from the severe emotional and behavioral problems caused by exposure to violence. These are called trauma-specific treatments. Trauma-specific treatments are similar to but also different in important ways from other mental health therapies or counseling for children and adolescents.[27,29,31]

Violence requires children to become survivors in order to cope with the social-emotional impact of experiencing extreme fear, loss, powerlessness, immobilization, and ultimately betrayal at the hands of their trusted loved ones or caretakers or both. When children become focused on survival, they are likely to develop mental health and behavioral problems as a byproduct of feeling extreme fear, being torn apart from loved ones or betrayed by their loved ones, and being powerless to prevent or undo the harm that results from being immobilized and unable to escape the abuse or the witnessing of violence.

Tragically, living in a state of fear, grief, and helpless immobilization requires the child to cope by worrying and constantly watching for the next danger (a state of anxiety and hypervigilance), by giving up on the hope of a safe and happy life and having trustworthy relationships (grief and depression), by fighting back to protect them-selves and those they care about (anger and aggression), by acting without taking the time to think (impulsivity), by never letting down their guard (hyperactivity and sleep problems), and by trying to stay safe by avoiding anything that re-minds them of the violence and taking whatever they can get from life to provide some relief (inter-rupted development: substance use, high-risk or disruptive behaviors, relationship avoidance, school avoidance, delinquency, aggression against peers and authority figures). Standard treatments that do not include trauma-informed care components for these social-emotional and behavioral problems are most often not effective.[19,27] Current treatment mod-els, void of trauma-informed care components, in fact may actually exacerbate the child's symptoms, causing further harm to the child survivor of violence exposure. In order to heal and sustain recovery, these children need trauma-focused services and trauma-specific treatment.

> "If one accepts [the ACE Study] data…one recognizes that this calls for a paradigm shift in primary care medical practice, moving from our current symptom-responsive mode to the more comprehensive style that we originally conceived for primary care but clearly never attained."
>
> **— Dr. Vincent Felitti, Co-Principal Investigator of the ACE Study; President and CEO, California Institutes of Preventive Medicine; Clinical Professor of Medicine at the University of California, San Diego; and Fellow of the American College of Physicians**

Trauma-specific treatment adds three key ingredients that are missing in other standard treatments for children[24,31]:

- First, children and their parents or other caregivers are provided with down-to-earth but state-of-the art education about how violence leads to the emotional and behavioral problems that have led them to need treatment.

- Second, the child and parents/caregivers are helped to use psychological or behavioral skills that enable them to feel sufficiently safe and effective enough to be able to confidently deal with reminders or distressing memories of past violence instead of being perpetually trapped in a state of fear, anger, grief, or depression as a result of their exposure to violence.

- Third, the child and parents/caregivers are provided with ways of helping, supporting, and feeling close to one another that are designed specifically to reduce distressing reminders of trauma and memories of violence, and to enable them to feel secure in their relationship together when they encounter reminders or memories of trauma and violence.

These ingredients can be provided in multiple settings with numerous service and treatment methods that can be customized to the age, gender, and ethnocultural background of the survivors of exposure to violence and psychological trauma. Trauma-informed care allows trauma-specific treatments to be delivered effectively to help children of different ages and stages of psychological development, as well as to be acceptable to and beneficial for both girls and boys, children of different ethnocultural backgrounds and sexual identities, and children who have different physical or emotional disabilities or who have experienced different types of violence.

In order to ensure that all children exposed to violence have a genuine chance to recover and heal from the emotional, social, and physical wounds they experience, the task force proposes the following recommendations to develop, support, and sustain existing trauma-informed care, trauma-specific treatments, and trauma-focused services as the standard of care nationwide for children exposed to violence and psychological trauma.

3.1 Provide all children exposed to violence access to trauma-informed services and evidence-based trauma-specific treatment.

Trauma-specific treatments are being provided to thousands of children in this country as the result of efforts of government and foundation-funded initiatives — for example, the Administration on Children, Youth and Families' (ACYF's) Initiative Addressing Trauma Among Children and Youth[32] and the Substance Abuse and Mental Health Services Administration's National Child Traumatic Stress Network (NCTSN).[22] The ACYF initiative leverages regulations and funding from many federal programs, links resources to private initiatives sponsored by foundations such as the MacArthur and Annie E. Casey foundations and organizations such as the Child Welfare League of America with a blueprint for mandating and fully funding trauma-specific treatment for children exposed to abuse and violence. The NCTSN's more than 75 centers nationally support tens of thousands of providers in the healthcare, juvenile justice, law enforcement, child welfare, education, foster care, mental health, education, law enforcement, and military service systems with education and technical assistance on trauma-informed care, trauma-specific treatments, and trauma-focused services.

Despite these important efforts, thousands of communities and millions of children exposed to violence and psychological trauma in this country do not have access to trauma-focused or evidence-based trauma-specific treatment. Most services and treatment providers in this country who help children and their families exposed to violence and psychological trauma do not provide trauma-informed care, trauma-specific treatment, or trauma-focused services.[1,2] This must be changed. Many scientifically proven approaches to trauma-informed care, trauma-specific treatments, and trauma-focused services exist for these children, but to fully address the epidemic of children exposed to violence and psychological trauma these services and treatments must be made available in every community and to every child and family exposed to violence and psychological trauma.

In addition, the challenges of effectively providing services and treatment to these children are immense because the emotional wounds and behavioral problems caused by violence are severe. To ensure that the best possible services and treatment are received by every child exposed to violence, refinements and new models of services and treatment are still greatly needed in order to address the complex needs of this population. This requires systematic programs of research that are fully funded in order to complete studies that adequately address the complexity of the impact of violence exposure and psychological trauma.

The greatest challenge, however, is to drastically increase the number of treatment providers who have the expertise to provide trauma-specific treatment and trauma-focused services to the millions of children exposed to violence who currently do not receive trauma-informed care.[30] Meeting this important challenge will require coordinated action by government at all levels, by organizations and professionals currently providing services and treatment to children and families, and by the professional societies and educational programs that ensure that the necessary workforce is available, fully prepared, and consistently and continuously trained.

3.2 Adapt evidence-based treatments for children exposed to violence and psychological trauma to the cultural beliefs and practices of the recipients and their communities.

Treatment for the various forms of exposure to violence is not monolithic. Although the number of trauma-specific treatments (designed specifically to heal the psychological trauma that results from exposure to violence) with clinical and scientific evidence of safety and effectiveness (an "evidence base") is large and continues to grow, few have been tested and proven safe and effective specifically with children exposed to violence.[17,18,20,24,33,34] Fewer still have been adapted and targeted for children exposed to different forms of violence, although we know that different types of violence have very different adverse aftereffects and therefore require treatments adapted to address those specific aftereffects.[24,33,34] We also know that children of different developmental stages, different gender (girls versus boys), and children and families of different ethnocultural backgrounds and sexual orientations are best helped by treatments that are adapted to be consistent with their personal, family, or cultural beliefs and practices.[35–46] Federal, regional, and state funding should be dedicated to the development, testing, adaptation, and distribution of carefully adapted, evidence-based, trauma-specific treatments in order to reach the millions of children currently in need.

Unfortunately, some of the most effective treatments are very difficult or impossible to implement in remote rural or highly stressed urban areas or with children and families struggling with adversities such as homelessness or addictions. These treatments also may be partly or wholly incompatible with the cultural beliefs and practices in American Indian/Alaska Native, Asian-Pacific, African-American, Latino/Hispanic, or other ethnocultural minority communities. The problem is that many of these communities and groups have large numbers of children exposed to violence and extreme stress and psychological trauma while having few, if any, services.

Many of the existing trauma-focused services simply have not been implemented in remote and underserved locales or have not been translated or adapted to be consistent with the cultural beliefs and practices and language(s) of members of those communities. Federal and public-private partnership funding should be allocated or developed to establish national, regional, state, or tribal task forces and technical assistance centers that engage experts in violence and trauma and members of these communities (youth as well as adults) in adapting and delivering evidence-based trauma-specific treatments to underserved communities and populations, including children and families of color, Native American children and families, children and families seeking asylum or that are immigrants, homeless children and their families, lesbian-gay-bisexual-transgender-questioning sexual orientation (LGBTQ) families and children, and children and families with physical and psychological disabilities.

"The implementation of cultural relevancy and sensitivity increases the effectiveness of the practitioner, program, and treatment by giving a sense of trust, respect, humility, and identity. Recommendation: Increase support and incentives for programs that are culturally relevant, sensitive, and balanced."

— Lyle Claw, President of Changing Lives Around the World

Treatments adapted to be acceptable and effective in underserved communities remain generally inaccessible to these communities because of shortages in funding, trauma-informed professionals, and the technology needed to reach sparsely populated or otherwise inaccessible communities.[39-46] We must develop portable trauma-informed treatments, harness the power of digital technologies, and use other strategies to deliver treatment in communities that lack a social services infrastructure. The federal government, states, and private philanthropic entities all have a role to play in supporting this crucial area of work.

3.3 Develop and provide trauma-informed care in all hospital-based trauma centers and emergency departments for all children exposed to violence.

In 1998, the U.S. Department of Justice's Office for Victims of Crime (OVC), responding to an American Academy of Pediatrics report on youth violence,[47] recommended that "hospital-based counseling and prevention programs be established in medical facilities that provide services to gang violence victims." Injured youth arrive in trauma rooms bearing tattoos that read "Born to be hated, dying to be loved"; "Living is hard, dying is easy"; and "Death is nothing, but to live defeated is to die every day." Injury and death are the norm for children living in violent families and communities. The first (and often only) place where they go for any kind of help is the hospital emergency department (ED) for urgent medical care.

Professionals and staff in emergency medical services are uniquely positioned to engage children who have been exposed to violence and prolonged extreme psychological trauma who may otherwise never be identified.

At the ED, professionals and staff can provide adult mentoring, needs assessment, and immediate access to mental health services with trauma-specific treatments. Model programs now in place demonstrate how partnerships sustained between EDs and trauma clinicians; hospital-based peer educators; mental health, counseling, and social work professionals; and community organizations and public health agencies can use a trauma-informed approach to change these children's lives.[48–54] Trauma-informed ED services can empower victimized children and youth and their families with skills, support, and resources so that they can return to their communities, reject or stand strong in the face of violence, strengthen others who have been affected by violence, and contribute to building safer and healthier communities.

The National Network of Hospital-based Violence Intervention Programs (NNHVIP) is an initiative that should be expanded beyond the 20 member programs currently funded in U.S. cities to involve EDs across the country in delivering: (1) a comprehensive trauma-informed care service model for all youth and their families that begins in the ED, and (2) education to prepare emergency physicians and staff to offer trauma-informed health care, trauma-specific treatments, and trauma-focused services.

"Without intervention, hospitals discharge violently injured patients to the same violent environments where they were injured, without a prescription for staying safe and with community pressure to seek revenge. Too often, this results in a revolving door of violence, causing even more injuries, arrests, incarcerations, and, sadly, deaths."

— **Dr. Theodore Corbin, Medical Director of Healing Hurt People, and Co-Director of the Center for Nonviolence and Social Justice**

3.4 Share information and implement coordinated and adaptive approaches to improve the quality of trauma-specific treatments and trauma-focused services and their delivery by organizations and professionals across settings and disciplines to children exposed to violence.

To be effective, trauma-specific treatments and trauma-focused services must be provided in a consistent manner across the many systems, programs, and professions dedicated to helping children exposed to violence.[22] However, these services and treatments must never be conducted in a one-size-fits-all manner that fails to fit the individual needs and circumstances of diverse children and their families and communities.

Services and treatment for children exposed to violence and psychological trauma require constant adaptation in order to reach and benefit traumatized children of different ethnocultural backgrounds, types of communities (rural, urban, suburban), gender, sexual orientation, developmental stage, and types of exposure to violence. Even this brief listing — which is only the very beginning of the preliminary and essential factors that must be addressed in order to make services and treatment responsive to the needs and circumstances of the many different children, families, and communities that are affected by violence — highlights the crucial importance of developing coordinated and adaptive approaches to high-quality services and treatments across the wide range of systems and professionals working with children exposed to violence.

At the federal and state government level, funding for services and treatment for children exposed to violence and psychological trauma should include the requirement that all providers develop, implement, and demonstrate the success of collaborative planning and services or treatment delivery with other providers and programs locally and nationally.

Providers also should be required to demonstrate that their delivery of services and treatment is accomplished with a high level of quality and fidelity to evidence-based principles of trauma-informed care and to the practice guidelines of evidence-based trauma-specific treatments and trauma-focused services. A template for these requirements developed by the ACYF can serve as a useful model for these initiatives.[32]

Within the professions whose members deliver services and treatment to children exposed to violence, mechanisms need to be developed to ensure that preprofessional education, continuing professional education, and standards and guidelines for professional practice explicitly mandate the delivery of trauma-specific treatments and trauma-focused services in collaboration with professionals from other professions in a multidisciplinary approach.[30]

All national, regional, and state associations of provider organizations serving children and their families exposed to violence and psychological trauma should establish standards mandating adherence by all participating providers to government regulations and professional ethical and practice guidelines for the coordinated and collaborative delivery of trauma-specific treatments and trauma-focused services.

3.5 Provide trauma-specific treatments in all agencies and organizations serving children and families exposed to violence and psychological trauma that are suitable to their clinicians' and staff members' professional and paraprofessional roles and responsibilities.

The task force recommends that all agencies and organizations serving children and families exposed to violence and trauma undertake a systematic implementation of evidence-based trauma-specific treatments that follows the guidelines of dissemination science.[55–57] This includes providing intensive training and ongoing quality assurance monitoring and quality improvement activities to ensure that all providers of psychological, psychiatric, counseling, social work, addiction treatment, and marriage and family therapy services consistently and effectively utilize those treatments.[58,59]

The most recent Issue Brief from the Safe Start Center on Children Exposed to Violence, "Victimization and Trauma Experienced by Children and Youth: Implications for Legal Advocates" (see http://www.safestartcenter.org/pdf/issue-brief_7_courts.pdf), describes several widely available trauma-specific treatments that have been shown scientifically to be effective with young children, school-aged children, and adolescents. These and a number of other evidence-based or promising trauma-specific treatments have been identified by national organizations such as the NCTSN (www.nctsnet.org), the National Registry of Evidence-based Practices and Programs, the Department of Justice Office of Justice Programs (www.crimesolutions.gov), and the Office of Juvenile Justice and Delinquency Prevention (www.ojjdp.gov/mpg). The task force recommends that agencies and providers utilize trauma-specific treatments that have a demonstrated scientific and dissemination evidence base that is consistent with these consensus guidelines when treating children exposed to violence and the families of these children.

3.6 Ensure that every professional and advocate serving children exposed to violence and psychological trauma learns and provides trauma-informed care and trauma-focused services.

Every day, tens of thousands of children who have been exposed to violence receive treatment across the nation in hospitals, clinics, child guidance and counseling centers, community mental health centers, therapeutic group homes and residential programs, school-based clinics, or the offices of private practitioners.[60] They are treated by professionals from many disciplines, including psychologists, psychiatrists, social workers, mental health counselors, substance abuse counselors, school counselors, in-home therapists, family therapists, and psychiatric nurses. These treatment providers work in every setting in which children spend their days — schools, youth centers, even the family's home — as well as where children receive care — clinics, hospitals, counseling centers, child protective services offices, homeless shelters, and domestic violence programs — and where they encounter the legal system: on the street with police officers, in the courts, and in probation and detention centers. The task force recommends that each of these treatment providers in all of these settings develops expertise in helping the children whom they treat to recover from violence and psychological trauma by providing trauma-informed care and trauma-focused services.

3.7 Grow and sustain an adequate workforce of trauma-informed service providers, with particular attention paid to the recruitment, training, and retention of culturally diverse providers.

In order to support the recommended mandate for all child- and family-serving treatment providers to use trauma-informed approaches to their services and to employ trauma-specific treatment if they conduct psychosocial treatment, the task force recommends that a national effort be undertaken by professional and educational organizations and institutions in order to build a workforce of sufficient size and capacity to achieve this goal. There is a significant but addressable gap between the overall number of providers of trauma-informed care services and the large number of children and families exposed to violence and psychological trauma who do not, or cannot, access evidence-based treatment services. However, there are hundreds of graduate and undergraduate professional education programs in colleges, universities, medical and law schools, freestanding programs of higher education, and technical or vocational schools where tens of thousands of students each year are being prepared for careers in the healthcare and human services, public health, child welfare, and criminal justice systems that serve children and families. *Courses in trauma-informed care and trauma-focused services should be a required part of the curriculum for each program and all students.*[30]

Continuing technical and professional training as well as certification is required or recommended for providers in all of these systems, and there are thousands of continuing education courses offered online, at training sites in most communities, and in regional and national conventions and meetings. Courses in trauma-informed care and trauma-focused services should be required for all child- and family-serving providers as a part of their continuing education and recertification. In addition, providers who supervise other professionals or staff should be provided with training and required to regularly update their skills and knowledge in trauma-informed supervision and in ensuring that supervisees provide trauma-informed services to all children exposed to violence and the families of these children.

Additionally, there is a substantial gap between the small number of service providers who are from minority ethnocultural groups and the large number of children and their families exposed to violence who are of minority backgrounds.[61] Professions and technical vocations that serve children and their families exposed to violence should monitor, document, and take steps to increase the ethnocultural diversity of their membership.[62]

"Augment the workforce of tribal people to become mental health professionals with an early childhood specialty by providing tuition supports, student loan forgiveness, and promotion of mental health professions by the Indian Health Service."

— **Maria Brock, LISW, Tribal Home Visiting Project Director, Native American Professional Parent Resources, Inc.**

It is crucial that our country, at multiple levels, increase and support access to providers for children and families of ethnocultural minority backgrounds.[61] *It is also crucial to develop and support the education and advancement of service providers who share the same ethnocultural heritage, practices, and languages of the minority service recipients. It is essential that all providers serving children and their families who are exposed to violence and psychological trauma be respectful of, and take responsibility for becoming informed about, the language, values, beliefs, and both cultural and traumatic history of every client whom they serve.*[63]

This will require substantial investment by a cross section of strategic funders and providers of technical and professional training in order to recruit and successfully prepare students of diverse ethnocultural backgrounds. Equally important, educational and training programs must develop socially just protocols that will systematically recruit students from racial, ethnic, and cultural minority groups to build a workforce of treatment providers that reflects the population of children and families exposed to violence and psychological trauma.

3.8 Ensure that professional societies develop, adopt, disseminate, and implement principles, practices, and standards for comprehensive evidence-based treatment of children exposed to violence or psychological trauma.

Every professional society in the United States and their international partners representing providers of services for children exposed to violence recognize that evidence-based treatment is the standard for both ethical and effective medical and psychological services, but few have developed, formally adopted, and disseminated to their memberships specific principles, practice guidelines, and standards for evidence-based trauma-informed care, trauma-specific treatments, and trauma-focused services for violence-exposed children and their families.

Sections or divisions within major professional societies, such as the American Psychological Association's Division of Trauma Psychology, and specialized cross-disciplinary professional societies focused on treatment of traumatized children and adults, such as the International Society for Traumatic Stress Studies, the International Society for the Study of Trauma and Dissociation, and the American Professional Society on the Abuse of Children, have developed, adopted, and disseminated detailed practice standards and guidelines that should serve as examples for all professional societies and their members that provide services to children and their families exposed to violence.

A federally funded network (or public-private partnership) of regional clearinghouses and resource centers on evidence-based treatment for children and families exposed to violence and psychological trauma should be established in collaboration with the national centers of excellence on children exposed to violence proposed in Chapter 1's recommendations.

This network of clearinghouses and resource centers must coordinate closely with the NCTSN and other federally funded networks and technical assistance centers engaged in educating, training, and disseminating information about evidence-based trauma-informed care, trauma-specific treatments, and trauma-focused services.

3.9 Provide research funding to continue the clinical and scientific development of increasingly effective evidence-based treatments for children exposed to violence.

It is expensive, but absolutely necessary, to develop and test new evidence-based practices and treatments.[44] We must now develop research and funding infrastructures that encourage the creation and testing of innovative practices and programs that allow for the evolution of increasingly effective new evidence-based treatments.

Federal government funding through the departments of Health and Human Services, Education, Justice, and Defense for research on treatments for children exposed to violence and psychological trauma must be either maintained without reductions or increased. To fully achieve the greatly needed advancements in this field, state and federal government agency partnerships, and public and private foundation and organization partnerships, must be encouraged and assisted in developing funding programs specifically designed to sponsor continued clinical and scientific innovations in the treatment of children exposed to violence.

Additionally, state and federal government agency partnerships, and public and private foundation and organization partnerships, must be encouraged and assisted in developing funding programs specifically designed to partner with higher educational institutions in their role as trainers of service providers in evidence-based trauma-informed care, trauma-specific treatments, and trauma-focused services.

"While there is some evidence for the use of evidence-based treatments among ethnic minority youth, these findings are very preliminary.… More work is necessary to evaluate the efficacy of additional interventions, including those for violence-exposed youth, with children from a broader range of cultural groups."

— Dr. Michael de Arellano, National Crime Victims Research and Treatment Center, Department of Psychiatry and Behavioral Sciences, Medical University of South Carolina

3.10 Provide individuals who conduct services and treatment for children exposed to violence with workforce protection to prepare them for the personal impact of this work and to assist them in maintaining a safe and healthy workplace.

Providing evidence-based trauma-informed care, trauma-specific treatments, and trauma-focused services brings professionals face-to-face with the pain, suffering, betrayal, and isolation that children and families experience when they are victimized by violence.[64] For most providers, this is highly stressful and requires careful attention to maintaining their own emotional and physical health and professional and personal support systems. Some professionals, often (but not only) those who have experienced violence themselves, can experience deep emotional distress that requires personal healing for themselves. These emotional wounds are not caused by the children and families they treat — with rare exceptions — but are old wounds that are inadvertently opened by the intense emotional work involved in providing evidence-based trauma-informed care, trauma-specific treatments, and trauma-focused services. These wounded healers can nevertheless be highly effective because they have a personal understanding of trauma and a unique degree of empathy for the wounded children and families they treat.

Graduate professional training programs often prepare their students to take proactive steps to maintain their emotional health and heal emotional wounds that emerge in the course of providing treatment, and this should be mandatory in all professional and paraprofessional education programs. However, in most settings where treatment is provided to children who are exposed to violence and psychological trauma, little or no time, funding, or therapeutic services or supervision is provided to help professionals (and also affected paraprofessionals) to care for themselves or to recognize and deal with the inevitable emotional impact of vicarious exposure to violence and psychological trauma.

Federal, state, and local funding for organizations, agencies, and contract professionals who treat children exposed to violence and psychological trauma, and public and private health insurance that covers this treatment, should designate funds on an ongoing basis to cover financial costs to programs and practitioners of therapeutic supervision and support services for all professionals treating children exposed to violence and psychological trauma.

3.11   Incentivize healthcare providers and insurance providers to reimburse trauma-focused services and trauma-specific treatment.

Even evidence-based treatments will fail if poorly implemented.[56,57,65] Treatment providers must be prepared in their professional education and required and incentivized in their practices to routinely monitor and report on the quality, reach, and outcomes of the evidence-based or evidence-informed services they provide using established methods for doing so. And the most promising new treatments for children exposed to violence and psychological trauma must be subject to rigorous evaluations to test their effectiveness.[19]

The Centers for Medicare & Medicaid Services should work with consumers and professional societies and experts to design (and provide technical support to) provider systems in order to encourage rigorous ongoing evaluation of the delivery, quality, and effectiveness of the implementation of trauma-informed care, trauma-specific treatments, and trauma-focused services for children exposed to violence.

National professional standards established by a partnership of the federal government and all major child- and family-serving professions should be used as benchmarks for evaluations of delivery and outcomes of evidence-based trauma-specific treatments and trauma-focused services for children and their families exposed to violence and psychological trauma.

Federal agencies should also fund and facilitate impact evaluations that can reveal the strengths, weaknesses, and ultimate merits of new treatment programs and lead to timely improvements. Government should expand state block grants and Medicaid and CHIP (Children's Health Insurance Program) programs to reimburse for trauma-informed care, trauma-specific treatments, and trauma-focused services.

Treatment is more successful when all of the professionals involved in a child's life share information as appropriate and coordinate services. Child- and family-serving professionals from the mental health, substance abuse, child welfare, juvenile justice, education, and social services systems often simultaneously provide services for children exposed to violence and their families. However, collaboration across systems and providers typically is done on an ad hoc rather than systematic basis, leading to fragmented, incomplete, inefficient, and ineffective services that also result in unnecessary costs and unnecessary re-traumatization.

Professional policy institutes should be mandated and funded by federal and state legislation to bring together professional experts, advocates, and affected children and families in order to design and set benchmarks for the implementation and monitoring of standards for cross-system collaboration in services for children and their families exposed to violence and psychological trauma.

References

1. U.S. Health Resources and Services Administration, *Child Health 2011.*

2. U.S. Department of Health and Human Services Administration for Children and Families Children's Bureau, *Child Maltreatment 2010.*

3. Yanos, P. T., Czaja, S. J., & Widom, C. S. (2010). A prospective examination of service use by abused and neglected children followed up into adulthood. *Psychiatric Services, 61*(8), 796–802.

4. Wells, R., et al. (2009). Health service access across racial/ethnic groups of children in the child welfare system. *Child Abuse & Neglect, 33*(5), 282–92.

5. Kolko, D. J., et al. (2009). Community treatment of child sexual abuse: a survey of practitioners in the National Child Traumatic Stress Network. *Administration and Policy in Mental Health, 36*(1), 37–49.

6. Harris, W. W., Lieberman, A. F., & Marans, S. (2007). In the best interests of society. *Journal of Child Psychology and Psychiatry and Allied Disciplines, 48*(3–4), 392–411.

7. Ford, J. D. (2009). Neurobiological and developmental research: clinical implications. In C. A. Courtois & J. D. Ford (Eds.), *Treating complex traumatic stress disorders: an evidence-based guide* (pp.31–58). New York, NY: Guilford Press.

8. Lieberman, A. F. (2007). Ghosts and angels: Intergenerational patterns in the transmission and treatment of the traumatic sequelae of domestic violence. *Infant Mental Health Journal, 28*(4), 422–439.

9. Anda, R. F., et al. (2006). The enduring effects of abuse and related adverse experiences in childhood: A convergence of evidence from neurobiology and epidemiology. *European Archives of Psychiatry and Clinical Neuroscience, 256*(3), 174–86.

10. Felitti, V. J., et al. (1998). Relationship of childhood abuse and household dysfunction to many of the leading causes of death in adults. The Adverse Childhood Experiences (ACE) Study. *American Journal of Preventive Medicine, 14*(4), 245–58.

11. Perepletchikova, F., & Kaufman, J. (2010). Emotional and behavioral sequelae of childhood maltreatment. *Current Opinion in Pediatrics, 22*(5), 610–5.

12. Fargo, J. D. (2009). Pathways to adult sexual revictimization: direct and indirect behavioral risk factors across the lifespan. *Journal of Interpersonal Violence, 24*(11), 1771–91.

13. Barnes, J. E., et al. (2009). Sexual and physical revictimization among victims of severe childhood sexual abuse. *Child Abuse & Neglect, 33*(7), 412–20.

14. Rheingold, A. A., et al. (2012). Prevalence and mental health outcomes of homicide survivors in a representative US sample of adolescents: data from the 2005 National Survey of Adolescents. *Journal of Child Psychology and Psychiatry and Allied Disciplines, 53*(6), 687–94.

15. Zinzow, H. M., et al. (2012). Prevalence and risk of psychiatric disorders as a function of variant rape histories: results from a national survey of women. *Social Psychiatry and Psychiatric Epidemiology, 47*(6), 893–902.

16. McCauley, J. L., et al. (1997). Clinical characteristics of women with a history of childhood abuse: Unhealed wounds. *Journal of the American Medical Association, 277*(17), 1362–1368.

17. Cohen, J. A., et al. (2012). Trauma-focused CBT for youth with complex trauma. *Child Abuse & Neglect, 36*(6), 528–41.

18. Cohen, J. A., Mannarino, A. P., & Murray, L. K. (2011). Trauma-focused CBT for youth who experience ongoing traumas. *Child Abuse & Neglect, 35*(8), 637–46.

19. Ford, J. D., & Cloitre, M. (2009). Best practices in psychotherapy for children and adolescents. In C. A. Courtois & J. D. Ford (Eds.), *Treating complex traumatic stress disorders: an evidence-based guide* (pp. 59–81). New York, NY: Guilford.

20. Ghosh Ippen, C., et al. (2011). Traumatic and stressful events in early childhood: can treatment help those at highest risk? *Child Abuse & Neglect, 35*(7), 504–13.

21. Marrow, M., et al. (2012). The value of implementing TARGET within a trauma-informed juvenile justice setting. *Journal of Child & Adolescent Trauma, 5*, 257–270.

22. Ko, S. J., et al. (2008). Creating trauma-informed systems: Child welfare, education, first responders, health care, juvenile justice. *Professional Psychology: Research and Practice, 39*(4), 396–404.

23. Fallot, R., & Harris, M. (2008). Trauma-informed services. In G. Reyes, J.D. Elhai, & J. Ford (Eds.), *The Encyclopedia of Psychological Trauma* (pp. 660–662). Hoboken, NJ: Wiley.

24. Berkowitz, S. J., Stover, C. S., & Marans, S. R. (2011). The Child and Family Traumatic Stress Intervention: secondary prevention for youth at risk of developing PTSD. *Journal of Child Psychology and Psychiatry, 52*(6), 676–85.

25. Pilnik, L., & Kendall, J. (2012). Victimization and trauma experienced by children and youth: Implications for legal advocates. *Safe Start Center Series on Children Exposed to Violence, 7.*

26. Vickerman, K. A., & Margolin, G. (2007). Posttraumatic stress in children and adolescents exposed to family violence: II. Treatment. *Professional Psychology: Research and Practice, 38*(6), 620–628.

27. Harvey, S. T., & Taylor, J. E. (2010). A meta-analysis of the effects of psychotherapy with sexually abused children and adolescents. *Clinical Psychology Review, 30*(5), 517–35.

28. Saxe, G., MacDonald, H., & Ellis, H. (2007). Psychosocial approaches for children with PTSD. In E. B. Foa, et al. (Eds.), *Handbook of PTSD: Science and practice* (pp.359–375). New York, NY: Guilford.

29. Ford, J. D., and Courtois, C. A. (Eds.). (2013). *Treating complex traumatic stress disorders in children and adolescents: Scientific foundations and therapeutic models.* New York, NY: Guilford.

30. Courtois, C. A., & Gold, S. (2009). The need for inclusion of psychological trauma in the professional curriculum. *Psychological Trauma, 1*(1), 3–23.

31. Cohen, J. A., & Mannarino, A. P. (2010). Psychotherapeutic options for traumatized children. *Current Opinion in Pediatrics, 22*(5), 605–9.

32. Samuels, B. (2012). *Promoting Social and Emotional Well-Being for Children and Youth Receiving Child Welfare Services. 2012.*

33. Cohen, J. A., Mannarino, A. P., & Iyengar, S. (2011). Community treatment of posttraumatic stress disorder for children exposed to intimate partner violence: a randomized controlled trial. *Archives of Pediatric and Adolescent Medicine, 165*(1), 16–21.

34. Ford, J. D., et al. (2012). Randomized trial comparison of emotion regulation and relational psychotherapies for PTSD with girls involved in delinquency. *Journal of Clinical Child Adolescent Psychology, 41*(1), 27–37.

35. Ford, J. D. (2008). Trauma, posttraumatic stress disorder, and ethnoracial minorities: Toward diversity and cultural competence in principles and practices. *Clinical Psychology: Science and Practice, 15*(1), 62–67.

36. Hwang, W. C. (2006). The psychotherapy adaptation and modification framework – Application to Asian Americans. *American Psychologist, 61*(7), 702–715.

37. Andres-Hyman, R. C., et al. (2006). Culture and clinical practice: Recommendations for working with Puerto Ricans and other Latinas(os) in the United States. *Professional Psychology: Research and Practice, 37*(6), 694–701.

38. Kataoka, S. H., et al. (2003). A school-based mental health program for traumatized Latino immigrant children. *Journal of the American Academy of Child & Adolescent Psychiatry, 42*(3), 311–318.

39. Sareen, J., et al. (2007). Perceived barriers to mental health service utilization in the United States, Ontario, and the Netherlands. *Psychiatric Services, 58*(3), 357–64.

40. Borntrager, C. F., et al. (2009). Provider attitudes toward evidence-based practices: are the concerns with the evidence or with the manuals? *Psychiatric Services, 60*(5), 677–81.

41. Chorpita, B. F., Daleiden, E. L. (2009). Mapping evidence-based treatments for children and adolescents: application of the distillation and matching model to 615 treatments from 322 randomized trials. *Journal of Consulting and Clinical Psychology, 77*(3), 566–79.

42. Rodriguez, M., et al. (2009). Intimate partner violence and barriers to mental health care for ethnically diverse populations of women. *Trauma, Violence, & Abuse, 10*(4), 358–74.

43. Ahmed, A. T., & McCaw, B. R. (2010). Mental health services utilization among women experiencing intimate partner violence. *American Journal of Managed Care, 16*(10), 731–8.

44. Chorpita, B. F., Bernstein, A., & Daleiden, E. L. (2011). Empirically guided coordination of multiple evidence-based treatments: an illustration of relevance mapping in children's mental health services. *Journal of Consulting and Clinical Psychology, 79*(4), 470–80.

45. Williams, D. R., & Marks, J. (2012). Community development efforts offer a major opportunity to advance Americans' health. *Health Affairs, 30*(11), 2052–5.

46. Williams, D. R., McClellan, M. B., & Rivlin, A. M. (2012). Beyond the affordable care act: achieving real improvements in Americans' health. *Health Affairs, 29*(8), 1481–8.

47. American Academy of Pediatrics Task Force on Violence. (1999). The role of the pediatrician in youth violence prevention in clinical practice and at the community level. *Pediatrics, 103*(1), 173–181.

48. Berkowitz, S. J., & Marans, S. (2003). The traumatized child at the emergency department. *Child and Adolescent Psychiatric Clinics of North America, 12*(4), 763–77.

49. MacMillan, H. L., et al. (2009). Screening for intimate partner violence in health care settings: a randomized trial. *Journal of the American Medical Association, 302*(5), 493–501.

50. Shepherd, J. (2007). Preventing alcohol-related violence: a public health approach. *Criminal Behaviour and Mental Health, 17*(4), 250–64.

51. Swahn, M. H., & Potter, L. B. (2001). Factors associated with the medical severity of suicide attempts in youths and young adults. *Suicide and Life-Threatening Behavior, 32*(1 Suppl), 21–9.

52. Zatzick, D. F., et al. (2006). Predicting posttraumatic stress symptoms longitudinally in a representative sample of hospitalized injured adolescents. *Journal of the American Academy of Child & Adolescent Psychiatry, 45*(10), 1188–95.

53. Daviss, W. B., et al. (2000). Predicting posttraumatic stress after hospitalization for pediatric injury. *Journal of the American Academy of Child & Adolescent Psychiatry, 39*(5), 576–583.

54. Daviss, W. B., et al. (2000). Acute stress disorder symptomatology during hospitalization for pediatric injury. *Journal of the American Academy of Child & Adolescent Psychiatry, 39*(5), 569–575.

55. Sexton, T. L., et al. (2010). Action brief: future directions in the implementation of evidence based treatment and practices in child and adolescent mental health. *Administration and Policy in Mental Health, 37*(1–2), 132–4.

56. Proctor, E. K., et al. (2009). Implementation research in mental health services: an emerging science with conceptual, methodological, and training challenges. *Administration and Policy in Mental Health, 36*(1), 24–34.

57. Schoenwald, S. K., et al. (2008). A survey of the infrastructure for children's mental health services: implications for the implementation of empirically supported treatments (ESTs). *Administration and Policy in Mental Health, 35*(1–2), 84–97.

58. Henggeler, S. W., et al. (2008). Promoting the implementation of an evidence-based intervention for adolescent marijuana abuse in community settings: testing the use of intensive quality assurance. *Journal of Clinical Child and Adolescent Psychology, 37*(3), 682–9.

59. Lang, J. M., Ford, J. D., & Fitzgerald, M. M. (2011). An algorithm for determining use of trauma-focused cognitive-behavioral therapy. *Psychotherapy, 47*(4), 554–69.

60. Fairbank, J. A., & Fairbank, D. W. (2009). Epidemiology of child traumatic stress. *Current Psychiatry Reports, 11*(4), 289–95.

61. Kataoka, S. H., Zhang, L., & Wells, K. B. (2002). Unmet need for mental health care among U.S. children: variation by ethnicity and insurance status. *American Journal of Psychiatry, 159*(9), 1548–55.

62. Pole, N., Gone, J. P., & Kulkarni, M. (2008). Posttraumatic stress disorder among ethnoracial minorities in the United States. *Clinical Psychology: Science and Practice, 15*(1), 35–61.

63. Brown, L. (2009). Cultural competence. In C. A. Courtois & J. D. Ford (Eds.), *Treatment of complex traumatic stress disorders* (pp. 166–182). New York, NY: Guilford.

64. Pearlman, L. A., & Caringi, J. (2009). Living and working self-reflectively to address vicarious trauma. In C. A. Courtois and J. D. Ford (Eds.), *Treating complex traumatic stress disorders: an evidence-based guide* (pp. 202–222). New York, NY: Guilford Press.

65. Chorpita, B. F., & Regan, J. (2009). Dissemination of effective mental health treatment procedures: Maximizing the return on a significant investment. *Behaviour Research and Therapy, 47*(11), 990–3.

CHAPTER FOUR:
Creating Safe and Nurturing Homes

CHAPTER FOUR:
Creating Safe and Nurturing Homes

E ach year, millions of children in this country are exposed to violence and abuse in their homes and families. This exposure can take many forms, including experiencing physical and sexual abuse; witnessing domestic violence (also known as intimate partner violence) and violence among family members, including siblings, grandparents, and extended family; and losing family members due to lethal or criminal violence.

The National Survey of Children's Exposure to Violence, supported by the Department of Justice Office of Juvenile Justice and Delinquency Prevention and the Centers for Disease Control and Prevention, provides scientific evidence that millions of children in this country are exposed to violence in their families each year. More than 1 in 9 U.S. children were exposed to some form of family violence in the past year, including 1 in 15 exposed to intimate partner violence between their parents or between a parent and that parent's partner. Overall, more than one in every four children have been exposed to at least one form of family violence before they reach adolescence. By the time children have grown into adolescence — specifically, between the ages of 14 to 17 years old — almost half (40%) of youths in the United States have been exposed to family violence. Exposure to violence in the family is not a rare event that happens to only a few highly vulnerable children. It is a crisis that can happen to any child, and it happens too often to far too many children.

Children who are exposed to violence in their homes often experience multiple forms of violence concurrently and over the course of their lives.[1] Child sexual abuse often occurs alongside physical assault and other forms of maltreatment,[2] and tragically, children are most often sexually abused by family members or family friends they know and trust.[3] Research tells us that in the United States, one in four girls and one in six boys are sexually abused before their 18th birthdays.[4]

Each form of violence in the family or home or through close relationships has distinct adverse effects on children. To preserve and support safe and nurturing homes for all children, we must understand how violence of different types harms children when it happens in the home or family.

Family violence refers to any form of violence by or toward members of a family. Children may be direct victims of physical assault or sexual abuse, or they may witness domestic violence. These children develop levels of anxiety and fear that are much higher than normal and experience consistent difficulties in learning how to manage anger and other forms of emotional distress.[5–12] As a result, they may have problems in school, difficulty making and keeping friends, and significant challenges feeling safe and loved in their families even when the violence has stopped. As they grow into adolescence and adulthood, children who were victims of violence in their homes are more likely than others to have problems with impulsive behavior; addictions; depression; conflict and emotional detachment in their relationships with peers, family members, and primary partners; and difficulties in school and at work.[11,13–33]

Sexual abuse by caregivers has been found to place children at risk for additional sexual and physical victimization; homelessness; and involvement with peers who use or sell drugs, drop out of school, steal, and engage in other delinquent behaviors.[5,34,35] Nightmares, anxiety, distrust, isolation, problems expressing feelings, dissociation, medical problems, substance abuse, self-harm, and difficulty concentrating are just some of the effects of child sexual abuse.[6,7,28,36–57] One of the most immediate consequences of child sexual abuse is the emergence of serious problems at school, including sharply deteriorating grades and performance, behavior problems, and an attitude of apparent disinterest in learning or abiding by rules in school (this has been described as a disinvestment in education).[2,15,58] In addition, sexual abuse is often cited as a reason children and adolescents run away from home.[28,55–57,59]

The effects of child sexual abuse can persist into and throughout adulthood. Multiple studies show that childhood sexual abuse can put children at significant risk for a wide range of medical, psychological, behavioral, social, economic, legal, and other struggles over their lifetimes. Research also shows that childhood sexual abuse often leads to commercial sexual exploitation and substance abuse.[6,36,38,41,60–69] Several studies have found that child sexual abuse is a common occurrence for homeless women, men, and adolescents and that sexually abused children or adolescents often are re-victimized later in life.[24,43,70–92]

Children also are exposed to violence as witnesses to domestic violence — a pattern of assaultive and coercive behaviors — including physical, sexual, and emotional abuse that an adult uses against an intimate partner. This pattern of violence and abuse typically is used as a tactic by men against their female partners and sometimes against their children,[93–95] and it can also arise in same-sex relationships. Witnessing domestic violence can destroy a child's core sense of security and trust and can create deep feelings of helplessness, guilt, and shame when children cannot make the violence stop or protect the non-offending parent. Children raised in homes with domestic violence are at risk for becoming either victims or perpetrators of violence in intimate and family relationships as adults.[80,84,89,96–100] Witnessing domestic violence has a profound impact on a child's view of intimate relationships, making future relationships seem untrustworthy and undependable at best and like dangerous struggles at worst. This perception can lead to a lifetime of avoidance of intimacy or conflict in intimate relationships, which is detrimental not only to the child but also to the child's extended family and future generations.

Tragically, these varied forms of family violence often occur together. Scientific studies have repeatedly demonstrated that children who witness domestic violence are more likely than other children to be physically or sexually abused and that children who are abused or neglected also are at high risk for witnessing intimate partner or other forms of violence within their families.[1,101,102] Children whose parents or other primary caregivers are impaired by untreated mental health disorders, substance abuse, or legal problems also have been shown to be at significant risk for abuse, neglect, and witnessing domestic violence.[12,103–116] Therefore, any form of exposure to violence in a family should be considered a warning sign that the children in that family are at high risk. These children should be assessed for all of the types of violence to which they may be exposed. Too often it is assumed that a child has been exposed to only one or a few types of violence when they may actually be polyvictims and in need of protection or healing from exposure to several types of violence in their families and communities (see Chapter 5).

Every form of family violence can cause severe disruption in or loss of essential relationships. This is particularly true when violence is lethal, resulting in the permanent loss of a family member or loved one. An estimated 3,500–4,000 children witness *fatal family violence* each year in this country.[117–120] Children in families in which one parent kills another parent suffer unique and severe trauma.[121–125] The surviving children may lack official status as a victim. Although much has been learned about how to help these children (including evidence-based trauma-specific therapy for complicated grief; trauma-informed support for grief and mourning; and participation in funerals, grave visitation, and social gatherings to remember the homicide victim),

"The event that affected me the most was when my sister was shot and killed by her son's father while her three children (ages 9 months, 2, and 5) and other nieces and nephews watched. On March 24, 2007, I lost my sister to domestic violence."

— Aisha Stubbs, Struggling Youth Into Successful Adults

they are not typically identified or served. Children who survive fatal family violence are often forgotten in the aftermath of such tragedies. And when they are remembered, attention to the surviving children may be focused on the few who provide witness testimony. The traumatic grief these children experience can remain an unresolved emotional injury for the rest of their lives,[126–128] because it compromises their core sense of psychological security — a sense of emotional well-being that is crucial for every child's healthy development. If caregivers or family members inflict violence, they become sources of fear and anger for children. If caregivers or family members are victims of violence in the home, this also impacts children. Simply put, the well-being of a child is inextricably linked to the well-being of the adults in his or her life, and when these adults harm or kill one another, the child is left with a deep sense of betrayal that quickly erodes a foundation for trusting the surviving parent or any caregiver or intimate partner.

Moving forward, we need to deepen our understanding about the loss of a core sense of security and the rapid progression of developmental risks that exposure to family violence poses to children and adolescents. We also need to improve our knowledge about how prevention, intervention, and resilience can be integrated to improve life success for children victimized by and exposed to family violence. Most urgently, we need to re-energize our prevention efforts, public service and awareness campaigns, and other critical teaching initiatives that build on and enhance each family's, parent's, and caregiver's knowledge and ability to protect and nurture children through warm, supportive, loving, and nonviolent relationships.

Recognizing that the best place for children and adolescents to not just survive but thrive is in families that keep them safe and nurture their development, the task force offers the following recommendations:

4.1 Expand access to home visiting services for families with children who are exposed to violence, focusing on safety and referral to services.

Help for families experiencing or at risk for violence is most accessible when it is brought directly to the family in their own home. Home visitation programs bring professionals, such as nurses, social workers, family educators, and mental health professionals, to meet regularly in the home to help parents and children develop ways of communicating together, managing the basic routines that are essential to daily family life and healthy growth, and participating in medical and mental health treatment. These home visiting programs show considerable promise in reducing child abuse and promoting healthy development of children in families that are at risk due to poverty and lack of access to resources.[129–132] However, with one recent exception,[133] home visiting programs have not been found to reduce family or domestic violence or to help children in violent or abusive families heal and recover.[134] This may be for many reasons, but a crucial limitation in most home visiting interventions is that the staff lack specialized training on identifying children who have been exposed to violence and assisting in their recovery.[135,136]

The task force recommends that home visitation programs be expanded to address the dynamics of child abuse and domestic violence and to provide evidence-based safety planning for parents, including pregnant mothers who are victims of domestic violence and sexual assault. It also recommends that home visitation programs be designed to strengthen the connections between children and their non-offending and protective parents, recognizing that a child's well-being is inextricably linked to the well-being of parents and caregivers and that maintaining a strong connection between parent and child is a strategy for healing and resilience.[137]

"Early childhood, and particularly the perinatal phase of life, represents a wholly unique and consequential window of both risk and opportunity when we consider policies and strategies to reduce crime, protect children from violence and harm, and strive to preserve health and strengthen the wider social fabric."

— Dr. Neil Guterman, Mose and Sylvia Firestone Professor, Director of the Beatrice Cummings Mayer Program in Violence Prevention, and Dean of the School of Social Service Administration, University of Chicago

Home visiting programs and programs that specialize in providing services to children and families experiencing domestic violence should collaborate to devise new strategies that integrate home visiting with trauma-specific interventions.[138] In addition, home visitors should be trained to identify children who have been exposed to traumatic abuse, neglect, domestic violence, or other forms of family violence, as well as parents and caregivers who may be impaired because they were sexually abused or exposed to violence as children themselves.

4.2 Increase collaborative responses by police, mental health providers, domestic violence advocates, child protective service workers, and court personnel for women and children who are victimized by intimate partner violence.

Every day, law enforcement agencies around the country respond to calls for service that are initiated by intimate partner violence and domestic disturbances. In fact, such calls constitute 30 to 40 percent of all police calls for service nationally. When trained and partnered with other service providers, police are perfectly placed to identify children who are traumatized by domestic violence, assess immediate and future threats, and follow up with visits to evaluate victims' safety and other concerns. This kind of engagement delivers a message to victims that they are not alone in facing the traumatic aftermath of intimate partner violence or in confronting the threat of further violence. In addition, follow-up visits from police and their partners, when accepted by victims, may also demonstrate to perpetrators that their abusive behavior is no longer hidden and cannot continue in the shadows of the family's isolation. As a result, women are more likely to reach out to law enforcement before violence escalates and to feel supported and strengthened as they move forward in addressing their families' needs for safety, security, and psychological recovery.[139–141] Effective collaborative strategies for responding to domestic violence must involve and capitalize on the role of law enforcement.

4.3 Ensure that parents who are victims of domestic violence have access to services and counseling that help them protect and care for their children.

Victims of domestic violence need access to resources that can help them safely explore how to protect themselves and their children and how to stabilize the family once the violence has subsided.[93,142,143] Substantial evidence shows that mothers who have been battered by their partners develop symptoms of post-traumatic stress, depression, and anxiety.[106,144–151] Research is providing growing evidence that children and parents benefit from relationship-based interventions that help them communicate with each other about the violence they endured.[152–154] These interventions give children the tools to show their parents how frightening the experience of violence was for them, and they help parents understand their children's experience of violence and learn strategies to recover from their own traumatic stress reactions. Parents who have experienced intimate partner violence are much more likely to be able to provide their children emotional security and encourage their development if they receive trauma-informed services and treatment.

"We need to take a multiple-generation approach to ending abuse and violence. We know that children are more likely to experience or witness violence or abuse if their parents experienced it. Providing resources so parents can get the services they need to heal from childhood trauma is essential."

— Jeannette Pai-Espinosa, National Crittenton Foundation

4.4 When domestic violence and child sexual or physical abuse co-occur, ensure that the dependency and family courts, the child protection system, and domestic violence programs work together to create protocols and policies that protect children and adult victims.

When domestic violence and child abuse co-occur in a family, all victims need protection. Adult caregivers who are victimized and their children involved in custody and dependency cases should receive coordinated trauma-informed services and trauma-specific treatment appropriate to their circumstances and developmental stage. The courts; child welfare agencies; and gatekeepers such as custody evaluators, guardians ad litem, and court-appointed special advocates (CASAs) should be educated on the dynamics of domestic violence and child abuse; trauma-informed service models; and evidence-based screening, assessment, and treatments for adults and children that address the adverse impact of domestic violence and child abuse. They also should be educated on effective strategies for mediation or couples counseling and the considerations for safe access, visitation, and exchange of victimized children by their parents. All services provided to adult victims of domestic violence should be designed to support their relationships with their children, maintain or enhance their options for safety, and support their ability to protectively parent their children. Children recover most fully from exposure to violence if other family members who are victimized, especially their primary caregivers, receive timely evidence-based treatment and trauma-informed services.

The task force also recommends that every reasonable effort should be made in dependency courts to keep violence-exposed children and their non-offending parents or other family caregivers together. Even when children cannot safely remain in the home with their parents and siblings, their emotional security and ability to recover from violent trauma is greatest if they are able to be with other family members who safely care for them. This recommendation is consistent with federal regulations that require states to give preference to an adult relative over a nonrelated caregiver when determining placement for a child, provided that the relative caregiver meets all relevant state child protection standards.

Disruption of primary caregiving relationships worsens the impact of domestic violence and abuse on victimized children. It often occurs when domestic violence offenders are awarded custody or when children are reflexively or repeatedly placed outside the home by child protective services. Studies show that multiple out-of-home placements add to the severity of conduct, attention, and hyperactivity problems caused by physical abuse. Out-of-home placements put children at risk

"[When my father was arrested for abusing my mother] you ripped me away from the mother I wanted to protect and to be with [and] the siblings who I loved and wanted to protect…. You moved us into foster homes outside of our own community, which ripped me away from every teacher who supported me and understood what was going on, from any friends…who supported us and knew what was going on."

— Jim Henderson, Battered Women's Justice Project

for further victimization either directly or because non-kin caregivers fail to protect them from aggression or model aggressive behavior,[9,12,155,156] which increases the risk that the children will develop problems with depression, anxiety, impulsivity, and aggression.[157–167] Out-of-home placements also are associated with diminished self-esteem,[168] which can make a child vulnerable to coping by means of aggression, antisocial behavior, and delinquency.[10–12,169] Thus, despite being intended to enhance the safety and well-being of victimized children, placement away from the family and other primary caregivers can compound the adverse effects of children's exposure to violence.

Disruption in primary caregiving relationships also may occur with custody or visitation awards that promote contact between children and a violent parent or parent's ex-spouse. When the offender continues to use violence or coercion to control or intimidate the other parent or the children, physical or shared custody and visitation and exchanges of children create opportunities for renewed domestic violence or abuse. Research has shown that physical abuse, stalking, and harassment continue at significant rates post-separation and may even become more severe.[170–172] Legal policies and protocols must be designed to protect children from the damaging effects of continuing domestic violence or abuse.[173] They also must allow adult victims to get the help they need without losing custody of their children to the child protection system or their abusers.

4.5 Create multidisciplinary councils or coalitions to assure systemwide collaboration and coordinated community responses to children exposed to family violence.

The crisis of family violence is too widespread to be solved by a single provider, agency, or organization. Victims of family violence confront many legal, medical, housing, and safety issues, and find themselves at the door of multiple providers, repeatedly telling their stories and often receiving conflicting advice.[123,125,149,151,174–179]

The task force recommends that each city, county, and tribe establish and sustain a multidisciplinary council that includes every agency that may touch the life of children exposed to violence. These councils must ensure that violence-exposed children and families receive consistent messages and services, that information is shared by all relevant agencies and providers, and that services are integrated. They should involve service providers and key decision makers who can affect policy, programs, and case management. Multi-agency councils also provide opportunities for involved agencies to learn their different mandates and core responsibilities, thereby establishing an informed and cohesive response based on this knowledge. Such a multidisciplinary council of agencies and programs can enable children and families to receive more coordinated, humane, and effective services mitigating the long-term effects of witnessing or suffering violence. In addition, an established interagency council with identified multilevel support can address multiple issues through development of protocols and support of multidisciplinary teams, subgroups, and task forces focused on child fatality review, domestic violence, sexual assault, sexual trafficking/exploitation, cyber-crimes, abductions, substance abuse, and mental health. These groups are available in most communities with differing degrees of specialization depending upon the size and infrastructure of the community.

> "I think the nature of this problem really requires the different disciplines and fields to work together. It's not just a nice idea, it's a necessity."
>
> — **Dr. Howard Dubowitz, Professor of Pediatrics and Head, Division of Child Protection, and Director, Center for Families, University of Maryland School of Medicine**

Community collaboration and coordination across disciplines is critical to ensuring adequate identification, assessment, and screening; comprehensive service delivery; and improved policymaking on behalf of children and parents who experience family violence. The task force recommends active collaboration among mental health, pediatric, child welfare, social and family services, and community organizations, including domestic violence shelters; homeless shelters; schools; law enforcement; and the judiciary. These service providers and organizations should base their decisions on the goal of preventing further exposure to violence and promoting the healthy growth and development, and success in school, and peer relationships.

4.6 Provide families affected by sexual abuse, physical abuse, and domestic violence with education and services to prevent further abuse, to respond to the adverse effects on the family, and to enable the children to recover.

Families are the first line of defense against children's exposure to violence and the primary source of immediate day-to-day support and nurturance when children are recovering from exposure to violence. When families understand how sexual or physical abuse and domestic violence affect children and what each family member can do to reinstate the physical and emotional security that such violence takes away, they can provide the essential support that enables an abused child to begin to heal and recover. Family members also need information and guidance to help them deal with their own traumatic shock, fear, anger, and guilt when they learn that their child has been abused. Family members of physically or sexually abused children should receive trauma-informed education and support services and evidence-based trauma-specific treatment to help them recover from their own posttraumatic distress. They will then be better able to provide the abused children with a renewed sense of security and hope by modeling healthy relationships and behaviors that are grounded in respect and equality.

Programs that engage parents to help protect and support children, ideally working to stop child sexual or physical abuse before it occurs — and also enabling parents to assist their children in recovery if sexual abuse does occur — are key. Prevention programs that equip parents and other family members with the skills to establish healthy, supportive, proactive relationships with children should be available to all families in every community. Parents need knowledge, practical advice, and the skills needed to talk with confidence to their children about sexual development and healthy relationships. They need to know what to do when they suspect sexual or physical abuse and how to talk with other adults about child sexual or physical abuse, and they need to understand mandated reporting responsibilities. All child- and youth-serving agencies therefore should educate young parents and soon-to-be parents on strategies for recognizing and preventing physical abuse, sexual abuse, and domestic violence. Because parents may have been exposed to violence in their childhoods, they also should be educated on recognizing and getting help for their own posttraumatic reactions stemming from their own childhood exposure to violence, so that they can prevent those reactions from impairing their ability to safely and successfully parent their children.

When a child is sexually abused, family relationships can make a significant difference in how he or she heals. Connections to emotionally supportive adults within and outside of the family are critical to a child's resilience and coping mechanisms. Supportive families and, more specifically, healthy, supportive relationships between parents and children can help to prevent negative coping mechanisms, such as binge drinking and suicidal thoughts among adolescent survivors of sexual abuse. For this reason, the task force supports intervention services that recognize the parent-child relationship as a path toward healing, reflect an understanding of the complex trauma experienced by children who have been sexually abused, and tap children's innate sources of resilience and strength. Ensuring availability of early trauma-focused interventions and longer-term treatment for children seen in Child Advocacy Centers (which conduct forensic evaluations of abused children around the country) and Rape Crisis Centers, for example, would capitalize on the use of existing settings where abused children can be identified and receive the care that they need to recover.

4.7 Ensure that parenting programs in child- and family-serving agencies, including fatherhood programs and other programs specifically for men, integrate strategies for preventing domestic violence and sexual assault and include reparation strategies when violence has already occurred.

Fathers who perpetrate violence against their partners often are repeating a pattern of violence they witnessed while growing up. Many men who use violence are victims of the long-term effects of childhood exposure to violence.[112,124,180,181] Some men are receptive to programs that encourage an end to domestic violence. Whenever possible, agencies that work with affected children and families should include those men in their interventions. Help in understanding their children's experience of violence may increase some fathers' empathy for their children and promote motivation to change.

The task force recommends that all agencies, programs, and providers working with fathers who have been violent toward their family members provide in-depth assessment, diagnosis and treatment planning, education, and strategies that enhance adequate external controls to ensure that no further violence occurs. Too often, violent offenders are court ordered to undergo services such as anger management or batterer intervention before diagnostic evaluations have taken place. Without a clear link between identified underlying difficulties that lead to intimate partner violence and specific evidence-based treatment interventions, the strategies used to rehabilitate violent family members are likely to be ineffective because they are not matched to the specific problems of each offender. Intervention with fathers who use violence is not "one size fits all." Fathers who use violence also must be held accountable and monitored, because change does not always come easily or quickly. Every agency, program, or provider working with these fathers therefore must offer a complete and evidence-based array of services and treatments matched to the specific individual and designed to ensure that no further violence occurs.

"When we bring men together [who] are working on healing from past traumatic experience, they begin to recognize something that they know at their core: that they actually influence their children profoundly. And the question is how. And in those círculos [circles] where they get acknowledged, where their trauma is addressed and recognized, where they get a chance to decide what they want to move toward, do they want to remain stuck?"

— Héctor Sánchez-Flores, Executive Director, National Compadres Network

4.8 Provide support and counseling to address the unique consequences for children exposed to lethal violence, both in the home as a result of domestic violence homicides and suicides, and in the community.

When children lose a family member or other loved one, especially a primary caregiver, to a violent death or as a result of injuries from which the family member does not recover emotionally or physically, they can experience overwhelming grief. Studies have shown that grief that is compounded by violence leads children to feel not just sadness but also terror and horror.[127,182] Family members are irreplaceable, and their sudden loss due to violence leaves children with no way to say goodbye or to understand how or why such an unimaginable event could have happened. Traumatic loss leaves children burdened by guilt, believing they should have seen the loss coming and stopped it, and unsure about how to continue without that person's presence in their life.

Violent death of any family member is horrifying and debilitating. Each family member has a unique place in the child's life, and their loss leaves a hole that cannot be filled. When the lost family member was at the center of the child's life and a source of core security and nurturing, the grief and terror are not just about the violent death but also about the frightening prospect of having to go through life without this caregiver's unique love, guidance, and protection. The loss of a primary caregiver to lethal violence can lead children to withdraw from and distrust even healthy relationships with other current or future caregivers — having been hurt deeply once, children may detach from or reject other caregivers to protect themselves from any repetitions of the loss. They also may have substantial difficulty engaging in intimate relationships with partners or in the emotional intimacy of parenting their own children when they grow into adulthood.

Evidence-based treatments that have been developed specifically to help children recover from the traumatic grief of a violent death in their family[183–185] should be available to all children who experience a loss due to violence, in every community in this country. These treatments help children communicate the shock and terror that they experienced, first to a therapist and then to a supportive caregiver in their family.[183–185] They also help children remember their lost loved ones and their relationships in ways that enable them to hold on to memories that sustain their emotional connections despite their family members' no longer being physically present. When other family members or caregivers also have been traumatized by the violent loss, treatment helps them to go through a similar process of recovery and healing to enable them to support the child emotionally.

Every child and family exposed to violent death should be identified and provided with access to services not just in the immediate aftermath but also over time. Traumatic grief does not end quickly, and it often persists for years, although the severity of the emotional injury can be greatly diminished with proper treatment and trauma-informed services. Services for children and families who suffer traumatic losses due to violence must be designed to be readily accessible without arbitrary time limits.

Unfortunately, systems currently in place do not reliably track and provide services to children who perpetrate lethal violence. These children often are survivors of abuse or other family or community violence. They often become lost in many legal, family services, mental health, and child protection systems, and if not located and helped, they may return to inflict additional violence or turn to suicide. These child survivors present an ultimate challenge, but they also represent an opportunity to improve public safety by delivering services that help them recover from the effects of the violence they have done as well as the violence to which others have exposed them. Every community should have trauma-informed services in place to identify, track, and promote the recovery of all children who perpetrate lethal violence.

4.9 Develop interventions in all child- and family-serving agencies that build on the assets and values of each family's culture of origin and incorporate the linguistic and acculturation challenges of immigrant children and parents.

Children and families who immigrate to a new country often do so because they have faced violence as a result of war, political conflicts, ethnic cleansing or genocide, or natural disasters that has traumatized the whole family. Because they may have difficulty forming new social ties or face isolation and discrimination in their new communities, they are at risk for exposure to domestic and community violence and child abuse. Even if they did not experience violence previously, immigrant families often face cultural, language, and economic barriers and stressors as well as stigma and discrimination, which can place their children at risk for exposure to violence.

Evidence-based interventions created specifically for immigrant families and children exposed to violence provide them with a network of services and supports that are grounded in the beliefs and values of their cultures of origin rather than forcing them to renounce or relinquish those crucial ties and foundations. The task force recommends that all immigrant families receive these interventions from multidisciplinary collaborative teams and networks of providers who respect and are informed about the cultural beliefs and practices of the families they serve. These interventions can enable immigrant families to avoid or overcome the isolation, stigma, and practical barriers that otherwise could make them vulnerable to violence from outside or within the family.

4.10 Ensure compliance with the letter and spirit of the Indian Child Welfare Act (ICWA).

Children exposed to family violence particularly need to retain their connection with their cultures and communities, which is a key factor that can protect them from the psychological harm and insecurity caused by exposure to violence in their families. Remaining in their communities and staying involved with cultural, religious, and community activities provides children with an indirect connection to their families even when they cannot live in their family homes or with family members. This is particularly important but also particularly difficult when families live in isolated communities that have been subjected to trauma over many generations, such as AIAN communities.

AIAN women and children face family violence at rates far greater than other groups. This tragedy occurs on reservations, in Native communities, and in urban settings and results in AIAN children's experiencing out-of-home placement far more often than other children. In 1978, with the passage of ICWA, the federal government recognized the importance of keeping AIAN children with AIAN families and the important role tribal governments must play in protecting their children. ICWA clearly articulates placement preferences for AIAN children removed from their homes because of abuse or neglect and the efforts public agencies must make to keep AIAN children safe in their own homes, and it also sets clear requirements for public agencies and courts on communicating and working with tribal agencies and courts. These requirements apply to child custody proceedings regardless of where the AIAN child resides in the United States.

Thirty-four years after ICWA's passage, full implementation of the act remains elusive. Judges and attorneys in the state and the tribal court systems must educate each other and work together to ensure the ICWA requirements achieve the stated policy "to protect the best interests of Indian children and to promote the stability and security of Indian tribes and families." Tribes must receive direct access to federal foster care funds (Title IV-E) not only for the provision of foster care but also for the training of workers and administration of a system that will protect their most vulnerable and traumatized members. Movement toward full implementation of ICWA must be accompanied by technical assistance to tribes so they can effectively enlarge their capacity for family court systems, licensing and monitoring of foster homes, and participating in state child protective services cases that involve AIAN children. Because ICWA is a federal statute, successful implementation will be best ensured through strong, coordinated support from the Bureau of Indian Affairs in the Department of the Interior, the DHHS Administration for Children and Families, and the Office of Juvenile Justice and Delinquency Prevention within the Department of Justice.

4.11 Initiate a nationally sponsored program similar to the Department of Defense's community and family support programs that provides military families with specialized services focused on building strengths and resilience, new parent support, youth programs, and forging partnerships with communities.

Military families and their children face unique challenges related to violence, especially when a family member such as a father or mother is continually deployed to combat areas or other dangerous areas around the world where violence and death are an imminent threat or an immediate reality. Military violence can lead to post-traumatic stress problems that make parenting difficult even for the most resilient service members and spouses or partners. In some cases, it can result in chronic depression, addiction, domestic violence, child abuse, or traumatic loss for a child due to a parent's suicide. These challenges are widely recognized, and the Department of Defense has improved its community and family support programs in concert with the President's Strengthening Our Military Families initiative to oversee the safety and well-being of military families, especially their children. Because many military families reside in civilian communities, military leaders have fostered close partnerships with community leaders in coordinating complementary programs for both civilian and military families. These initiatives should be continued and expanded to reach the families of all military personnel and veterans.

References

1. Turner, H. A., Finkelhor, D., & Ormrod, R. (2010). Poly-victimization in a national sample of children and youth. *American Journal of Preventive Medicine, 38*(3), 323–30.

2. Finkelhor, D., et al. (2011). School, police, and medical authority involvement with children who have experienced victimization. *Archives of Pediatrics and Adolescent Medicine, 165*(1), 9–15.

3. Finkelhor, D., et al. (2009). Violence, abuse, and crime exposure in a national sample of children and youth. *Pediatrics, 124*(5), 1411–23.

4. Pereda, N., et al. (2009). The international epidemiology of child sexual abuse: a continuation of Finkelhor (1994). *Child Abuse & Neglect, 33*(6), 331–42.

5. Jones, D. J., et al. (2012). Linking childhood sexual abuse and early adolescent risk behavior: The intervening role of internalizing and externalizing problems. *Journal of Abnormal Child Psychology.*

6. Maniglio, R. (2011). The role of child sexual abuse in the etiology of substance-related disorders. *Journal of Addictive Disorders, 30*(3), 216–28.

7. Chen, L. P., et al. (2010). Sexual abuse and lifetime diagnosis of psychiatric disorders: systematic review and meta-analysis. *Mayo Clinic Proceedings, 85*(7), 618–29.

8. Maniglio, R. (2009). The impact of child sexual abuse on health: a systematic review of reviews. *Clinical Psychology Review, 29*(7), 647–57.

9. Ford, J. D., Wasser, T., & Connor, D. F. (2011). Identifying and determining the symptom severity associated with polyvictimization among psychiatrically impaired children in the outpatient setting. *Child Maltreatment, 16*(3), 216–26.

10. Ford, J. D., Fraleigh, L. A., & Connor, D. F. (2010). Child abuse and aggression among psychiatrically impaired children. *Journal of Clinical Child & Adolescent Psychology, 39*(1), 25–34.

11. Ford, J. D., et al. (2010). Poly-victimization and risk of posttraumatic, depressive, and substance use disorders and involvement in delinquency in a national sample of adolescents. *Journal of Adolescent Health, 46*(6), 545–52.

12. Ford, J. D., Connor, D. F., & Hawke, J. (2009). Complex trauma among psychiatrically impaired children: a cross-sectional, chart-review study. *Journal of Clinical Psychiatry, 70*(8), 1155–63.

13. Jun, H. J., et al. (2012). Growing up in a domestic violence environment: relationship with developmental trajectories of body mass index during adolescence into young adulthood. *Journal of Epidemiology and Community Health.*

14. Turner, H. A., Finkelhor, D., & Ormrod, R. (2010). The effects of adolescent victimization on self-concept and depressive symptoms. *Child Maltreatment, 15*(1), 76–90.

15. Voisin, D. R., Neilands, T. B., Hunnicutt, S. (2010). Mechanisms linking violence exposure and school engagement among African American adolescents: examining the roles of psychological problem behaviors and gender. *American Journal of Orthopsychiatry, 81*(1), 61–71.

16. Huang, S., et al. (2011). The long-term effects of childhood maltreatment experiences on subsequent illicit drug use and drug-related problems in young adulthood. *Addictive Behaviors, 36*(1–2), 95–102.

17. Lee, S., et al. (2011). The prevalence of family childhood adversities and their association with first onset of DSM-IV disorders in metropolitan China. *Psychological Medicine, 41*(1), 85–96.

18. Mallie, A., et al. (2011). Childhood abuse and adolescent sexual re-offending: A meta-analysis. *Child & Youth Care Forum, 40*(5), 401–417.

19. McKelvey, L. M., et al. (2011). Growing up in violent communities: Do family conflict and gender moderate impacts on adolescents' psychosocial development? *Journal of Abnormal Child Psychology, 39*(1), 95–107.

20. Boivin, S., et al. (2012). Past victimizations and dating violence perpetration in adolescence: the mediating role of emotional distress and hostility. *Journal of Interpersonal Violence, 27*(4), 662–84.

21. Calvete, E., & Orue, I. (2012). The impact of violence exposure on aggressive behavior through social information processing in adolescents. *American Journal of Orthopsychiatry, 81*(1), 38–50.

22. de Boer, S. B., et al. (2012). Childhood characteristics of adolescent inpatients with early-onset and adolescent-onset disruptive behavior. *Journal of Psychopathology and Behavioral Assessment, 34*(3), 415–422.

23. Goldsmith, R. E., Freyd, J. J., & DePrince, A. P. (2012). Betrayal trauma: associations with psychological and physical symptoms in young adults. *Journal of Interpersonal Violence, 27*(3), 547–67.

24. Hadland, S. E., et al. (2012). Suicide and history of childhood trauma among street youth. *Journal of Affective Disorders, 136*(3), 377–80.

25. Jaite, C., et al. (2012). Etiological role of childhood emotional trauma and neglect in adolescent anorexia nervosa: a cross-sectional questionnaire analysis. *Psychopathology, 45*(1), 61–6.

26. Jun, H. J., et al. (2012). Growing up in a domestic violence environment: relationship with developmental trajectories of body mass index during adolescence into young adulthood. *Journal of Epidemiology and Community Health, 66*(7), 629–35.

27. Konings, M., et al. (2012). Replication in two independent population-based samples that childhood maltreatment and cannabis use synergistically impact on psychosis risk. *Psychological Medicine, 42*(1), 149–59.

28. Meltzer, H., et al. (2012). Children who run away from home: risks for suicidal behavior and substance misuse. *Journal of Adolescent Health, 51*(5), 415–21.

29. Rosenkranz, S. E., Muller, R. T., & Henderson, J. L. (2012). Psychological maltreatment in relation to substance use problem severity among youth. *Child Abuse & Neglect, 36*(5), 438–48.

30. Shin, S. H., & Miller, D. P. (2012). A longitudinal examination of childhood maltreatment and adolescent obesity: results from the National Longitudinal Study of Adolescent Health (AddHealth) Study. *Child Abuse & Neglect, 36*(2), 84–94.

31. Shin, S. H., Miller, D. P., & Teicher, M. H. (2012). Exposure to childhood neglect and physical abuse and developmental trajectories of heavy episodic drinking from early adolescence into young adulthood. *Drug and Alcohol Dependence.*

32. Spann, M. N., et al. (2012). Childhood abuse and neglect and cognitive flexibility in adolescents. *Child Neuropsychology, 18*(2), 182–9.

33. Turner, H. A., et al. (2012). Recent victimization exposure and suicidal ideation in adolescents. *Archives of Pediatrics and Adolescent Medicine,* 1–6.

34. Murray, J., & Farrington, D. P. (2010). Risk factors for conduct disorder and delinquency: key findings from longitudinal studies. *Canadian Journal of Psychiatry, 55*(10), 633–42.

35. Jonas, S., et al. (2011). Sexual abuse and psychiatric disorder in England: results from the 2007 Adult Psychiatric Morbidity Survey. *Psychological Medicine, 41*(4), 709–19.

36. Meade, C. S., et al. (2012). Methamphetamine use is associated with childhood sexual abuse and HIV sexual risk behaviors among patrons of alcohol-serving venues in Cape Town, South Africa. *Drug and Alcohol Dependence, 126*(1–2), 232–9.

37. Dyer, A., et al. (2012). Body image in patients with posttraumatic stress disorder after childhood sexual abuse and co-occurring eating disorder. *Psychopathology.*

38. Wilson, H. W., & Widom, C. S. (2011). Pathways from childhood abuse and neglect to HIV-risk sexual behavior in middle adulthood. *Journal of Consulting and Clinical Psychology, 79*(2), 236–46.

39. Peltan, J. R., & Cellucci, T. (2011). Childhood sexual abuse and substance abuse treatment utilization among substance-dependent incarcerated women. *Journal of Substance Abuse Treatment, 41*(3), 215–24.

40. Bedi, S., et al. (2011). Risk for suicidal thoughts and behavior after childhood sexual abuse in women and men. *Suicide and Life-Threatening Behavior, 41*(4), 406–15.

41. Asgeirsdottir, B. B., et al. (2011). Associations between sexual abuse and family conflict/violence, self-injurious behavior, and substance use: the mediating role of depressed mood and anger. *Child Abuse & Neglect, 35*(3), 210–9.

42. Vrabel, K. R., et al. (2010). Co-occurrence of avoidant personality disorder and child sexual abuse predicts poor outcome in long-standing eating disorder. *Journal of Abnormal Psychology, 119*(3), 623–9.

43. Balsam, K. F., Lehavot, K., & Beadnell, B. (2010). Sexual revictimization and mental health: a comparison of lesbians, gay men, and heterosexual women. *Journal of Interpersonal Violence, 26*(9), 1798–814.

44. Paras, M. L., et al. (2009). Sexual abuse and lifetime diagnosis of somatic disorders: a systematic review and meta-analysis. *Journal of the American Medical Association, 302*(5), 550–61.

45. Sanci, L., et al. (2008). Childhood sexual abuse and eating disorders in females: findings from the Victorian Adolescent Health Cohort Study. *Archives of Pediatric and Adolescent Medicine, 162*(3), 261–7.

46. Rohde, P., et al. (2008). Associations of child sexual and physical abuse with obesity and depression in middle-aged women. *Child Abuse & Neglect, 32*(9), 878–87.

47. Klonsky, E. D., & Moyer, A. (2008). Childhood sexual abuse and non-suicidal self-injury: meta-analysis. *British Journal of Psychiatry, 192*(3), 166–70.

48. Afifi, T. O., et al. (2008). Population attributable fractions of psychiatric disorders and suicide ideation and attempts associated with adverse childhood experiences. *American Journal of Public Health, 98*(5), 946–52.

49. Dube, S. R., et al. (2005). Long-term consequences of childhood sexual abuse by gender of victim. *American Journal of Preventive Medicine, 28*(5), 430–8.

50. Ystgaard, M., et al. (2004). Is there a specific relationship between childhood sexual and physical abuse and repeated suicidal behavior? *Child Abuse & Neglect, 28*(8), 863–75.

51. Sar, V., et al. (2004). Childhood trauma, dissociation, and psychiatric comorbidity in patients with conversion disorder. *American Journal of Psychiatry, 161*(12), 2271–6.

52. Hillis, S. D., et al. (2004). The association between adverse childhood experiences and adolescent pregnancy, long-term psychosocial consequences, and fetal death. *Pediatrics, 113*(2), 320–7.

53. Dong, M., et al. (2003). The relationship of exposure to childhood sexual abuse to other forms of abuse, neglect, and household dysfunction during childhood. *Child Abuse & Neglect, 27*(6), 625–39.

54. Jones, L. M., Finkelhor, D., & Halter, S. (2006). Child maltreatment trends in the 1990s: why does neglect differ from sexual and physical abuse? *Child Maltreatment, 11*(2), 107–20.

55. Mueser, K. T., & Taub, J. (2008). Trauma and PTSD among adolescents with severe emotional disorders involved in multiple service systems. *Psychiatric Services, 59*(6), 627–634.

56. Thompson, S. J., et al. (2007). Predictors of posttraumatic stress symptoms among runaway youth utilizing two service sectors. *Journal of Traumatic Stress, 20*(4), 553–63.

57. Embry, L. E., et al. (2000). Risk factors for homelessness in adolescents released from psychiatric residential treatment. *Journal of the American Academy of Child and Adolescent Psychiatry, 39*(10), 1293–1299.

58. Holt, M. K., Finkelhor, D., & Kantor, G. K. (2007). Multiple victimization experiences of urban elementary school students: associations with psychosocial functioning and academic performance. *Child Abuse & Neglect, 31*(5), 503–15.

59. Stiffman, A. R. (1989). Physical and sexual abuse in runaway youths. *Child Abuse & Neglect, 13*(3), 417–26.

60. Breslau, J., et al. (2011). A multinational study of mental disorders, marriage, and divorce. *Acta Psychiatrica Scandinavica, 124*(6), 474–86.

61. Conroy, E., et al. (2009). Child maltreatment as a risk factor for opioid dependence: Comparison of family characteristics and type and severity of child maltreatment with a matched control group. *Child Abuse & Neglect, 33*(6), 343–52.

62. Anda, R. F., et al. (2008). Adverse childhood experiences and prescription drug use in a cohort study of adult HMO patients. *BMC Public Health, 8,* 198.

63. Edwards, V. J., et al. (2007). Adverse childhood experiences and smoking persistence in adults with smoking-related symptoms and illness. *Permanente Journal, 11*(2), 5–13.

64. Dube, S. R., et al. (2006). Adverse childhood experiences and the association with ever using alcohol and initiating alcohol use during adolescence. *Journal of Adolescent Health, 38*(4), 444 e1–10.

65. Dube, S. R., et al. (2003). Childhood abuse, neglect, and household dysfunction and the risk of illicit drug use: the adverse childhood experiences study. *Pediatrics, 111*(3), 564–72.

66. Hillis, S. D., et al. (2001). Adverse childhood experiences and sexual risk behaviors in women: a retrospective cohort study. *Family Planning Perspectives, 33*(5), 206–11.

67. Wilson, H. W., & Widom, C. S. (2010). The role of youth problem behaviors in the path from child abuse and neglect to prostitution: A prospective examination. *Journal of Research in Adolescence, 20*(1), 210–236.

68. Wilson, H. W., & Widom, C. S. (2009). A prospective examination of the path from child abuse and neglect to illicit drug use in middle adulthood: the potential mediating role of four risk factors. *Journal of Youth and Adolescence, 38*(3), 340–54.

69. Roxburgh, A., et al. (2008). Drug dependence and associated risks among female street-based sex workers in the greater Sydney area, Australia. *Substance Use and Misuse, 43*(8–9), 1202–17.

70. Andres-Lemay, V. J., Jamieson, E., & MacMillan, H. L. (2005). Child abuse, psychiatric disorder, and running away in a community sample of women. *Canadian Journal of Psychiatry, 50*(11), 684–9.

71. Tyler, K. A., Cauce, A. M., & Whitbeck, L. (2004). Family risk factors and prevalence of dissociative symptoms among homeless and runaway youth. *Child Abuse & Neglect, 28*(3), 355–66.

72. Bassuk, E. L., Perloff, J. N., & Dawson, R., Multiply homeless families: The insidious impact of violence. *Housing Policy Debate, 12*(2), 299–320.

73. Ryan, K. D., et al. (2000). Psychological consequences of child maltreatment in homeless adolescents: untangling the unique effects of maltreatment and family environment. *Child Abuse & Neglect, 24*(3), 333–52.

74. Whitbeck, L. B., Hoyt, D. R., & Yoder, K. A. (1999). A risk-amplification model of victimization and depressive symptoms among runaway and homeless adolescents. *American Journal of Community Psychology, 27*(2), 273–296.

75. Molnar, B. E., et al. (1998). Suicidal behavior and sexual/physical abuse among street youth. *Child Abuse & Neglect, 22*(3), 213–22.

76. Davies-Netzley, S., Hurlburt, M. S., & Hough, R. L. (1996). Childhood abuse as a precursor to homelessness for homeless women with severe mental illness. *Violence and Victimology, 11*(2), 129–42.

77. Simmel, C., Postmus, J. L., & Lee, I. (2012). Sexual revictimization in adult women: examining factors associated with their childhood and adulthood experiences. *Journal of Child Sexual Abuse, 21*(5), 593–611.

78. Loeb, T. B., et al. (2011). Associations between child sexual abuse and negative sexual experiences and revictimization among women: Does measuring severity matter? *Child Abuse & Neglect.*

79. Zinzow, H. M., et al. (2010). Drug- or alcohol-facilitated, incapacitated, and forcible rape in relationship to mental health among a national sample of women. *Journal of Interpersonal Violence, 25*(12), 2217–36.

80. Perepletchikova, F., & Kaufman, J. (2010). Emotional and behavioral sequelae of childhood maltreatment. *Current Opinion in Pediatrics, 22*(5), 610–5.

81. Messman-Moore, T. L., Walsh, K. L., & Dilillo, D. (2010). Emotion dysregulation and risky sexual behavior in revictimization. *Child Abuse & Neglect, 34*(12), 967–976.

82. Ullman, S. E., Najdowski, C. J., & Filipas, H. H. (2009). Child sexual abuse, post-traumatic stress disorder, and substance use: predictors of revictimization in adult sexual assault survivors. *Journal of Child Sexual Abuse, 18*(4), 367–85.

83. Lindhorst, T., et al. (2009). Mediating pathways explaining psychosocial functioning and revictimization as sequelae of parental violence among adolescent mothers. *American Journal of Orthopsychiatry, 79*(2), 181–90.

84. Fargo, J. D. (2009). Pathways to adult sexual revictimization: direct and indirect behavioral risk factors across the lifespan. *Journal of Interpersonal Violence, 24*(11), 1771–91.

85. Barnes, J. E., et al. (2009). Sexual and physical revictimization among victims of severe childhood sexual abuse. *Child Abuse & Neglect, 33*(7), 412–20.

86. Zinzow, H. M., et al. (2008). Sexual assault, mental health, and service use among male and female veterans seen in Veterans Affairs primary care clinics: a multi-site study. *Psychiatry Research, 159*(1–2), 226–36.

87. Widom, C. S., Czaja, S. J., & Dutton, M. A. (2008). Childhood victimization and lifetime revictimization. *Child Abuse & Neglect, 32*(8), 785–96.

88. Campbell, R., et al. (2008). The co-occurrence of childhood sexual abuse, adult sexual assault, intimate partner violence, and sexual harassment. *Journal of Consulting and Clinical Psychology, 76*(2), 194–207.

89. Kimerling, R., et al. (2007). Epidemiology and consequences of women's revictimization. *Womens Health Issues, 17*(2), 101–6.

90. Hosser, D., Raddatz, S., & Windzio, M. (2007). Child maltreatment, revictimization, and violent behavior. *Violence and Victims, 22*(3), 318–33.

91. Dietrich, A. (2007). Childhood maltreatment and revictimization: the role of affect dysregulation, interpersonal relatedness difficulties and posttraumatic stress disorder. *Journal of Trauma and Dissociation, 8*(4), 25–51.

92. Noll, J. G. (2005). Does childhood sexual abuse set in motion a cycle of violence against women? *Journal of Interpersonal Violence, 20*(4), 455–462.

93. Selic, P., Pesjak, K., & Kersnik, J. (2011). The prevalence of exposure to domestic violence and the factors associated with co-occurrence of psychological and physical violence exposure: a sample from primary care patients. *BMC Public Health, 11,* 621.

94. Stuart, G. L., et al. (2006). Examining a conceptual framework of intimate partner violence in men and women arrested for domestic violence. *Journal of Studies on Alcohol, 67*(1), 102–12.

95. Schechter, S. E. (2004). Domestic violence and poverty: Helping young children and their families. Available from http://www.ncdsv.org/images/UI-SSW_EarlyChildhoodDVandPoverty_1-2004.pdf

96. Krause, E. D., et al. (2008). Avoidant coping and PTSD symptoms related to domestic violence exposure: a longitudinal study. *Journal of Traumatic Stress, 21*(1), 83–90.

97. Noll, J. G., et al. (2003). Revictimization and self-harm in females who experienced childhood sexual abuse: results from a prospective study. *Journal of Interpersonal Violence, 18*(12), 1452–71.

98. Bohn, D. K. (2003). Lifetime physical and sexual abuse, substance abuse, depression, and suicide attempts among Native American women. *Issues in Mental Health Nursing, 24*(3), 333–52.

99. Gladstone, G. L., et al. (2004). Implications of childhood trauma for depressed women: an analysis of pathways from childhood sexual abuse to deliberate self-harm and revictimization. *American Journal of Psychiatry, 161*(8), 1417–25.

100. Dunkle, K. L., et al. (2004). Prevalence and patterns of gender-based violence and revictimization among women attending antenatal clinics in Soweto, South Africa. *American Journal of Epidemiology, 160*(3), 230–9.

101. Hamby, S., et al. (2010). The overlap of witnessing partner violence with child maltreatment and other victimizations in a nationally representative survey of youth. *Child Abuse & Neglect, 34*(10), 734–41.

102. Finkelhor, D., et al. (2010). Trends in childhood violence and abuse exposure: evidence from 2 national surveys. *Archives of Pediatric and Adolescent Medicine, 164*(3), 238–42.

103. Turner, H. A., et al. (2012). Family context, victimization, and child trauma symptoms: variations in safe, stable, and nurturing relationships during early and middle childhood. *American Journal of Orthopsychiatry, 82*(2), 209–19.

104. Boden, J. M., Fergusson, D. M., & Horwood, L. J. (2010). Risk factors for conduct disorder and oppositional/defiant disorder: evidence from a New Zealand birth cohort. *Journal of the American Academy of Child & Adolescent Psychiatry, 49*(11), 1125–33.

105. Wong, W. C., et al. (2009). Individual, familial and community determinants of child physical abuse among high-school students in China. *Social Science and Medicine, 68*(10), 1819–25.

106. Taylor, C. A., et al. (2009). Intimate partner violence, maternal stress, nativity, and risk for maternal maltreatment of young children. *American Journal of Public Health, 99*(1), 175–83.

107. Spriggs, A. L., et al. (2009). Family and school socioeconomic disadvantage: interactive influences on adolescent dating violence victimization. *Social Science & Medicine, 68*(11), 1956–65.

108. Spano, R., Vazsonyi, A. T., & Bolland, J. (2009). Does parenting mediate the effects of exposure to violence on violent behavior? An ecological-transactional model of community violence. *Journal of Adolescence, 32*(5), 1321–41.

109. Schechter, D. S., & Willheim, E. (2009). Disturbances of attachment and parental psychopathology in early childhood. *Child & Adolescent Psychiatric Clinics of North America, 18*(3), 665–86.

110. Rosen, L. H., et al. (2009). Persistent versus periodic experiences of social victimization: predictors of adjustment. *Journal of Abnormal Child Psychology, 37*(5), 693–704.

111. Mitchell, S. J., et al. (2009). Violence exposure and the association between young African American mothers' discipline and child problem behavior. *Academic Pediatrics, 9*(3), 157–63.

112. Margolin, G., et al. (2009). Youth exposed to violence: stability, co-occurrence, and context. *Clinical Child and Family Psychology Review, 12*(1), 39–54.

113. Fowler, P. J., et al. (2009). Community and family violence: indirect effects of parental monitoring on externalizing problems. *Journal of Prevention and Intervention in the Community, 37*(4), 302–15.

114. Elbogen, E. B., & Johnson, S. C. (2009). The intricate link between violence and mental disorder: results from the National Epidemiologic Survey on Alcohol and Related Conditions. *Archives of General Psychiatry, 66*(2), 152–61.

115. Afifi, T. O., et al. (2009). The relationship between child abuse, parental divorce, and lifetime mental disorders and suicidality in a nationally representative adult sample. *Child Abuse & Neglect, 33*(3), 139–47.

116. Dong, M., et al. (2004). The interrelatedness of multiple forms of childhood abuse, neglect, and household dysfunction. *Child Abuse & Neglect, 28*(7), 771–84.

117. Finkelhor, D., & Jones, L. (2012). Trends in child maltreatment. *Lancet, 379*(9831), 2048–9; author reply 2049.

118. Truman, J., & Smith, E. (2012). Prevalence of violent crime among households with children, 1993–2010. *Department of Justice Bureau of Justice Statistics Special Report 238799.*

119. U.S. Department of Health and Human Services Administration for Children and Families Children's Bureau. (2011). *Child Maltreatment 2010.*

120. Powers, R. A., & Kaukinen, C. E. (2012). Trends in intimate partner violence: 1980–2008. *Journal of Interpersonal Violence, 27*(15), 3072–90.

121. Garcia, L., Soria, C., & Hurwitz, E. L. (2007). Homicides and intimate partner violence: a literature review. *Trauma Violence & Abuse, 8*(4), 370–83.

122. Field, C. A., & Caetano, R. (2005). Intimate partner violence in the U.S. general population: progress and future directions. *Journal of Interpersonal Violence, 20*(4), 463–9.

123. Willis, D., et al. (2010). Children who witness violence: what services do they need to heal? *Issues in Mental Health Nursing, 31*(9), 552–60.

124. Israel, E., & Stover, C. (2009). Intimate partner violence: the role of the relationship between perpetrators and children who witness violence. *Journal of Interpersonal Violence, 24*(10), 1755–64.

125. Groves, B. M. (1999). Mental health services for children who witness domestic violence. *Future of Children, 9*(3), 122–32.

126. Lang, J., & Ford, J. D. (2008). Cognitive behavior therapy for childhood traumatic grief. In G. Reyes, J. D. Elhai, & J. D. Ford (Eds.), *Encyclopedia of psychological trauma* (pp. 135–138). Hoboken, NJ: John Wiley & Sons.

127. McClatchy, I. S., Vonk, M. E., & Palardy, G. (2009). The prevalence of childhood traumatic grief—a comparison of violent/sudden and expected loss. *Omega (Westport), 59*(4), 305–23.

128. Brown, E. J., et al. (2008). Childhood traumatic grief: a multi-site empirical examination of the construct and its correlates. *Death Studies, 32*(10), 899–923.

129. Eckenrode, J., et al. (2010). Long-term effects of prenatal and infancy nurse home visitation on the life course of youths: 19-year follow-up of a randomized trial. *Archives of Pediatrics and Adolescent Medicine, 164*(1), 9–15.

130. Zielinski, D. S., Eckenrode, J., & Olds, D. L. (2009). Nurse home visitation and the prevention of child maltreatment: impact on the timing of official reports. *Development and Psychopathology, 21*(2), 441–53.

131. Fergusson, D. M., et al. (2006). Randomized trial of the Early Start program of home visitation: parent and family outcomes. *Pediatrics, 117*(3), 781–6.

132. MacMillan, H. L., et al. (2005). Effectiveness of home visitation by public-health nurses in prevention of the recurrence of child physical abuse and neglect: a randomised controlled trial. *Lancet, 365*(9473), 1786–93.

133. Bair-Merritt, M. H., et al. (2010). Reducing maternal intimate partner violence after the birth of a child: a randomized controlled trial of the Hawaii Healthy Start Home Visitation Program. *Archives of Pediatrics and Adolescent Medicine, 164*(1), 16–23.

134. Paulsell, D., et al. (2010). *Home Visiting Evidence of Effectiveness Review.*

135. Davidov, D. M., et al. (2012). Mandatory reporting in the context of home visitation programs: intimate partner violence and children's exposure to intimate partner violence. *Violence Against Women, 18*(5), 595–610.

136. Jack, S. M., et al. (2012). Development of a nurse home visitation intervention for intimate partner violence. *BMC Health Services Research, 12,* 50.

137. National Advisory Committee on Violence Against Women. *Draft report of the National Advisory Committee on Violence Against Women.* Unpublished. 25.

138. Kahn, J., & Moore, K. A. (2010). What works for home visiting programs: Lessons from experimental evaluations of programs and interventions. *Child Trends Fact Sheet.*

139. Stover, C. S., Berkman, M., Desai, R., & Marans, S. (2010). The efficacy of a police-advocacy intervention for victims of domestic violence: 12-month follow-up data. *Violence Against Women, 16*(4), 410–425.

140. Stover, C. S., Poole, G., & Marans, S. (2009). The Domestic Violence Home-Visit Intervention: Impact on police-reported incidents of repeat violence over 12 months. *Violence and Victims, 24,* 591–606.

141. Stover, C. S., Rainey, A., Berkman, M., & Marans, S. (2008). Factors associated with engagement in a police-advocacy home-visit intervention to prevent domestic violence. *Violence Against Women, 14*(12), 1430–1450.

142. Ybarra, G. J., Wilkens, S. L., 7 Lieberman, A. F. (2007). The influence of domestic violence on preschooler behavior and functioning. *Journal of Family Violence, 22*(1), 33–42.

143. Sturge-Apple, M. L., et al. (2009). The role of mothers' and fathers' adrenocortical reactivity in spillover between interparental conflict and parenting practices. *Journal of Family Psychology, 23*(2), 215–25.

144. Johnson, D. M., & Zlotnick, C. (2007). Utilization of mental health treatment and other services by battered women in shelters. *Psychiatric Services, 58*(12), 1595–7.

145. Humphreys, J., et al. (2001). Psychological and physical distress of sheltered battered women. *Health Care for Women International, 22*(4), 401–14.

146. Gleason, W. J. (1993). Mental disorders in battered women: an empirical study. *Violence and Victims, 8*(1), 53–68.

147. Lacey, K. K., et al. (2012). The impact of different types of intimate partner violence on the mental and physical health of women in different ethnic groups. *Journal of Interpersonal Violence.*

148. Nathanson, A. M., et al. (2012). The prevalence of mental health disorders in a community sample of female victims of intimate partner violence. *Partner Abuse, 3*(1), 59–75.

149. Cho, H., & Kim, W. J. (2012). Intimate partner violence among Asian Americans and their use of mental health services: comparisons with white, black, and Latino victims. *Journal of Immigrant and Minority Health, 14*(5), 809–15.

150. Cerulli, C., et al. (2011). Co-occurring intimate partner violence and mental health diagnoses in perinatal women. *Journal of Women's Health (Larchmont), 20*(12), 1797–803.

151. Okuda, M., et al. (2011). Mental health of victims of intimate partner violence: results from a national epidemiologic survey. *Psychiatric Services, 62*(8), 959–62.

152. Ghosh Ippen, C., et al. (2011). Traumatic and stressful events in early childhood: can treatment help those at highest risk? *Child Abuse & Neglect, 35*(7), 504–13.

153. Lieberman, A. L., Ghosh Ippen, C., & Marans, S. (2009). Psychodynamic therapy for child trauma. In E. B. Foa, et al. (Eds.), *Effective treatments for PTSD* (pp. 370–387). New York, NY: Guilford.

154. Van Horn, P., & Lieberman, A. (2008). Using dyadic therapies to treat traumatized children. In D. Brom, R. Pat-Horenzcyk, & J. D. Ford (Eds.), *Treating traumatized children* (pp. 210–224). London: Routledge.

155. DeGue, S., & Spatz Widom, C. (2009). Does out-of-home placement mediate the relationship between child maltreatment and adult criminality? *Child Maltreatment, 14*(4), 344–55.

156. Taussig, H. N. (2002). Risk behaviors in maltreated youth placed in foster care: a longitudinal study of protective and vulnerability factors. *Child Abuse & Neglect, 26*(11), 1179–99.

157. Xing, X., et al. (2011). Gender differences in the reciprocal relationships between parental physical aggression and children's externalizing problem behavior in China. *Journal of Family Psychology, 25*(5), 699–708.

158. McKinney, C., Milone, M. C., & Renk, K. (2011). Parenting and late adolescent emotional adjustment: mediating effects of discipline and gender. *Child Psychiatry and Human Development, 42*(4), 463–81.

159. Siffert, A., & Schwarz, B. (2011). Parental conflict resolution styles and children's adjustment: children's appraisals and emotion regulation as mediators. *Journal of Genetic Psychology, 172*(1), 21–39.

160. Silver, R. B., et al. (2010). The impact of parents, child care providers, teachers, and peers on early externalizing trajectories. *Journal of School Psychology, 48*(6), 555–83.

161. McCoy, K., Cummings, E. M., & Davies, P. T. (2009). Constructive and destructive marital conflict, emotional security and children's prosocial behavior. *Journal of Child Psychology and Psychiatry and Allied Disciplines, 50*(3), 270–9.

162. Miner, J. L., & Clarke-Stewart, K. A. (2008). Trajectories of externalizing behavior from age 2 to age 9: relations with gender, temperament, ethnicity, parenting, and rater. *Developmental Psychology, 44*(3), 771–86.

163. Fite, J. E., et al. (2008). Adolescent aggression and social cognition in the context of personality: impulsivity as a moderator of predictions from social information processing. *Aggressive Behavior, 34*(5), 511–20.

164. Williams, S. T., Conger, K. J., & Blozis, S. A. (2007). The development of interpersonal aggression during adolescence: the importance of parents, siblings, and family economics. *Child Development, 78*(5), 1526–42.

165. Vaillancourt, T., et al. (2007). Trajectories and predictors of indirect aggression: results from a nationally representative longitudinal study of Canadian children aged 2–10. *Aggressive Behavior, 33*(4), 314–26.

166. Miller, C. J., et al. (2006). Family and cognitive factors: modeling risk for aggression in children with ADHD. *Journal of the American Academy of Child and Adolescent Psychiatry, 45*(3), 355–63.

167. Taussig, H. N., & Clyman, R. B. (2011). The relationship between time spent living with kin and adolescent functioning in youth with a history of out-of-home placement. *Child Abuse & Neglect, 35*(1), 78–86.

168. Raviv, T., et al. (2010). Cumulative risk exposure and mental health symptoms among maltreated youth placed in out-of-home care. *Child Abuse & Neglect, 34*(10), 742–51.

169. Hanson, R. F., et al. (2006). Relations among parental substance use, violence exposure and mental health: The national survey of adolescents. *Addictive Behaviors, 31*(11), 1988–2001.

170. Jaffee, S. R., et al. (2007). Individual, family, and neighborhood factors distinguish resilient from non-resilient maltreated children: a cumulative stressors model. *Child Abuse & Neglect, 31*(3), 231–53.

171. Jaffee, S. R., et al. (2004). Physical maltreatment victim to antisocial child: evidence of an environmentally mediated process. *Journal of Abnormal Psychology, 113*(1), 44–55.

172. Jaffee, S. R., et al. (2002). Influence of adult domestic violence on children's internalizing and externalizing problems: an environmentally informative twin study. *Journal of the American Academy of Child & Adolescent Psychiatry, 41*(9), 1095–103.

173. Taussig, H. N., Culhane, S. E., & Hettleman, D. (2007). Fostering healthy futures: an innovative preventive intervention for preadolescent youth in out-of-home care. *Child Welfare, 86*(5), 113–31.

174. Rose, D., et al. (2011). Barriers and facilitators of disclosures of domestic violence by mental health service users: qualitative study. *British Journal of Psychiatry, 198*(3), 189–94.

175. Spilsbury, J. C., et al. (2008). Profiles of behavioral problems in children who witness domestic violence. *Violence Victims, 23*(1), 3–17.

176. Cho, H. (2012). Use of mental health services among Asian and Latino victims of intimate partner violence. *Violence Against Women, 18*(4), 404–19.

177. Finkelhor, D., et al. (2011). School, police, and medical authority involvement with children who have experienced victimization. *Archives of Pediatric and Adolescent Medicine, 165*(1), 9–15.

178. Ahmed, A. T., & McCaw, B. R. (2010). Mental health services utilization among women experiencing intimate partner violence. *American Journal of Managed Care, 16*(10), 731–8.

179. Rodriguez, M., et al. (2009). Intimate partner violence and barriers to mental health care for ethnically diverse populations of women. *Trauma, Violence, & Abuse, 10*(4), 358–74.

180. Slep, A. M., & O'Leary, S. G. (2005). Parent and partner violence in families with young children: rates, patterns, and connections. *Journal of Consulting and Clinical Psychology, 73*(3), 435–44.

181. Schacht, P. M., Cummings, E. M., & Davies, P. T. (2009). Fathering in family context and child adjustment: a longitudinal analysis. *Journal of Family Psychology, 23*(6), 790–7.

182. Wittouck, C., et al. (2011). The prevention and treatment of complicated grief: a meta-analysis. *Clinical Psychology Review, 31*(1), 69–78.

183. Cohen, J. A., et al. (2012). Trauma-focused CBT for youth with complex trauma. *Child Abuse & Neglect, 36*(6), 528–41.

184. Cohen, J. A., et al. (2009). Cognitive-behavioral therapy for children and adolescents. In E. B. Foa, T. M. Keane, & M. J. Friedman (Eds.), *Effective treatments for PTSD* (pp. 223–244). New York, NY: Guilford.

185. Murray, L. K., et al. (2008). Cognitive behavioral therapy for symptoms of trauma and traumatic grief in refugee youth. *Child & Adolescent Psychiatric Clinics of North America, 17*(3), 585–604, ix.

CHAPTER FIVE:
Communities Rising Up Out of Violence

CHAPTER FIVE:
Communities Rising Up Out of Violence

Community violence affects millions of children in this country every year.[1-8] Such violence can occur in episodic incidents such as shootings in schools or other public places, causing children and families to feel terror in their own neighborhoods and schools and leaving them to recover from the traumatic grief of losing friends or peers who are killed or who never fully recover. Increasingly, children are being victimized as violence continues to be part of the fabric of American communities as a result of gangs, or when bullying or corporal punishment is tolerated or sanctioned in schools or youth activities.

Community violence affects child victims and witnesses and children whose family members, neighbors, friends, or coworkers are harmed or killed. Community violence is especially harmful for children and adolescents who are exposed to pervasive violence, such as those youth who experience gang intimidation or assaults, hear gunfire, or witness drive-by shootings and murders. In communities where violence is endemic, the cycle is perpetuated when child victims who are dealing with the fear, outrage, and grief of their own experiences with violence are drawn into delinquent and criminal behavior through their relationships or associations with violent peers, family members, or friends.[4,6,9-28]

Violence in the community or school can attract children into affiliating with peers or adults who use violence to intimidate, control, or harm other children. Violence can seem to children who are victimized to provide a source of power, prestige, security, or even belongingness when they feel powerless, rejected, unsafe, and alone. The negative

"As a teenager I joined one of the most organized and dangerous street gangs in Chicago because I wanted to be a part of something…. I remember the pain of having to cope with the deaths of my closest friends…. I also recall the cold sweats at night and being unable to sleep, and having to get high in order to better cope with the inner pain."

— **Alfredo Barraza, Youth Advocate, Latino Organization of the Southwest** consequences of exposure to violence in the community or school, however, extend well past the point of entering adulthood and may include negative outcomes such as disrupted education, lower job prospects, fragmented relationships, legal problems, incarceration, serious injury and illness, and even death.

Children can be exposed to community violence as innocent bystanders, but they also may be targeted by perpetrators because of their vulnerability. Children may be perceived as "different" based on their race or ethnicity, language, sexual orientation, physical or mental disabilities, physical characteristics (such as being small for their age or overweight), family economic status, either low or high academic involvement or achievement, or belonging to a marginalized peer group. Predatory violence toward children often occurs in secrecy — although, as evidenced by numerous revelations of institutionally tolerated sexual abuse in religious, educational, and youth activity organizations, violence can be a "secret" that is hidden in plain sight. Violence against children is especially difficult to detect when the predator is a trusted and institutionally protected caregiver outside the home or a community leader, such as a child care provider, teacher, coach, activity leader, or religious official. With the explosion of Internet media available to children, predators also increasingly target, recruit, and exploit children through online contacts.

> "Even many of those who acknowledge the existence of child abuse…fool themselves into thinking that these horrible crimes happen to somebody else's kids at the hands of some stranger, somebody unrecognized in their world. It's hard for people to realize the truth — that children from all sectors of society are abused every day by people they should be able to trust."
>
> — The Hon. John Romero, Children's Court Division, Second Judicial District Court, State of New Mexico

Entrapment and exploitation by predators who should be trusted caregivers and role models not only directly harms children but also likely leads them to develop severe trust issues even in trustworthy relationships because of the fear, anger, guilt, shame, and confusion caused by this betrayal of the fundamental assumption that adults are protectors.

Children also are exposed to community violence when adults or youth in their school or neighborhood engage in criminal violence using weapons or physical assault, such as in gang wars, or when these adults or youth assault children traveling to school or in the school itself. Less commonly, riots and terrorist attacks victimize children. Although rarely experienced by children in this country, many children who are immigrants from violence-torn countries have witnessed or been exposed to horrific community violence in the form of torture, bombings, wars, and ethnic cleansing.

Community networks and systems are integral to a child's development of psychological health and well-being, social opportunity, and a purposeful existence.[6,24,26,29–31] Beyond the immediate adverse impact on the individual child who is exposed, community violence can warp, fragment, or even destroy the child's community. This is important because effective interventions to reduce the occurrence or after-effects of community violence need to support the recovery of the entire community (or neighborhood, or school) in order to protect all affected children and help them to heal if actually exposed to violence.

Child survivors of community violence often struggle with rebuilding trust, finding meaning in life apart from the desire for safety and justice, finding realistic ways to protect themselves and their loved ones from danger, and dealing with feelings of guilt, shame, powerlessness, and doubt. There is also a concern that witnessing violence can lead children to identify with the aggressors and to turn to violence as a way to emulate the actions that perpetrators are modeling, or to try to protect themselves with aggressive coping behaviors: when children learn to use violence based on witnessing violence, this can perpetuate a cycle of escalating violent behavior, especially in intimate relationships.[6,7,17,18,20,29,32]

In addition, when children witness violence in their communities, it can become an accepted norm for them.[22] They can learn to think of danger, fear, injury, and death as normal. Instead of celebrating life, they too often must mourn losses, creating shrines for their many friends and family members who have been killed. These children wait nervously or helplessly for the next explosion of violence in their neighborhood or school, or they mourn the all-too-common deaths or devastated lives of their families, friends, and community members. Many feel they need to fight back against actual or potential perpetrators. These dynamics have become the "new normal" for far too many children and far too many communities.

Creating peaceful communities is essential to rescue children from being trapped in a life of violence and allowing them to live a full life free from exposure to violence. Youth exposed to community violence are at high risk for developing serious problems such as post-traumatic stress disorder (PTSD), depression, social isolation or conflicted relationships, underachievement and school dropout, addictions, and perpetrating violence themselves.[4,6,7,9–17,23,24,33–35] The combination of exposure to community violence and developing severe PTSD symptoms is particularly strongly associated with problems with aggression.[36] Unfortunately, children who cope with exposure to violence by engaging in violent behavior tend to be viewed as "deviant" or "future criminals" rather than as traumatized victims. As a consequence, they rarely receive support or assistance to address the trauma-related symptoms that often precipitate children's acts of violence or delinquency. Exposure to violence does not justify or excuse acts of violence, but with appropriate trauma-informed law enforcement and judicial responses, these children can reform their behavior and attitudes if they receive trauma-informed services and trauma-specific treatment (Chapter 2).

"When it comes to LGBT youth, the biggest thing that I find is a lot of these kids are looking for a straight ally out there, like straight role models, people who are going to say, 'It's okay, and I'm okay with it. I'm not going to condemn you, and I'm going to stick up for you when other people don't.'"

— Nate Monson, Executive Director, Iowa Safe Schools

Research indicates that although children of all ages are exposed to community violence, adolescence is the developmental period of greatest risk for witnessing or being involved in life-threatening community violence.[1,37,38] Adolescents are grappling with complex questions regarding their values and aspirations and are developing a worldview that they will retain for the rest of their adult lives. They are uniquely positioned, therefore, to be agents of positive change in their communities on behalf of ending violence and healing the harm caused to peers, siblings, and children of all ages when violence contaminates the community. Involving youth as positive agents of change is vital to all efforts to protect children from violence and to help victims to heal from its traumatic aftereffects.

Exposure to community violence also affects families in profound ways that can diminish their ability to provide a safe and nurturing home for their children (see Chapter 4). A common parental reaction to children being exposed to violence in their neighborhoods or schools is the development of anxiety concerning their children's health and well-being. Parents may blame themselves for not protecting their child adequately and become overprotective or use punitive discipline in response to their child's acting-out behavior. Parents also face the difficult task of reassuring their child while trying to cope with their own fears. This is especially difficult when community violence is chronic in their child's school or neighborhood. Thus, ending community violence is essential to the health and safety of families and to their ability to ensure the healthy development and safety of their children.

Reducing and preventing community violence depends on understanding its sources and perpetuating factors. Different communities face different challenges, and these unique challenges are best understood and addressed through collaborative problem assessment and strategy development. At the individual level, timely and sensitive care for children and families exposed to community violence is needed through trauma-informed psychoeducation, crisis hotlines, screening to identify violence-exposed children who are at high risk of developing PTSD and related psychosocial and behavioral problems, and referral for trauma-informed services and trauma-specific treatment. Progress has been made in developing violence prevention programs, especially for gang prevention and conflict resolution with high-risk youth. Public health approaches, such as those in the Centers for Disease Control and Prevention's UNITY (Urban Networks to Increase Thriving Youth) program, involve a comprehensive approach to community violence that incorporates prevention and treatment.

The science of treatment for children exposed to community violence has been developed over the past two decades. Trauma-specific therapeutic interventions for children and adolescents exposed to community violence have been shown to be effective when delivered in mental health clinics, in schools, and in home-based and residential programs.[7,39–47] Such treatments require continued development and should be conducted with children of all ages — including toddlers and preschool and elementary school students, for whom they can help build a foundation of psychological and interpersonal resilience when violence has occurred in their lives[48–51] — to heal the emotional, behavioral, and social wounds of violence.

In addition, programs that involve the family, school, and community services such as law enforcement, the courts, and child protection, have the strongest evidence base for developing children's resilience.[47,52–62] These programs provide supportive relationships and guidance not only for children but also for their parents and families. In addition, they are designed to increase community safety and to provide families with access to recreational facilities and health care. These multidimensional approaches to enhancing children's psychological strengths and social support networks have shown evidence of success with children and adolescents who are likely to have been exposed to violence.[39,43,47,63]

In order to both reduce the extent of this pandemic of children's exposure to community violence on behalf of children not yet exposed and help children who are victims to recover and heal from the trauma and grief caused by violence in their neighborhoods and schools, the task force proposes 11 recommendations that are described below.

5.1 Organize local coalitions in every community representing professionals from multiple disciplines and the full range of service systems (including law enforcement, the courts, health care, schools, family services, child protection, domestic violence programs, rape crisis centers, and child advocacy centers) as well as families and other community members, to assess local challenges and resources, develop strategies, and carry out coordinated responses to reduce violence and the number of children exposed to violence.

When children are exposed to community violence, the entire community is trau-matized and must join together to restore communal safety. No provider, agency, or program can be fully successful when acting alone to help a child recover from community violence. No community can rise up out of violence without the coordination of many disciplines, professionals, agencies, organizations, businesses, and concerned adults and children in coalitions that take a positive stand against violence. With concerted action, children's lives can be saved or reclaimed, and the entire community can be transformed and empowered. Pilot sites implementing the Department of Justice Office of Juvenile Justice and Delinquency Prevention's (OJJDP's) comprehensive strategy found that by developing coalitions of multidisciplinary stakeholders they gained a better understanding of their local problems of children exposed to violence and were able to comprehensively identify and address gaps in crucial services for these children and their families.

Community coalitions, like those formed through the National Forum on Youth Violence Prevention, show great promise for ending children's exposure to community violence. This forum is a vibrant national network of federal and local stakeholders that, through the use of multidisciplinary partnerships, has developed approaches that combine prevention, intervention, enforcement, reentry, and data-driven strategies to strengthen communities, to better prevent violence, and to promote the safety, health, and development of our nation's youth. Similarly, the demonstration sites participating in the U.S. Attorney General's Defending Childhood Initiative have embraced multi-agency and multidisciplinary action-oriented approaches to building and sustaining coordinated community responses to violence and to children's exposure to violence. Local efforts like these are designed to increase children's safety and well-being by changing behavior and attitudes while also providing intensive case management and wraparound support services as well as immediate access to services tailored to meet the individual needs of children and families exposed to violence. Across the country, we need to build coalitions like these while also emphasizing the need for delinquency prevention, legal services, housing services, mental health services, recreational programs, and transitional employment programs that provide on-the-job training with an intentional focus on building life skills.

5.2 Recognize and support the critical role of law enforcement's participation in collaborative responses to violence.

Law enforcement takes the lead when dealing with the perpetrators of violence, but law enforcement also can play a unique role in contributing to community coalitions that advocate for safety and nonviolence. The contribution that law enforcement can make to protecting and defending children against violence is under-utilized when this is limited to 9-1-1 crisis-driven responses. Models of community policing have enabled law enforcement to work collaboratively with concerned community members and constituencies in many cities, towns, and rural areas across the country. This approach recognizes law enforcement personnel as integral members of the community who bring special expertise to enhancing the well-being of everyone in that community as well as to ensuring public safety.

Successful national and local models for partnerships of child- and family-serving providers with law enforcement build on and expand upon principles of community policing. These model programs are a systematic partnership between law enforcement and community agencies and providers that bring expertise in child development, violence prevention, and treatment of children exposed to violence. The partnership includes an ongoing dialogue in which all of the participants share their experience and expertise while working collaboratively with one another on the streets, on police calls to respond to violence in homes and schools, and in open forums with youth, parents, educators, healthcare providers, child welfare workers, probation officers, judges, and other concerned citizens. The role of law enforcement is expanded to include serving as a protective source of security and as a gateway for connecting children and families to trauma-informed services and trauma-specific treatment.

The key elements of this collaboration between law enforcement, juvenile justice, domestic violence, medical and mental health professionals, child welfare agencies, schools, and other community agencies include cross-training for police as well as mental health and other professional specialists on child development, trauma, and policing strategies; acute-response services that provide coordinated police and clinical response to violent events; regular interdisciplinary case conferencing for case planning, review, and monitoring; follow-up home visits by police officers, clinicians, and domestic violence advocates; and evidence-based trauma-specific treatment and trauma-informed services that are available to children and families exposed to violence in their homes, neighborhoods, or schools.[64-70]

"A sense of safety is paramount in having a safe community. The police have always dealt with the children exposed to the violence and trauma, but we needed help when it came to saving them from the harm caused by this exposure…. Together we can help restore a sense of safety in children's lives, so they can grow to be happy and productive members in society."

— Major Eddie Levins, Charlotte-Mecklenburg Police Department

Research and program evaluation studies demonstrate that these partnerships of child-serving professionals and law enforcement professionals effectively provide protection and help in recovery and healing for children exposed to violence.[1-6,24,65] They also have helped to mobilize community coalitions by bringing together youth and adults from all parts of the community and its public and private agencies, institutions, and constituencies to stand up for the safety of children on behalf of the entire community.

Reconfiguring law enforcement's role to include participation in community coalitions requires assigning officers to nontraditional roles. This involves fiscal costs and the increased staffing levels needed to fulfill all public safety responsibilities, especially the priority of responding to emergency calls for service. Community policing often requires a shift in deployment that can reduce the law enforcement agency's patrol function. It also requires additional time and expertise for specialized training of the participating officers, supervisors, and managers. Funding through the Department of Justice Community Oriented Policing Services (COPS) Office should be expanded to enable every community's law enforcement agency to undertake this shift in responsibilities. This change in perspective can enable both new and veteran officers to more fully serve their community by contributing to a community-wide multi-agency initiative to maintain public safety and enhance the well-being of all children and adults.

5.3 Involve men and boys as critical partners in preventing violence.

While men are more likely than women to perpetrate violence,[71-74] men are also leaders and the models for changing norms of masculinity that currently tolerate and at times condone violence. While some forms of male violence stem from traditional notions that men must prove their strength through fighting or that they are entitled to keep women and children in subservient roles, some of the violence perpetrated against women and girls, as well as other men and boys, may stem from deep-seated suffering and despair, a desire to demonstrate power in the face of life circumstances that feel hopeless and depleting. Most men and boys who use violence have suffered from abuse themselves.

"In a previous time, men were linked by our connectedness and reliance on one another in order to raise and nurture our children and families and prepare them for an evolving future. In many communities…these attributes have been replaced with complete opposite notions of maleness that are rooted in the struggle for power, dominance, and control over the children and partners we say we love. And our children suffer."

— Héctor Sánchez-Flores, Executive Director, National Compadres Network

In communities across the country, groups of men are organizing to support one another in using nonviolence to build healthy communities through civic programs, schools, sports, arts programs, businesses, and public-private partnerships. These men are going out on the streets, onto the playing fields and recreation centers, into the schools, and into faith-based organizations to teach boys as well as other men that violence does not equal strength. These initiatives, however, remain isolated and are too often built around the determination of a few individuals. The men doing this work need human and financial capital from both public and private sources. With those resources, initiatives involving men and boys as critical partners in preventing violence can grow from isolated islands of change into a substantial, growing network of men and boys across the country committed to creating widespread change and helping break the cycle of violence in our homes, schools, and communities.

5.4 Foster, promote, and model healthy relationships for children and youth.

Abuse within adolescent relationships is a critical, but often overlooked, type of violence that young people experience and to which they are exposed at alarming rates. Research suggests that one in five adolescent women have been abused by their dating partners, and two-thirds of youth who act violently in dating relationships report witnessing assaults between family members.[75–81] In addition to the harm that youth may experience as victims, we know that exposure to abuse within adolescent relationships and witnessing family violence (Chapter 4) increase the risk for violence in adulthood among the children involved. Therefore, it is critical that we deepen our understanding of the safety and developmental risks that exposure to abuse in adolescent relationships poses to adolescents, and we must improve our knowledge about how prevention, intervention, and resilience can be integrated to improve the chances of life success for youth. Community and school-based programs and policies that work in tandem to prevent relationship abuse and, just as importantly,

"Adolescence is a time when young people are gaining their independence. They're beginning these relationships that will form what their relationships look like in the future. Middle school is an absolutely critical time to engage parents, teens, caregivers, and other adults to support the development of healthy relationships."

— **Annie Pelletier Kerrick, Program Manager, Idaho Teen Dating Violence Awareness & Prevention Project**

to promote healthy relationships, have shown great promise.[82–86] These programs, guided by caring adults and communities and with shared leadership from youth as role models for younger children, are succeeding in changing social norms that tolerate and at times condone abuse.

Working collaboratively with young people, adults who are involved in the lives of children can take action against all forms of community violence by consciously serving as positive role models and engaging children and youth in healthy, nonviolent relationships. Healthy relationships are based on mutual respect, honest and sensitive communication, gender and racial equity, empathy, compassion, recognition of the different needs and abilities of people of different ages and backgrounds, and shared responsibility for success. Modeling healthy relationships, and helping youth to develop them with peers and their families, is a direct antidote for violence and its toxic effects. Youth-led community and school-based programs guided by conscientious adults are succeeding in communities across the country in mobilizing children and youth to invest themselves in healthy relationships.[87,88] These local initiatives need public and private support and sponsorship in order to become the rule rather than the exception in communities throughout our nation.

5.5 Develop and implement policies to improve the reporting of suspected child sexual abuse in every institution entrusted with the care and nurturing of children.

When children are sexually or physically abused, the harm that this violence causes is greatly exacerbated if the abuse and the perpetrator are not publicly identified and the perpetrator is not immediately prevented from further abusing that child or other children.

Communities must work particularly hard to break the silence and secrecy that shroud child sexual abuse. When community members talk about sexual violence and ask the right questions, they help to break the isolation that many children experience. When community members have the skills to identify and report child sexual abuse, they open doors of justice, healing, and support that had once been closed for many children. If community members intervene when they witness sexual violence, they not only help to prevent that specific occurrence; they also protect the abused child victim or other children from further victimization and help set social norms and create environments in which sexual violence is not tolerated. When community members talk about healthy sexuality and model positive, nurturing, respectful relationships and communication, they can work to ultimately prevent sexual violence from occurring.

Institutional protections that shield perpetrators of sexual or physical abuse or other forms of violence against children violate both the letter and the spirit of the law as well as moral and ethical principles that condemn such violence. When officials in an organization or system excuse or condone known acts of abuse or violence against children, they are indirectly but substantially contributing to the harm caused to children, past and future, who are exposed to violence.

Most, if not all, of the institutions in this country that are entrusted with the care and nurturing of children have policies and procedures for reporting the suspected abuse of children. All of these institutions must review these policies and procedures and modify them wherever necessary to eliminate their points of uncertainty. In addition, reviews should be undertaken in areas where there have been or potentially could be a failure of the institution's officials, employees, and other participating individuals and entities (such as volunteers, contractors, and consultants) to comply fully with the specific responsibilities for protecting children defined by these policies and procedures.

The education and supervision provided by the institution to all officials, employees, and other participants concerning their specific responsibilities in reporting all forms of suspected child abuse or other ways in which children are exposed to violence are an essential but often unfulfilled responsibility of every institution in our country, especially those entrusted with the care, education, supervision, and nurturing of children. Every institution must provide timely, ongoing education and supervision to its agents at all levels to ensure that all incidents of suspected child abuse are reported without delay and that appropriate legal authorities outside the institution who are responsible for children's safety and welfare are fully and immediately informed.

5.6 Train and require child care providers to meet professional and legal standards for identifying young children exposed to violence and preventing violence from occurring to any child for whom they are responsible.

Child care providers in center-based programs and in their own or the child's home have a unique opportunity to protect children from exposure to violence. Child care providers must be trained and provided with ongoing supervision and continuing education in order to be able to recognize children in their care who have been exposed to violence. National, state, local, and tribal child welfare departments that set standards for child care providers' reporting of abuse and neglect must establish clear and specific guidelines for all providers of child care and monitor adherence to these guidelines. In addition, professional organizations and regional and local agencies and programs that train child care providers and set standards for them must monitor adherence to these standards, which should be mandatory for all providers and should take the form of clear and specific guidelines for identifying and reporting suspected child abuse and other forms of exposure to violence.

Sadly, child care providers can themselves inflict violence on children or expose children to violence by perpetrating or condoning physical violence, sexual abuse, or child-to-child bullying in the child care setting. Governmental, professional, and private for-profit or nonprofit agencies and organizations that oversee child care providers must require all providers to complete preservice and ongoing continuing education and supervision in order to prevent the use of corporal punishment and incidents of sexually, physically, or emotionally abusive behavior toward children in center-based or home-based child care.

5.7 Provide schools with the resources they need to create and sustain safe places where children exposed to violence can get help.

Violence can spill over from families and the larger community into schools, but it also can be inadvertently fostered in schools when students are not taught how to handle conflict and build relationships in healthy ways that do not involve violence. Schools play an essential role in creating and establishing an environment for healthy and nonviolent behaviors that are both taught and modeled on the playground, in the food court, on the playing fields and in the locker rooms, in extracurricular activities, and in the classroom. Every adult in our schools is a potential positive — or negative — role model for hundreds or thousands of children every day. Programs that train all school staff — from teachers, administrators, and personnel to maintenance workers to school bus drivers to workers in the food court — to interact with students and one another in trauma-informed ways have been developed, scientifically tested, and widely disseminated in dozens of rural, urban, and suburban communities in our country.[89–98] Every school in the U.S. and all of their educational and support personnel should be provided with training and ongoing supervision in order to provide trauma-informed school services.

Schools also are a critical place for the identification of children exposed to violence who need immediate help (see Chapter 2) and where evidence-based trauma-specific treatment can be provided efficiently and in a timely and accessible manner (see Chapter 3) for those children. Every school in our country should have trained trauma-informed professionals on staff or working collaboratively as consultants to provide school-based, trauma-specific treatment and to assist children who have been exposed to violence and have chronic or severe problems to access evidence-based school- or clinic- or home-based treatment.

Corporal punishment is permitted in some schools in this country although it represents the use of violence as a means of changing behavior and enforcing discipline. Every school in which corporal punishment continues to be used should be provided with education and training for all administrators, teachers, and staff on trauma-informed alternatives to corporal punishment that have been shown to be effective in maintaining discipline without violence.

5.8 Provide children, parents, schools, and communities with the tools they need to identify and stop bullying and to help children who have been bullied — including the bullies themselves — to recover from social, emotional, and school problems.

Bullying is a form of violence that increasingly is recognized as a serious problem for teens and for school-age children as young as preschoolers. Bullying can involve verbal as well as physical violence and threats. Victims of bullying often are isolated by their peer group and shamed and humiliated not only by the bullies but also by other peers and adults (including their teachers, coaches, and even their own parents and other family members). Victims of bullying also commonly experience serious problems with depression, anxiety, loneliness, and hopelessness as well as with school achievement and attendance. For girls, physical, verbal, and social bullying have been found to be associated with subsequent body dissatisfaction, particularly when verbal bullying led them to experience anxiety and depression.[99]

Some bullying victims attempt to turn the tables and regain a sense of power, control, and peer acceptance by bullying other children. Bullies are not typically cruel or mean children by nature, but they can become cruel and hurtful toward other children as a form of self-protective reactive aggression. Children or youth who are bullies may appear successful and popular, but often they have been victims of bullying or violence in their own families and are troubled by serious emotional problems that can result in serious danger to themselves (such as substance abuse or suicidality) as well as to the children whom they bully.

Providing trauma-informed services and support to children who are bullies as well as to those who are victims of bullying is an essential step in stopping the spread of emotional and physical violence toward children in our schools and communities.

"Kids can't go to school ready to learn when they're full of fear or they're dealing with the emotional baggage of what violence has brought to their life. They can't concentrate when they're being bullied."

— Janell Regimbal, Senior Vice President, Children and Family Services, Lutheran Social Services of North Dakota

Programs designed based on the guidelines described in this chapter's previous recommendations — building multi-stakeholder community and school coalitions, providing healthy adult and peer role models, and teaching children healthy and safe ways to build and sustain relationships — have been shown to be successful in restoring safety and healthy development to the lives of children who are bullied and those who are bullies.[100,101] One study in 10 public middle schools found evidence of benefits primarily for White children but not for African-American or Hispanic youth, suggesting a need for careful ethnocultural adaptation of bullying-prevention programs.[102] These programs embody the principles of restorative justice, which can instill individual and community-level accountability and positive action to support healing and resilience as well as demonstrate the potential value of meaningful restitution.

5.9 Put programs to identify and protect children exposed to community violence who struggle with suicidality in place in every community.

The most tragic and severe consequence of children's exposure to violence is a combination of profound hopelessness and suicidality.[103,104] Children exposed to violence as a result of physical or sexual assault or abuse, pervasive criminal violence committed by gangs in their schools and neighborhoods, or bullying by peers or older children can become isolated and tormented by anxiety and depression. The violence can seem to be a prison or trap from which the only relief or escape is death — directly by self-harm, or indirectly by using drugs or alcohol or engaging in reckless, risky behavior in ways that are life-threatening.

"How does suicide intertwine with violence? Sometimes youth turn to suicide to escape the violence that exists in their families and between their peers…. These perpetuating cycles of violence lead to depression and destructive behaviors that oftentimes have violent endings…. Suicide, in times like this, is one of the first things to come to the mind of most Native youth."

— Coloradas Mangas, Mescalero Apache Tribe and Youth Board Member for the Center for Native American Youth

Suicide prevention programs for children and youth have been shown to be successful in a small number of community research studies,[96–98] but these programs are not available in most of our country's communities. Evidence-based, trauma-informed suicide prevention programs and trauma-specific treatments for children and youth who are at high risk due to severe suicidality should be adapted for children and communities of varied backgrounds and made accessible immediately to every child and family in every community in our country. These programs provide education, counseling, support from caring adults, healthy opportunities for restorative contacts with peers, and help from a network of multiple providers and agencies working as a coalition to protect children exposed to violence who are struggling with suicidality.

5.10 Support community programs that provide youth with mentoring as an intervention and as a prevention strategy, to reduce victimization by and involvement in violence and to promote healthy development by youths.

Adults are crucial role models for nonviolence in many walks of life in every child's community. A meaningful relationship with a positive adult role model has been shown repeatedly in scientific studies to be a protective factor against violence even for youth who are growing up in very difficult circumstances and violent environments.[105–111] Both informally, and formally in structured programs, an adult mentor can be the one adult who makes a difference in a child's life — including protecting that child or youth from violence and serving as a role model for achieving success without violence. Mentoring programs in the civilian and military communities have shown promise in reducing youth victimization by violence as well as the involvement of youth in violence and by improving youth's social, emotional, and behavioral well-being.[112–116]

Mentoring is not a panacea, however. It cannot replace interventions for children exposed to violence that are provided by multi-provider coalitions and support to the family as well as the child. Nor can it replace evidence-based treatment and trauma-informed services for children exposed to community violence. However, when included in community-wide programs that provide professional services and treatments, mentoring can make a unique contribution both to preventing children from being exposed to violence and to the recovery of children who are victimized by violence.

"If you are going to recommend more mentoring… I really encourage you to look at the social and emotional connections between trauma and adult outcomes and the programs that you are likely to support, so that, in combination, they produce outcomes that individually they could not."

— Bryan Samuels, Commissioner, Administration on Children, Youth and Families, U.S. Department of Health and Human Services

Mentoring requires great skill, integrity, and patience when provided to children or youth who have been victimized by violence. All mentoring programs for children exposed to violence should provide trauma-informed training and ongoing supervision to each adult who serves as a mentor in order to ensure the safety of the children they monitor and maximize the benefits of mentoring that the children receive.

5.11 Help communities learn and share what works by investing in research.

Research and program evaluations have immeasurably benefitted the existing interventions and programs that scientists, clinicians, and advocates have developed and that communities have adapted and put into practice to protect their children from exposure to violence and to help victims heal, regain their childhoods, and reclaim their right to develop a healthy, productive, and meaningful life.

Much more research will be needed to build the evidence base as communities adopt, adapt, and implement trauma-informed services and trauma-specific treatments for children who have been exposed to violence. Services and treatments cannot remain static, or they will become stagnant and obsolete. On the other hand, when research infuses services and treatments with new knowledge and improved practices, communities can update, refine, or change their programs for children exposed to violence based on what works rather than on parochial opinions or preferences.

Scientific research on the causes of children's exposure to community violence and ways to prevent and treat its adverse effects requires a coordinated national initiative to develop public-private partnerships and funding in order to ensure that the most effective and efficient interventions are available to, and used successfully in, every community in our country.

References

1. Fairbank, J. A., & Fairbank, D. W. (2009). Epidemiology of child traumatic stress. *Current Psychiatry Reports, 11*(4), 289–95.

2. Costello, E. J., et al. (2002). The prevalence of potentially traumatic events in childhood and adolescence. *Journal of Traumatic Stress, 15*(2), 99–112.

3. Finkelhor, D., et al. (2010). Trends in childhood violence and abuse exposure: evidence from 2 national surveys. *Archives of Pediatrics and Adolescent Medicine, 164*(3), 238–42.

4. Zinzow, H. M., et al. (2009). Prevalence and mental health correlates of witnessed parental and community violence in a national sample of adolescents. *Journal of Child Psychology and Psychiatry, 50*(4), 441–450.

5. Margolin, G., et al. (2009). Youth exposed to violence: stability, co-occurrence, and context. *Clinical Child and Family Psychology Review, 12*(1), 39–54.

6. Horowitz, K., McKay, M., & Marshall, R. (2005). Community violence and urban families: experiences, effects, and directions for intervention. *American Journal of Orthopsychiatry, 75*(3), 356–68.

7. Sieger, K., et al. (2004). The effects and treatment of community violence in children and adolescents: what should be done? *Trauma, Violence, & Abuse, 5*(3), 243–59.

8. Stein, B. D., et al. (2003). Prevalence of child and adolescent exposure to community violence. *Clinical Child and Family Psychology Review, 6*(4), 247–64.

9. Turner, H. A., et al. (2012). Recent victimization exposure and suicidal ideation in adolescents. *Archives of Pediatrics & Adolescent Medicine,* 1–6.

10. Miller, E., et al. (2012). Exposure to partner, family, and community violence: gang-affiliated Latina women and risk of unintended pregnancy. *Journal of Urban Health, 89*(1), 74–86.

11. McKelvey, L. M., et al. (2011). Growing up in violent communities: Do family conflict and gender moderate impacts on adolescents' psychosocial development? *Journal of Abnormal Child Psychology, 39*(1), 95–107.

12. Hunt, K. L., Martens, P. M., & Belcher, H. M. (2011). Risky business: trauma exposure and rate of posttraumatic stress disorder in African American children and adolescents. *Journal of Traumatic Stress, 24*(3), 365–9.

13. Voisin, D. R., Neilands, T. B., & Hunnicutt, S. (2010). Mechanisms linking violence exposure and school engagement among African American adolescents: examining the roles of psychological problem behaviors and gender. *American Journal of Orthopsychiatry, 81*(1), 61–71.

14. Garrido, E. F., et al. (2010). Does community violence exposure predict trauma symptoms in a sample of maltreated youth in foster care? *Violence and Victims, 25*(6), 755–69.

15. Zinzow, H. M., et al. (2009). Witnessed community and parental violence in relation to substance use and delinquency in a national sample of adolescents. *Journal of Traumatic Stress, 22*(6), 525–33.

16. Shields, N., Nadasen, K., & Pierce, L. (2009) Posttraumatic stress symptoms as a mediating factor on the effects of exposure to community violence among children in Cape Town, South Africa. *Violence and Victims, 24*(6), 786–99.

17. Fowler, P.J., et al. (2009). Community violence: a meta-analysis on the effect of exposure and mental health outcomes of children and adolescents. *Development and Psychopathology, 21*(1), 227–59.

18. Foster, H., & Brooks-Gunn, J. (2009). Toward a stress process model of children's exposure to physical family and community violence. *Clinical Child and Family Psychology Review, 12*(2), 71–94.

19. Fincham, D. S., et al. (2009). Posttraumatic stress disorder symptoms in adolescents: risk factors versus resilience moderation. *Comprehensive Psychiatry, 50*(3), 193–9.

20. Fredland, N. M., Campbell, J. C., & Han, H. (2008). Effect of violence exposure on health outcomes among young urban adolescents. *Nursing Research, 57*(3), 157–65.

21. Aisenberg, E., Ayon, C., & Orozco-Figueroa, A. (2008). The role of young adolescents' perception in understanding the severity of exposure to community violence and PTSD. *Journal of Interpersonal Violence, 23*(11), 1555–78.

22. McCart, M. R., et al. (2007). Do urban adolescents become desensitized to community violence? Data from a national survey. *American Journal of Orthopsychiatry, 77*(3), 434–42.

23. Denson, T. F., et al. (2007). Predictors of posttraumatic distress 1 year after exposure to community violence: the importance of acute symptom severity. *Journal of Consulting and Clinical Psychology, 75*(5), 683–92.

24. Scarpa, A., Haden, S. C., & Hurley, J. (2006). Community violence victimization and symptoms of posttraumatic stress disorder: the moderating effects of coping and social support. *Journal of Interpersonal Violence, 21*(4), 446–69.

25. Kennedy, A. C., & Bennett, L. (2006). Urban adolescent mothers exposed to community, family, and partner violence: is cumulative violence exposure a barrier to school performance and participation? *Journal of Interpersonal Violence, 21*(6), 750–73.

26. Rosenthal, B. S., & Wilson, W. C. (2003). The association of ecological variables and psychological distress with exposure to community violence among adolescents. *Adolescence, 38*(151), 459–79.

27. Evans, G. W., & English, K. (2002). The environment of poverty: multiple stressor exposure, psychophysiological stress, and socioemotional adjustment. *Child Development, 73*(4), 1238–48.

28. Rosenthal, B. S., & Wilson, W. C. (2001). Relationship between exposure to community violence and psychological distress: linear or curvilinear? *Psychological Reports, 88*(3 Pt 1), 635–40.

29. Brown, J. R., Hill, H. M., & Lambert, S. F. (2005). Traumatic stress symptoms in women exposed to community and partner violence. *Journal of Interpersonal Violence, 20*(11), 1478–94.

30. Bradshaw, C. P., & Garbarino, J. (2004). Social cognition as a mediator of the influence of family and community violence on adolescent development: implications for intervention. *Annals of the New York Academy of Sciences, 1036*, 85–105.

31. Kataoka, S. H., et al. (2003). A school-based mental health program for traumatized Latino immigrant children. *Journal of the American Academy of Child & Adolescent Psychiatry, 42*(3), 311–318.

32. Garrido, E. F., et al. (2011). Psychosocial consequences of Intimate Partner Violence (IPV) exposure in maltreated adolescents: Assessing more than IPV occurrence. *Journal of Family Violence, 26*(7), 511–518.

33. Ford, J. D., et al. (2008). Traumatic victimization, posttraumatic stress disorder, suicidal ideation, and substance abuse risk among juvenile justice-involved youths. *Journal of Child & Adolescent Trauma, 1,* 75–92.

34. Ford, J. D., et al. (2010). Poly-victimization and risk of posttraumatic, depressive, and substance use disorders and involvement in delinquency in a national sample of adolescents. *Journal of Adolescent Health, 46*(6), 545–52.

35. Gagne, M. H., Lavoie, F., & Hebert, M. (2005). Victimization during childhood and revictimization in dating relationships in adolescent girls. *Child Abuse & Neglect, 29*(10), 1155–72.

36. Ford, J. D., et al. (2012). Complex trauma and aggression in secure juvenile justice settings. *Criminal Justice & Behavior, 39*(5), 695–724.

37. Saigh, P. A., et al. (2008). Posttraumatic stress disorder in children and adolescents: History, risk, and cognitive behavioral treatment. In R. J. Morris & T. R. Kratochwill (Eds.), *The practice of child therapy* (pp. 433–454). Mahwah, NJ: Lawrence Erlbaum Associates Publishers.

38. Fairbank, J. A., Putnam, F. W., & Harris, W. W. (2007). The prevalence and impact of child traumatic stress. In M. J. Friedman, T. M. Keane, & P. A. Resick (Eds.), *Handbook of PTSD* (pp. 229–251). New York, NY: Guilford Press.

39. Cohen, J. A., Mannarino, A. P., & Murray, L. K. (2011). Trauma-focused CBT for youth who experience ongoing traumas. *Child Abuse & Neglect, 35*(8), 637–46.

40. Ford, J. D., et al. (2012). Randomized trial comparison of emotion regulation and relational psychotherapies for PTSD with girls involved in delinquency. *Journal of Clinical Child & Adolescent Psychology, 41*(1), 27–37.

41. Ford, J. D., & Hawke, J. (2012). Trauma affect regulation psychoeducation group and milieu intervention outcomes in juvenile detention facilities. *Journal of Aggression, Maltreatment & Trauma, 21*(4), 365–384.

42. Cohen, J. A., et al. (2012). Trauma-focused CBT for youth with complex trauma. *Child Abuse & Neglect, 36*(6), 528–41.

43. Cohen, J. A., Mannarino, A. P., & Iyengar, S. (2011). Community treatment of posttraumatic stress disorder for children exposed to intimate partner violence: a randomized controlled trial. *Archives of Pediatric & Adolescent Medicine, 165*(1), 16–21.

44. Marrow, M., et al. (2012). The value of implementing TARGET within a trauma-informed juvenile justice setting. *Journal of Child & Adolescent Trauma, 5,* 257–270.

45. Jaycox, L. H., Stein, B. D., & Amaya-Jackson, L. (2009). School-based treatment for children and adolescents. In E. B. Foa, et al. (Eds.), *Effective Treatments for PTSD (2nd Ed)* (pp. 327–345). New York, NY: Guilford.

46. Stein, B. D., et al. (2003). A mental health intervention for schoolchildren exposed to violence: a randomized controlled trial. *Journal of the American Medical Association, 290*(5), 603–11.

47. Berkowitz, S. J., Stover, C. S., & Marans, S. R. (2011). The Child and Family Traumatic Stress Intervention: secondary prevention for youth at risk of developing PTSD. *Journal of Child Psychology and Psychiatry, 52*(6), 676–85.

48. Briggs-Gowan, M. J., Carter, A. S., & Ford, J. D. (2012). Parsing the effects violence exposure in early childhood: modeling developmental pathways. *Journal of Pediatric Psychology, 37*(1), 11–22.

49. Briggs-Gowan, M. J., et al. (2011). Prevalence of exposure to potentially traumatic events in a healthy birth cohort of very young children in the northeastern United States. *Journal of Traumatic Stress, 23*(6), 725–33.

50. Briggs-Gowan, M. J., et al. (2010). Exposure to potentially traumatic events in early childhood: differential links to emergent psychopathology. *Journal of Child Psychology and Psychiatry, 51,* 1132–1140.

51. Mongillo, E. A., et al. (2009). Impact of traumatic life events in a community sample of toddlers. *Journal of Abnormal Child Psychology, 37*(4), 455–68.

52. Nakamura, B., et al. (2011). Large-scale implementation of evidence-based treatments for children 10 years later. *Clinical Psychology: Science and Practice, 18*(1), 24–35.

53. Lowell, D. I., et al. (2011). A randomized controlled trial of Child FIRST: a comprehensive home-based intervention translating research into early childhood practice. *Child Development, 82*(1), 193–208.

54. Chorpita, B. F., Bernstein, A., & Daleiden, E. L. (2011). Empirically guided coordination of multiple evidence-based treatments: an illustration of relevance mapping in children's mental health services. *Journal of Consulting and Clinical Psychology, 79*(4), 470–80.

55. Harvey, S. T., & Taylor, J. E. (2010). A meta-analysis of the effects of psychotherapy with sexually abused children and adolescents. *Clinical Psychology Review, 30*(5), 517–35.

56. Cohen, J. A., & Mannarino, A. P. (2010). Psychotherapeutic options for traumatized children. *Current Opinion in Pediatrics, 22*(5), 605–9.

57. Trosper, S. E., et al. (2009). Emotion regulation in youth with emotional disorders: implications for a unified treatment approach. *Clinical Child and Family Psychology Review, 12*(3), 234–54.

58. Ehrenreich, J. T., et al. (2009). Development of a Unified Protocol for the Treatment of Emotional Disorders in Youth. *Child and Family Behavior Therapy, 31*(1), 20–37.

59. Huey, S. J., Jr., & Polo, A. J. (2008). Evidence-based psychosocial treatments for ethnic minority youth. *Journal of Clinical Child & Adolescent Psychology, 37*(1), 262–301.

60. Chorpita, B. F., Becker, K. D., & Daleiden, E. L. (2007). Understanding the common elements of evidence-based practice: misconceptions and clinical examples. *Journal of the American Academy of Child & Adolescent Psychiatry, 46*(5), 647–52.

61. Kazdin, A. E., & Wassell, G. (2000). Therapeutic changes in children, parents, and families resulting from treatment of children with conduct problems. *Journal of the American Academy of Child & Adolescent Psychiatry, 39*(4), 414–20.

62. Henggeler, S. W., et al. (2008). Promoting the implementation of an evidence-based intervention for adolescent marijuana abuse in community settings: testing the use of intensive quality assurance. *Journal of Clinical Child & Adolescent Psychology, 37*(3), 682–9.

63. Ford, J. D., & Courtois, C. A. (Eds.). (2013). *Treating complex traumatic stress disorders in children and adolescents: Scientific foundations and therapeutic models.* New York, NY: Guilford.

64. Stover, C. S., et al. (2008). Factors associated with engagement in a police-advocacy home-visit intervention to prevent domestic violence. *Violence Against Women, 14*(12), 1430–50.

65. Harpaz-Rotem, I., et al. (2007). Clinical epidemiology of urban violence: responding to children exposed to violence in ten communities. *Journal of Interpersonal Violence, 22*(11), 1479–90.

66. Murphy, R. A., et al. (2005). Acute service delivery in a police-mental health program for children exposed to violence and trauma. *Psychiatric Quarterly, 76*(2), 107–21.

67. Marans, S., Berkowitz, S. J., & Cohen, D. J. (1998). Police and mental health professionals. Collaborative responses to the impact of violence on children and families. *Child & Adolescent Psychiatric Clinics of North America, 7*(3), 635–51.

68. Marans, S., Smolover, D., & Hahn, H. (2012). Responding to child trauma: Theory, programs, and policy. In E. L. Grigorenko (Ed.), *Handbook of Juvenile Forensic Psychology and Psychiatry* (pp. 453–466). New York, NY: Springer.

69. Marans, S., & Berkman, M. (2006). Police–mental health collaboration on behalf of children exposed to violence: The Child Development–Community Policing program model. In A. Lightburn, & P. Sessions (Eds.), *Handbook of Community-Based Clinical Practice* (pp. 426–439). Cary, NC: Oxford University Press.

70. Marans, S., et al. (1995). *The police-mental health partnership: a community-based response to urban violence.* New Haven, CT: Yale University Press.

71. Kessler, R. C., et al. (2011). Childhood adversities and adult psychopathology in the WHO World Mental Health Surveys. *British Journal of Psychiatry, 197,* 378–85.

72. Kessler, R. C., et al. (1995). Posttraumatic stress disorder in the National Comorbidity Survey. *Archives of General Psychiatry, 52*(12), 1048–60.

73. McLaughlin, K. A., et al. (2010). Childhood adversities and adult psychopathology in the National Comorbidity Survey Replication (NCS-R) III: associations with functional impairment related to DSM-IV disorders. *Psychological Medicine, 40*(5), 847–59.

74. Perkonigg, A., et al. (2000). Traumatic events and post-traumatic stress disorder in the community: Prevalence, risk factors and comorbidity. *Acta Psychiatrica Scandinavica, 101*(1), 46–59.

75. Makin-Byrd, K., Bierman, K. L., & Conduct Problems Prevention Research Group. (2012). Individual and Family Predictors of the Perpetration of Dating Violence and Victimization in Late Adolescence. *Journal of Youth and Adolescence.*

76. Ellis, W. E., Chung-Hall, J., & Dumas, T. M. (2012). The Role of Peer Group Aggression in Predicting Adolescent Dating Violence and Relationship Quality. *Journal of Youth and Adolescence.*

77. Khubchandani, J., et al. (2012). Adolescent dating violence: a national assessment of school counselors' perceptions and practices. *Pediatrics, 130*(2), 202–10.

78. Martsolf, D. S., et al. (2012). Patterns of dating violence across adolescence. *Qualitative Health Research, 22*(9), 1271–83.

79. Alleyne-Green, B., Coleman-Cowger, V. H., & Henry, D. B. (2012). Dating violence perpetration and/or victimization and associated sexual risk behaviors among a sample of inner-city African American and Hispanic adolescent females. *Journal of Interpersonal Violence, 27*(8), 1457–73.

80. Jouriles, E. N., et al. (2012). Youth experiences of family violence and teen dating violence perpetration: cognitive and emotional mediators. *Clinical Child and Family Psychology Review, 15*(1), 58–68.

81. Boivin, S., et al. (2012). Past victimizations and dating violence perpetration in adolescence: the mediating role of emotional distress and hostility. *Journal of Interpersonal Violence, 27*(4), 662–84.

82. Miller, E., et al. (2012). "Coaching boys into men": a cluster-randomized controlled trial of a dating violence prevention program. *Journal of Adolescent Health, 51*(5), 431–8.

83. Noonan, R. K., & Charles, D. (2009). Developing teen dating violence prevention strategies: formative research with middle school youth. *Violence Against Women, 15*(9), 1087–105.

84. Jaycox, L. H., et al. (2006). Impact of a school-based dating violence prevention program among Latino teens: randomized controlled effectiveness trial. *Journal of Adolescent Health, 39*(5), 694–704.

85. Foshee, V. A., et al. (2005). Assessing the effects of the dating violence prevention program "safe dates" using random coefficient regression modeling. *Prevention Science, 6*(3), 245–58.

86. Wolfe, D. A., et al. (2003). Dating violence prevention with at-risk youth: a controlled outcome evaluation. *Journal of Consulting and Clinical Psychology, 71*(2), 279–91.

87. Gestsdottir, S., & Lerner, R. M. (2007). Intentional self-regulation and positive youth development in early adolescence: Findings from the 4-h study of positive youth development. *Developmental Psychology, 43*(2), 508–521.

88. Kia-Keating, M., et al. (2011). Protecting and promoting: an integrative conceptual model for healthy development of adolescents. *Journal of Adolescent Health, 48*(3), 220–8.

89. Crooks, C. V., et al. (2011). Impact of a universal school-based violence prevention program on violent delinquency: distinctive benefits for youth with maltreatment histories. *Child Abuse & Neglect, 35*(6), 393–400.

90. Walker, S. L., & Smith, D. J., Jr. (2009). "Children at risk": development, implementation, and effectiveness of a school-based violence intervention and prevention program. *Journal of Prevention & Intervention in the Community, 37*(4), 316–25.

91. Park-Higgerson, H. K., et al. (2008). The evaluation of school-based violence prevention programs: a meta-analysis. *Journal of School Health, 78*(9), 465–79; quiz 518–20.

92. Multisite Violence Prevention Project. (2008). The multisite violence prevention project: impact of a universal school-based violence prevention program on social-cognitive outcomes. *Prevention Science, 9*(4), 231–44.

93. Gorman, D. M., Conde, E. (2007). Conflict of interest in the evaluation and dissemination of "model" school-based drug and violence prevention programs. *Evaluation and Program Planning, 30*(4), 422–9.

94. Task Force on Community Preventive Services. (2007). A recommendation to reduce rates of violence among school-aged children and youth by means of universal school-based violence prevention programs. *American Journal of Preventive Medicine, 33*(2 Suppl), S112–3.

95. Modzeleski, W. (2007). School-based violence prevention programs: offering hope for school districts. *American Journal of Preventive Medicine, 33*(2 Suppl), S107–8.

96. Freedenthal, S. (2010). Adolescent help-seeking and the Yellow Ribbon Suicide Prevention Program: an evaluation. *Suicide and Life-Threatening Behavior, 40*(6), 628–39.

97. Wyman, P. A., et al. (2010). An outcome evaluation of the Sources of Strength suicide prevention program delivered by adolescent peer leaders in high schools. *American Journal of Public Health, 100*(9), 1653–61.

98. Waldvogel, J. L., Rueter, M., & Oberg, C. N. (2008). Adolescent suicide: risk factors and prevention strategies. *Current Problems in Pediatric and Adolescent Health Care, 38*(4), 110–25.

99. Farrow, C. V., & Fox, C. L. (2011). Gender differences in the relationships between bullying at school and unhealthy eating and shape-related attitudes and behaviours. *British Journal of Educational Psychology, 81*(Pt 3), 409–20.

100. Ttofi, M. M., & Farrington, D. P. (2012). Risk and protective factors, longitudinal research, and bullying prevention. *New Directions for Youth Development, 2012*(133), 85–98.

101. Schroeder, B. A., et al. (2012). The implementation of a statewide bullying prevention program: preliminary findings from the field and the importance of coalitions. *Health Promotion Practice, 13*(4), 489–95.

102. Bauer, N. S., Lozano, P., & Rivara, F. P. (2007). The effectiveness of the Olweus Bullying Prevention Program in public middle schools: a controlled trial. *Journal of Adolescent Health, 40*(3), 266–74.

103. Turner, H. A., et al. (2012). Recent Victimization Exposure and Suicidal Ideation in Adolescents. *Archives of Pediatrics & Adolescent Medicine,* 1–6.

104. Belshaw, S. H., et al. (2012). The relationship between dating violence and suicidal behaviors in a national sample of adolescents. *Violence and Victims, 27*(4), 580–91.

105. Hawkins, J. D., et al. (2012). Sustained decreases in risk exposure and youth problem behaviors after installation of the Communities That Care prevention system in a randomized trial. *Archives of Pediatrics & Adolescent Medicine, 166*(2), 141–8.

106. Fagan, A. A., et al. (2011). Effects of Communities That Care on the adoption and implementation fidelity of evidence-based prevention programs in communities: results from a randomized controlled trial. *Prevention Science, 12*(3), 223–34.

107. Fagan, A. A., et al. (2009). Translational research in action: implementation of the Communities That Care prevention system in 12 communities. *Journal of Community Psychology, 37*(7), 809–829.

108. Hawkins, J. D., Catalano, R. F., & Miller, J. Y. (1992). Risk and protective factors for alcohol and other drug problems in adolescence and early adulthood: implications for substance abuse prevention. *Psychological Bulletin, 112*(1), 64–105.

109. Hawkins, J. D., Von Cleve, E., & Catalano, R. F., Jr. (1991). Reducing early childhood aggression: results of a primary prevention program. *Journal of the American Academy of Child & Adolescent Psychiatry, 30*(2), 208–17.

110. Shaw, D. S., et al. (2006). Randomized trial of a family-centered approach to the prevention of early conduct problems: 2-year effects of the family check-up in early childhood. *Journal of Consulting and Clinical Psychology, 74*(1), 1–9.

111. Dishion, T. J., & McMahon, R. J. (1998). Parental monitoring and the prevention of child and adolescent problem behavior: a conceptual and empirical formulation. *Clinical Child and Family Psychology Review, 1*(1), 61–75.

112. Black, D. S., et al. (2010). The influence of school-based natural mentoring relationships on school attachment and subsequent adolescent risk behaviors. *Health Education Research, 25*(5), 892–902.

113. Horner, M. S., et al. (2008). Mentoring increases connectedness and knowledge: a cross-sectional evaluation of two programs in child and adolescent psychiatry. *Academic Psychiatry, 32*(5), 420–8.

114. Black, M. M., et al. (2006). Delaying second births among adolescent mothers: a randomized, controlled trial of a home-based mentoring program. *Pediatrics, 118*(4), e1087–99.

115. DuBois, D. L., & Silverthorn, N. (2005). Characteristics of natural mentoring relationships and adolescent adjustment: evidence from a national study. *Journal of Primary Prevention, 26*(2), 69–92.

116. DuBois, D. L., & Silverthorn, N. (2005). Natural mentoring relationships and adolescent health: evidence from a national study. *American Journal of Public Health, 95*(3), 518–24.

CHAPTER SIX:

Rethinking Our Juvenile Justice System

CHAPTER SIX:
Rethinking Our Juvenile Justice System

The vast majority of children involved in the juvenile justice system have survived exposure to violence and are living with the trauma of that experience. If we are to fulfill the goals of the juvenile justice system — to make communities and victims whole, to rehabilitate young offenders while holding them accountable, and to help children develop skills to be productive and succeed — we must rethink the way the juvenile justice system treats, assesses, and evaluates the children within it.

By the time children come into contact with the juvenile justice system, they have almost always been exposed to several types of traumatic violence over a course of many years. In a study conducted at a juvenile detention center in Cook County, Illinois, 90 percent of the youth reported past exposure to traumatic violence, which included being threatened with weapons (58 percent)[1] and being physically assaulted (35 percent).[2] Another study, this one conducted in juvenile detention centers in Connecticut, found that 48 percent of similar youth had experienced a traumatic loss.[3] Finally, according to a recent study that used a national sample of youth for comparison, youth in detention were three times as likely as those in the national sample to have been exposed to multiple types of violence and traumatic events.[2]

The relationship between exposure to violence and involvement in the justice system is not a coincidence. Exposure to violence often leads to distrust, hypervigilance, impulsive behavior, isolation, addiction, lack of empathy or concern for others, and self-protective aggression. When young people experience prolonged or repeated violence, their bodies and brains adapt by becoming focused on survival. This dramatically reduces their ability to delay impulses and gratification, to a degree even beyond that of normal adolescents. Youth who are trying to protect themselves from more violence, or who do not know how to deal with violence they have already

"When you live in a world that is never safe, where you feel abandoned and uncared for, numbing the pain and finding some kind of support becomes an essential survival skill. This is how I became, and how many children today become, easy prey for pedophiles. This is why our young people create the nurturance they so desperately need by forming and joining gangs. This is why many children enter into the drug world at an early age. This is why the sex trade begins to seem like a viable option. And this is how we lose our nation's future."

— Sonja Sohn, actor and founder of ReWired for Change

experienced, may engage in delinquent or criminal behavior as a way to gain a sense of control in their chaotic lives and to cope with the emotional turmoil and barriers to security and success that violence creates.

Research on brain development over the past two decades has shown that the areas of the prefrontal cortex responsible for cognitive processing and the ability to inhibit impulses and weigh consequences before taking action are not fully developed until people reach their mid-20s.[3,4] Adolescents experience heightened emotions and are more vulnerable to stress and prone to react without thinking than are adults.[5,6] The United States Supreme Court's recent groundbreaking decision to ban the death penalty for juveniles was due in large part to the advances in scientific understanding of how a normal adolescent's brain develops. This decision, and the rulings of other landmark Supreme Court cases, acknowledged the fundamental developmental differences between the brains of children and adolescents and those of adults.[7] Consistent with these legal decisions, science reveals that the developing brain, in early childhood and throughout adolescence, is very sensitive to harsh physical and environmental conditions.[8] Traumatic violence, in particular, can delay or derail brain development, leaving even the most resilient and intelligent child or adolescent with a severely diminished capacity to inhibit strong impulses, to delay gratification, to anticipate and evaluate the consequences of risky or socially unacceptable behavior, and to tolerate disagreement or conflict with other persons.

Children exposed to violence, who desperately need help, often end up alienated. Instead of responding in ways that repair the damage done to them by trauma and violence, the frequent response of communities, caregivers, and peers is to reject and ostracize these children, pushing them further into negative behaviors. Often the children become isolated from and lost to their families, schools, and neighborhoods and end up in multiple unsuccessful out-of-home placements and, ultimately, in correctional institutions.

Many youth in the justice system appear angry, defiant, or indifferent, but actually they are fearful, depressed, and lonely. They hurt emotionally and feel powerless, abandoned, and subject to double standards by adults in their lives and in "the system." These children are often viewed by the system as beyond hope and uncontrollable, labeled as "oppositional," "willfully irresponsible," or "unreachable." What appears to be intentional defiance and aggression, however, is often a defense against the despair and hopelessness that violence has caused in these children's lives. When the justice system responds with punishment, these children may be pushed further into the juvenile and criminal justice systems and permanently lost to their families and society.

By failing to correctly identify and treat children exposed to violence, the system wastes an opportunity to alter the delinquent or criminal conduct of the children. This failure makes our communities less safe and results in the loss of the valuable contributions of these children — in youth and into adulthood — to their communities.

This is not inevitable. These youth are not beyond our ability to help if we recognize that exposure to violence causes many children to become desperate survivors rather than hardened criminals. There are evidence-based interventions that can help to repair the emotional damage done to children as a result of exposure to violence and that can put them on a course to be well-adjusted, law-abiding, and productive citizens. Too often, these interventions are not used simply because they are not known or appreciated.[2,9,10]

"We need to redefine the terms that can lead a young person into a correctional facility and protect the public by detaining the most violent felons, not the young people who, with the proper supports, could be promising members of the next generation."

— Dr. Patrick McCarthy, President and CEO, Annie E. Casey Foundation

Rethinking how we approach young people in the justice system requires participation from everyone in the system. Law enforcement, judges, prosecutors, defense attorneys, probation officers, providers, and policymakers must all understand the data about children's exposure to violence that is contained in the ACE (Adverse Childhood Experiences)[11] and NatSCEV (National Survey of Children's Exposure to Violence)[12] studies as well as the latest research about what works for kids.[2,13] It also requires people outside the system to accept that children in the justice system are not "bad kids" but, instead, are traumatized survivors who have made bad decisions but can still turn things around if they have help. The problem is not just confined to boys of color in urban communities — it affects youth of varying racial and ethnic backgrounds in rural, suburban, and tribal communities as well as girls and LGBTQ (lesbian-gay-bisexual-transgender-questioning) youth.[14–17] While the challenges of developing services for children in small communities are often great, the needs of children in those communities make it imperative that every community get involved in addressing the need for trauma-informed assessment and care in its justice system.

"If our aim is to nurture healthy children within safe communities, we need to change our approach and the values that drive our responses to violence. The reliance on highly punitive approaches [is] not working — they make people more alienated and angry, they feed cycles of revenge, and, as if that is not enough, they are costly."

— Dr. Lauren Abramson, Executive Director, Community Conferencing Center, Baltimore

We must help children in the justice system to heal by responding in developmentally appropriate ways and by ensuring that the system itself does no harm. When traumatized children break the law and engage in delinquent conduct, even repeatedly, they still need and deserve help from adults. The system must recognize the heavy burdens that most young offenders carry and help them move into a healthy and productive adulthood by providing services that address the damage done by exposure to violence. Too often, the justice system relies on judgmental, punitive responses that are both harmful and ineffective.

Fortunately, the juvenile justice system has undergone tremendous change in recent years, as cross-systems collaboration,[18–20] evidence-based practices,[21,22] and "programs that work"[23] have moved the system towards better outcomes for children and their communities. An important next step in the improvement of the overall justice system is to incorporate what is known about children who have been exposed to violence into every facet of the system — juvenile and adult — and to incorporate trauma-informed care into decision-making responses for children throughout the system.

Trauma-informed screening and treatment are just as vital, if not more so, for children who have committed serious violent offenses. By eliminating the death penalty and an automatic life sentence without parole for juveniles, the Supreme Court has created a pathway for children who are found guilty of homicide or other very serious violent offenses to be thoroughly assessed to determine the causes of their violent conduct. Many of the children who have been convicted as adults have experienced tremendous damage from violence that, in the past, would have gone unaddressed once they were incarcerated. Providing opportunities for assessment and trauma-informed care in both the juvenile and adult justice systems will help to repair the damage done by exposure to violence, improve the safety of everyone within the system, and increase the safety of communities to which incarcerated and detained children are released.

Unfortunately, residential juvenile justice facilities, which should have the most comprehensive services for youth, often lack staff with professional training in mental health or substance abuse services.[24,25] Research studies show that 65 percent of girls and 70 percent of boys in detention have been diagnosed with multiple mental health disorders,[26] and nearly a quarter of youth in residential placements have attempted suicide.[27] These young people have significant needs, and yet most secure facilities are not designed and staffed to meet those needs, and for some young people, their problems worsen in harsh environments.[28] Confinement has been shown to exacerbate the symptoms of posttraumatic stress disorder (PTSD) through experiences that reactivate memories of past traumatic violence, such as being handcuffed, restrained, and searched.[29,30] Staff and administrators in juvenile justice programs, however, vary in their willingness to even acknowledge the need for mental health and related services.[31] Everyone in the juvenile justice system, including program staff and administrators, judges, attorneys, and probation officers, must be educated about the importance and benefits of providing appropriate trauma-informed services to youth in the system.

At worst, involvement in the juvenile justice system does additional harm to children. In one study, more than a third of young people in juvenile placement were found to fear attacks from staff or other youth.[27] Elsewhere, an analysis of data from state agencies responsible for overseeing juvenile detention facilities found that between 2004 and 2007 there were roughly 12,000 documented reports of physical, sexual, or emotional abuse by staff members — nearly 10 assaults a day, on average.[32] And because children are often afraid to report abuse by staff, and as facilities may not consistently document the reports they do receive, the actual number of assaults is undoubtedly higher.

Moreover, detention facilities and the justice system, through their routine practices, can bring additional harm to already traumatized youth. For example, the use of solitary confinement, isolation, and improper restraints can have devastating effects on these youth.[33,34] Detention facilities must maintain safety without relying on practices that are dangerous and that compromise the mental and physical well-being of the youth in their care.

"In one particularly brutal and corrupt private, for-profit prison that houses young men ages 13 to 22 who were tried and convicted as adults, young men endure particularly unspeakable abuses. Staff physically assault youth and sexually abuse them. Youth who are handcuffed and defenseless have been kicked, punched, and beaten all over their bodies."

— Sheila Bedi, Deputy Legal Director, Southern Poverty Law Center

The harm done to traumatized youth by the justice system is not limited to juvenile facilities. As one example, youth who have been forced into the sex trade and trafficked are often arrested and criminalized instead of being treated as the victims they are. We must develop trauma-informed services unique to these problems so that we can more effectively separate young boys and girls from their exploiters and help these youth transition to productive lives. These young people should not have to be caught in the justice system and risk further victimization in order to get the services they need. Unfortunately, sexually trafficked or exploited children and young adults often are not identified unless they come to the attention of law enforcement, and so it is essential that judicial and law enforcement professionals have trauma-informed options for young people built into their respective obligations to uphold the law and protect public safety.

A trauma-informed approach to juvenile justice does not require wholesale abandonment of existing programs; instead, it can be used to make many existing programs more effective and cost-efficient. By correctly assessing the needs of youth in the justice system, including needs reflecting their exposure to violence, and matching services directly to those needs, the system can help children recover from the effects of trauma and become whole.

As a guide to addressing the needs of the vast majority of at-risk and justice-involved youth who have been exposed to violence, the task force offers nine recommendations, which are described below.

6.1 Make trauma-informed screening, assessment, and care the standard in juvenile justice services.

All children who enter the juvenile justice system should be screened for exposure to violence. The initial screening should take place upon first contact with the juvenile justice system and should include youth who meet the criteria for diversion from the system. Where feasible, juvenile justice stakeholders should develop trauma-informed care and treatment for children diverted to prevention, mental health, or dependency programs.

"A judicial system that understands the effects of trauma will render very different disposition decisions and effect different and individualized services at an early point of contact."

— Tadarial Sturdivant, Director, Wayne County (Michigan) Child and Family Services

Research shows that youth involved in,[1,35] and at risk for involvement in,[36] juvenile justice can provide a thorough description of their exposure to violence and related posttraumatic problems when screened with brief, carefully developed, and behaviorally specific questionnaires. These include self-report trauma history screens, such as the Traumatic Events Screening Instrument (TESI),[36] and measures of PTSD symptoms such as the UCLA PTSD Reaction Index[37] as well as event and symptom screening questionnaires such as the Massachusetts Youth Screening Instrument-2 (MAYSI-2), which assesses "traumatic experiences" as well as symptoms such as physical health problems, anger and aggression, depression and anxiety, and substance abuse.

Many youth involved in juvenile justice are not maliciously aggressive but in fact are reacting defensively because of their exposure to violence. It is important to screen these youth for reactive aggression using a validated measure such as the Inventory of Callous-Unemotional (C-U) Traits.[38] Those who score below the threshold for severe C-U traits are good candidates for therapeutic intervention. However, those who score in the severe range for these traits may be youth who are still using aggression systematically but reactively as a way of defending themselves. These youth may benefit from interventions that help them develop skills for dealing with fear and hopelessness and from behavior management programs that engage them actively in making their lives and environments safer.

6.2 Abandon juvenile justice correctional practices that traumatize children and further reduce their opportunities to become productive members of society.

Juvenile justice programs have long struggled with "best practices" for addressing the needs of detained and adjudicated youth.[24,39] The most recent census of young people in residential placement, conducted in 2010, counted roughly 71,000 children nationwide living in juvenile institutions.[40,41] The total number of juveniles nationally who spend some amount of time in a locked facility over the course of a year is much larger, however. Many of these children are living with the effects of exposure to traumatic violence, but they are often not given the help they need to recover while in custody.

Most of the young people in custody during the 2010 census were not incarcerated for violent offenses. They were highly likely to have been exposed to violence, but most had not become perpetrators of violence. Sixty-three percent were confined for committing nonviolent offenses, technical violations of probation, or so-called status offenses such as truancy and underage drinking.[40] It is crucial that incarceration of juveniles not involve sanctions that subject them to additional violence, both to protect them from further harm and to avoid teaching them by example that violence is an appropriate means to control other people's behavior. This is also important for the slightly more than one-third of confined juveniles who committed a crime against another person, mainly robbery or assault, in order to avoid inadvertently strengthening the belief of these offenders that using violence is acceptable or effective.[40] Establishing firm and fair discipline, rules, and standards is an effective way to hold juveniles responsible while also teaching them through actions and words that violence is neither an acceptable nor viable way to achieve their life goals.

Juvenile justice programs have historically had three primary goals: increasing safety in juvenile justice facilities and in the community, bringing about justice for crimes committed, and rehabilitation of the youth in the care of these programs. With the growing recognition that many youth in these programs have significant exposure to violence and mental health problems,[42] a fourth goal has emerged: addressing youths' mental health needs to enable juvenile justice programs and facilities to successfully achieve their original goals of safety, justice, and rehabilitation.[24,43,44] Despite efforts to foster collaboration between mental health and juvenile justice leaders, programs, and providers,[43,45] numerous barriers have impeded the progress of mental health initiatives in juvenile justice facilities.[24,46,47] Funding for mental health services often is better in the juvenile justice system than in the community,[48,49] and yet only one in three youths is identified by juvenile probation officers as needing mental health services[49] — a proportion that is only half that of youth in juvenile justice programs who have a psychiatric disorder (close to 70 percent) and well below the proportion of youth who have two or more psychiatric disorders (approximately 45 percent).[42,50] Similarly, in an Australian study, less than half (18 percent overall) of the 40 percent of youth who reported substance abuse received a referral for drug or alcohol abuse treatment.[51] The importance of providing effective treatment for such youth is underscored by findings from the Cook County (Illinois) study that, 5 years after being assessed in detention, 40 percent of boys and 30 percent of girls still had psychiatric or substance abuse disorders.[52]

Punitive sanctions and practices used by law enforcement or juvenile justice personnel lead youth who have survived violence in their homes and communities to perceive adults from these sectors as a threat rather than a legitimate authority or role model. When these sanctions threaten adolescents' autonomy and personal space, they may fall back on "street rules" and resort to aggression, secrecy, deception, and avoidance instead of responsible and safe behavior.

When stressed by scarce resources, rapid staff turnover, threats of lawsuits, and negative publicity, juvenile justice and law enforcement personnel can become trapped in a survival mindset similar to that of the traumatized child. Preservation of the status quo may become their only priority, leading to the use of punitive correctional methods that damage youth rather than helping them.

Nowhere is the damaging impact of incarceration on vulnerable children more obvious than when it involves solitary confinement. A 2002 investigation by the U.S. Department of Justice showed that juveniles experience symptoms of paranoia, anxiety, and depression even after very short periods of isolation.[33] Confined youth who spend extended periods isolated are among the most likely to attempt or actually commit suicide. One national study found that among the suicides in juvenile facilities, half of the victims were in isolation at the time they took their own lives, and 62 percent of victims had a history of solitary confinement.[34]

Given the environment in most secure facilities for young offenders — the dangers, the lack of meaningful activities, and the failure to help these children deal with past trauma — it is not surprising that these youth are ill-equipped to change their behavior when they leave. Indeed, one longitudinal study following more than a thousand young offenders for 7 years after conviction concluded that longer stays in juvenile institutions do not reduce recidivism.[53] Some studies have even found that incarceration increases recidivism among juveniles who have lower-risk profiles and less-serious offending histories.[53,54]

Facilities and practices can change, however, without any loss of effectiveness. The task force heard of examples where dangerous, damaging practices were abandoned and replaced with comprehensive trauma-informed programming designed to meet the needs of young residents. Facilities must screen the young people who are referred to their care to determine their needs and vulnerabilities and must then address those needs with trauma-informed programs.

Juvenile justice officials should rely on detention as a last resort, and only for youth who pose a safety risk or who cannot receive effective treatment in the community. When children are in facilities, independent monitors should ensure that they are not abused by peers or staff and that they are receiving appropriate services to meet their needs. A clear system for grievances should be in place to address concerns of mistreatment or abuse in facilities.

> "I've always felt that one of the problems with the way the public experiences these types of institutional abuses is that the public experiences them episodically, when, in fact, there is ample and growing evidence that they are endemic to the very nature of large, distant, locked training schools for delinquent youth."
>
> **— Vincent Schiraldi, Commissioner, New York City Department of Probation**

6.3 Provide juvenile justice services appropriate to children's ethnocultural background that are based on an assessment of each violence-exposed child's individual needs.

In jurisdictions across the nation, racial and ethnic minority youth are overrepresented in the juvenile justice system, resulting in disproportionate minority contact with that system.[55] Involvement of minority youth with the justice system not only potentially perpetuates societal stigma and cultural trauma but also places such youth at higher risk for illness[55] and violent death.[56]

The backgrounds and experiences of youth who come into the system can affect the degree to which they experience trauma. Furthermore, cultural norms and practices influence how youth and families define a traumatic event and posttraumatic symptoms.[57] Although most studies do not report significant differences in the degree to which youth of different ethnic or racial backgrounds have been exposed to violence,[1,35] there are differences by background in how youth experience and respond to prior trauma. In one study, Hispanic/Latino youth were approximately twice as likely as White or Black youth to report a history of traumatic loss, neglect, or community violence. In that study, however, White youth reported more risk of suicide and of alcohol abuse than did either Black or Hispanic/Latino youth.

Results from two recent epidemiological studies based on reports from teachers[58] and youth[59] suggest that urban African-American youth may be more likely to be chronically engaged in physical aggression than youth of other groups. These differences emerge as early as kindergarten, and they likely coincide with exposure to violence in early childhood.[58] If these children become involved in the justice system, it is vital that they be screened and treated for prior exposure to violence to help militate against the negative effects of prior trauma.

Given the overrepresentation of Latino/Hispanic and African-American youth in the juvenile justice system and the often-associated negative stereotypes of minority youth, it is imperative that those who work with minority youth have respect for and understanding of the cultural differences between themselves and these youth. All youth involved in juvenile justice with prior exposure to violence should be identified and provided with help, but to be most effective, services and treatment should be adapted to the ethnocultural backgrounds of these youth.

Not only race/ethnicity per se but also the degree to which ethnic/racial minority youth assimilate into the majority culture or identify with their culture of origin may play a role in aggressive behavior. When ethnic/racial minority adolescents are in settings of mixed ethnicity (as is typical in juvenile justice), they often engage in bullying as a defensive behavior.[60] When youth engage in cross-ethnic/racial bullying or aggression, it is crucial to assess the potential influence of past exposure to violence, which may have led to fears about the threat posed by youth from other ethnic and racial groups. The system will be most effective if it identifies ethnic/racial trauma and fear and provides youth with skills for managing their stress reactions as a way to reduce reactive aggressive behavior.

The degree to which services and treatments are culturally sensitive influences the expectations of both youth and caregivers as well as their acceptance and rejection of those services.[58] Accordingly, culture-sensitive role models, practices, and programs aimed at healing traumatized youth and preventing youth who are within the system or at risk for entering it from being further exposed to violence are being developed nationwide[19] and incorporated into statewide juvenile justice systems.[61] The importance of integrating widely available and culturally adaptive interventions for traumatized children,[62] especially those involved in,[63,64] or at risk for becoming involved in,[65] the juvenile justice system cannot be overstated.

6.4 Provide care and services to address the special circumstances and needs of girls in the juvenile justice system.

According to a recently released report by the Georgetown Center on Poverty, Inequality, and Public Policy, "girls make up the fastest growing segment of the juvenile justice system. As a group, they are disproportionately 'high need' and 'low risk,' meaning that they face a host of challenges and have a critical need for services, but for the most part do not pose a significant threat to the public. The differences between the profiles and service needs of girls and boys entering the juvenile justice system present a significant challenge to the professionals who serve them. Many girls in the system have experienced traumatic events, including sexual and physical abuse and neglect, which have deeply wounded them emotionally and physically."[66] In fact, we know that a high percentage of girls in the juvenile justice system have been exposed to significant violence and trauma. Ninety percent of incarcerated girls report having experienced emotional, physical, and/or sexual abuse.[67]

The Georgetown Center report continues to say: "Overall, the juvenile justice system is ill-equipped to serve girls effectively — particularly those who have been exposed to violence — having failed to implement the reforms called for by a growing body of research on the needs of the girls in its care."[66] Involvement in the justice system may penalize girls by exacerbating existing health and family problems while failing to address underlying issues.[68–70] Twenty percent of youth in custody have or are expecting children. Girls who are pregnant or parenting within the juvenile justice system present their own set of needs. They are more likely to be parents than their non-justice-involved peers. Nine percent of girls in custody report that they have children, compared to six percent of girls in the general population.[71] Further, a Crittenton Foundation 2012 report on young mothers in the juvenile justice system found that of the girls sampled, 49 percent had experienced sexual abuse, 35 percent had experienced physical neglect, 67 percent had alcoholism or drug use in their home of origin, 83 percent had experienced the loss of a biological parent from home, 46 percent had depression or mental illness in their home, 56 percent reported that their mother treated them violently, and 49 percent reported that a member of their household had been imprisoned.

Girls present to the juvenile justice system with high rates of mental health problems and depression. In their adolescence, girls are more likely than boys to attempt suicide and to self-mutilate. Negative body image, low self-concept, and acute substance abuse aimed at self-medication, which so often result from stress or trauma, are issues that must be addressed differently in the future.

Girls in the juvenile justice system are in critical need of programming, facilities, and staff that are gender responsive. Most youth in the juvenile justice system are detained for nonviolent and status offenses. This is particularly true of girls, who are slightly more likely than boys to enter the system for minor offenses. Girls are also detained for longer periods of time than are their male counterparts when they commit the same crimes.[72]

Most youth, and most girls in particular, do not pose a significant public safety risk and would be far better served in nonresidential treatment facilities close to their own homes. However, for those who pose a serious societal risk, we recommend the utilization of small (i.e., no more than 20 beds) gender-responsive, culturally competent residential facilities that are staff secure. Additionally, there is a need for small, family-style group-living facilities for pregnant and parenting girls. Whenever possible, the child should be allowed to reside with the mother, ensuring safeguards for the child. Although allowing the mother to be with her child is clearly beneficial for the mother, it is even more beneficial for the long-term health and development of the child.

"A comprehensive continuum of care must be available to girls and young women who are survivors of violence or abuse. Services must be gender and culturally responsive, trauma-informed, age-appropriate, and strength-based. A variety of settings…must be offered. Services must focus on mental and physical recovery, health, self-esteem building, life skills development, academic achievement, career development, and more. For young parents, bonding and attachment programs, parenting skills, and childhood education are essential pieces of the puzzle."

— Jeannette Pai-Espinosa, National Crittenton Foundation

The key elements to trauma-informed, gender-responsive juvenile justice programs exist in every community. Very simply, programs that are good for girls, especially those recovering from exposure to violence, weave together family, community, and systems of care. These programs promote healing from trauma caused by physical and psychological abuse. In addition, they address the needs of girls while encouraging them to take leadership roles. Further, they promote the personal development of girls' individual strengths. They are community-based to help foster healthy family relationships and sustainable community connections, and they support ongoing, positive relationships between girls and older women, family, and community.[73]

6.5 Provide care and services to address the special circumstances and needs of LGBTQ youth in the juvenile justice system.

Lesbian, gay, bisexual, and transgender youth, as well as youth questioning their sexual orientations (LGBTQ youth), are often targeted by other youth for bullying, increasing their likelihood of experiencing despair, isolation, suicidal ideation, and chronic violence in the form of bullying. When these youth become involved with law enforcement or the courts, they are often placed in close, unsupervised contact with other youth, which in turn often leads to harassment, bullying, or assault. The same staff charged with monitoring and protecting these youth may exacerbate their trauma by joining in the harassment and assaults as an expression of their own homophobia. In order to have the best outcomes for these young people, the justice system must respond to their past exposure to violence and trauma in ways that do not perpetuate stereotypes or the use of stigma against LGBTQ youth. This includes providing services and treatment that support their sexual orientation, lifestyle, and peer group choices while helping them to establish a sense of security within themselves and their relationships, enabling them to make responsible and safe choices that enhance their development and protect them from violence.

In an effort to protect LGBTQ youth in their care, facilities often isolate them. This can directly traumatize these youth, however, or greatly worsen their posttraumatic symptoms from past exposure to violence. All juvenile justice personnel and facilities must provide consistent therapeutic supervision to ensure the safety of LGBTQ youth and thus protect them from further exposure to violence by peers or adults, but without resorting to isolation. Those who work with youth in juvenile justice programs and facilities must be trained to deliver trauma-informed care while demonstrating respect and support for the sexual orientation of these young people in order to end norms based on stigma.

> "The goal is to ensure that institutions serving youth (and the communities and families in which they live) are safe for and promote the healthy development of all young people. LGBT youth do not have 'special needs' requiring 'special treatment' or separate systems; their needs are the same as all other youth, but they are faced with unique challenges as a result of living with a stigmatized identity."
>
> — **Carolyn Reyes, Senior Staff Attorney, Legal Services for Children**

6.6 Develop and implement policies in every school system across the country that aim to keep children in school rather than relying on policies that lead to suspension and expulsion and ultimately drive children into the juvenile justice system.

Many children enter the juvenile justice system because schools rely on that system to enforce discipline. Harsh, exclusionary school discipline policies funnel children into the justice system in large numbers: Of the 3.3 million children suspended from school each year, 95 percent are sanctioned for nonviolent offenses like disruptive behavior and violating dress codes.[74] Moreover, according to the American Psychological Association (APA) Zero Tolerance Task Force, these policies do not result in improved safety in schools. Especially troubling is the fact that the APA task force found that children with emotional disturbances are disciplined under zero-tolerance policies at a disproportionally high rate. Interestingly, when harsh exclusionary policies are discontinued in schools, referrals to juvenile correctional facilities also decrease.[28]

School should be a safe place for all children to learn and develop. For children who are exposed to violence, schools may be one of the few safe places available to them. Children who have been exposed to violence should be able to receive support and healing measures in school rather than being subjected to harsh discipline for failing to adhere to school norms. Too many vulnerable children who have been exposed to violence are unnecessarily removed from schools through school discipline and referrals to the juvenile justice system. As described by the Department of Justice, Office of Juvenile Justice and Delinquency Prevention (OJJDP): "Without the structure and supervision that school provides, truants and dropouts often turn to delinquent or criminal behavior. A child's lack of commitment to school has been established as a risk factor for a variety of negative outcomes including: substance abuse, teen pregnancy, school dropout, and delinquency."

> "As public schools increasingly adopt harsh and extreme disciplinary policies and practices, greater numbers of boys and young men of color fill the ranks of suspended and ultimately expelled students. Once suspended and/or expelled, many boys seem to vanish into thin air and don't show up on anybody's radar screen again until they resurface, all too often, in the criminal justice system, branded as predators and sent to adult jails."
>
> — Mary Lee, Deputy Director, PolicyLink

The OJJDP has called for changes in school programs to stop the "school-to-prison pipeline," helping all students, including juvenile offenders, "to access quality education, and advancing the use of positive discipline and learning policies and practices" on a school-wide basis in every classroom and activity. Promising approaches to improving attendance, reducing truancy, and preventing dropout must be adopted by all school systems. So, too, must schools develop and implement innovative approaches to identify and help students who are at risk for dropping out, academic failure, behavioral problems, substance abuse, gang involvement, and depression that could lead to thoughts of suicide.

Optimally, academic environments and communities will provide youth with activities and feedback that highlight their strengths and teach them skills to manage intense stress reactions without hurting others or themselves. This rarely occurs in practice, however. While existing programs show promise in reducing bullying and substance abuse, they alone are insufficient to reduce the ultimate involvement of the at-risk students in the juvenile justice system. Most school intervention models do not teach students or school personnel how to create a trauma-informed school environment by understanding traumatized students' aggressive, avoidant (absenteeism, failure to complete schoolwork), or impulsive behavior as traumatic stress reactions, nor do they provide practical skills to enable youth and adults to recognize, prevent, or manage stress reactions. As a result, youth who are disruptive in school as an aftereffect of exposure to violence often are referred to the juvenile justice system.

Successful school-based programs help students develop better ways of handling emotional distress, peer pressures, and problems in their family and peer relationships. These programs translate research in brain science into practical knowledge and skills that school personnel and students can use in order to achieve the mindfulness and restraint necessary to make good choices and decisions.[75] The programs integrate trauma recovery into existing school curricula and activities, decrease the frequency and severity of dangerous, disruptive, or delinquent behavior among youth, reduce disciplinary interventions by staff, and increase students' abilities to have positive experiences with education, recreation, peer relationships, and the larger community.

6.7 Guarantee that all violence-exposed children accused of a crime have legal representation.

All children who enter the juvenile or adult justice system should be screened for exposure to violence and provided access to trauma-informed services and treatment. Defense attorneys who represent children in both systems are in a unique position to help identify prior exposure to violence in the lives of their clients and to help identify and prevent abuses of children in detention and placement programs.

The confidential attorney-client relationship can create a safe place for young people and their families to talk about past experiences or ongoing abuse.[76] While trust is not built up overnight, as attorneys work with their clients to prepare a defense, children often develop a relationship of openness and trust. As a result, clients and their families often disclose information about past or ongoing abuse and exposure to violence that they would not share with others in the justice system. Defense attorneys must be properly trained to respond to these disclosures of psychological trauma and exposure to violence so that they can both maintain their ethical obligations and help their clients obtain the services they need.

All children who appear in juvenile and adult proceedings have a constitutionally guaranteed right to counsel.[77] This is a right that all judges, prosecutors, and defense attorneys are sworn to uphold. Defense counsel plays an important role in ensuring fairness and equity in the juvenile justice system and protecting children from abuses of power by judges, prosecutors, probation officers, and correctional officials. In addition, defense attorneys are the only parties in the proceedings required by law to represent the *expressed interest* of the child.[76] They protect the due process rights of their clients by filing pretrial motions, petitions for habeas corpus, challenges to evidence, and appeals.

Unfortunately, the right to counsel is often restricted during the process of appointing counsel or denied through waiver of counsel. In many jurisdictions, the right to counsel for children is determined by family income tests that are established and administered by the offices of public defenders.[78] Public defenders and government officials should recognize the enormous difficulties facing children entering the justice system who are exposed to violence and the large number of children affected by exposure to violence. "Financial means" tests for the appointment of counsel for children in the adult and juvenile systems should be set aside, and all children — especially those exposed to violence — should be presumed indigent for the purpose of appointment of counsel.[79]

The rates at which children give up their right to counsel vary dramatically across jurisdictions. Some systems ensure that every child in the system is represented, while others allow 80–90 percent of youth who are charged with offenses to appear without counsel.[80] In many jurisdictions, children and their families opt to proceed without counsel because they believe that the child will receive a more lenient disposition if she/he appears unrepresented or that the case is not serious. Most of these decisions are made without an attorney to explain to the child or the family the risks or the potential consequences. In some very serious cases, such waivers could lead to lengthy periods of incarceration, lifetime registration for sex offenders, or even deportation. In especially troubling cases, parents may pressure their child to waive counsel because the parent does not want abuse in the home to be discovered or because the parent wishes the child to be sent to placement.

Defense attorneys also have a vital role in protecting youth from abuse and other forms of violence that are often found within the justice system. In the earliest stages of the process, it is the role of the defense attorney to ensure that the underlying facts are investigated and that children who are wrongly accused are able to challenge the case against them. Defense attorneys also ensure that children with legal defenses and mitigating circumstances are not coerced into admissions without advice about their legal options. Protecting the due process rights of youth at trial is integral to ensuring that children are not further traumatized.

Some cases involving children's exposure to violence are better addressed in the mental health or child protection system. In appropriate cases, defense attorneys can alert probation officers, prosecutors, and judges to such cases and request that their clients be diverted to alternative systems that can provide better trauma-informed care and services for youth.

One of the most vital roles of counsel is to protect children against unjustified placement and incarceration and to guard against abuses within facilities. In some states, counsel's legal obligation to represent children terminates upon disposition. But a rethinking of juvenile justice requires that serious thought be given to the representation of juveniles as long as they are under court supervision. The presence of counsel could help ensure successful placements and aftercare programming. When exposure to violence is discovered, defense counsel would have the ability to file legal motions to stop the abuse and to remove the child from the facility where it is occurring. Children who do not have these protections have no recourse when they are mistreated in facilities where they are cut off from their families and other caring adults.

6.8 Help, do not punish, child victims of sex trafficking.

Each year, thousands of American children, mainly girls, are coerced into commercial sex trafficking. These children are traumatized and exploited through prostitution and pornography. Many are compelled to perform sex acts for drugs, shelter, and food. "Sex traffickers frequently target vulnerable people with histories of abuse and then use violence, threats, lies, false promises, debt bondage, or other forms of control and manipulation to keep victims involved in the sex industry."[81]

Research shows that the vast majority of victims of domestic minor sex trafficking (DMST) — between 70 percent and 90 percent — have a prior history of sexual abuse.[82] The resulting exploitation is considered a modern-day form of slavery, as human trafficking victims are subjected to sexual exploitation or forced labor. The victims' fear of retribution through physical and sexual violence or by threat to families or significant others often prevents them from escaping or reporting to authorities.

While many trafficking networks operate out of urban areas, other traffickers seek the seclusion of rural and remote areas to operate without detection. Estimates of the dimensions of the problem vary dramatically. According to one estimate, approximately

"These kids are bought and sold, used and abused. For the vast majority of these children, the violence of prostitution — the daily rapes by customers, beatings by police, harassment by bystanders, and control by pimps — is not their first experience of violence."

— **Pamela Shifman, Director, Initiatives for Girls and Women, NoVo Foundation**

100,000 to 300,000 American children are sold for sex each year, with the average age of entry into the commercial sex industry between 12 and 14 years.[83]

The true dimensions of the problem internationally and within the United States are difficult to determine because of the underground nature of the trade. In March 2012, President Obama directed his Cabinet to redouble the administration's efforts to eliminate human trafficking abroad and in communities at home through several initiatives: an executive order strengthening protections in federal contracts, tools and training to identify and assist trafficking victims; increased resources for victims of human trafficking; and a comprehensive plan for future action. On September 25, 2012, the President announced further efforts to combat human trafficking. At that time he stated: *"It ought to concern every person, because it's a debasement of our common humanity. It ought to concern every community, because it tears at the social fabric. It ought to concern every business, because it distorts markets. It ought to concern every nation, because it endangers public health and fuels violence and organized crime. I'm talking about the injustice, the outrage of human trafficking, which must be called by its true name — modern slavery. Our fight against human trafficking is one of the great human causes of our time, and the United States will continue to lead it ...."*

Today, there is a national spotlight on the newest form of human trafficking, known as DMST as indicated above or as CSEC (commercial sexual exploitation of children). Traffickers in these crimes are pimps who have increasingly moved away from adult prostitution to the more financially lucrative crime of forcing minor children into prostitution. While many of these traffickers have a local gang affiliation, increasingly one sees organized crime syndicates begin to enter this criminal trade to sexually exploit children. The traffickers have evolved to using social network media sites and other technology-facilitated methods to find a steady flow of perpetrators who sexually assault these minor victims. They have also become more sophisticated in increasing their criminal clientele by transporting U.S. minors to multiple "tracks" in and out of other cities, counties, states, and countries. Many travel with their victims to cities that are hosting major sporting events or other popular media attractions for the sole purpose of prostituting and exploiting the children.

Unfortunately, many child victims do not seek help or resist intervention from law enforcement or social service organizations because they do not know their rights, they feel ashamed, they are reluctant to admit to victimization, or they fear their traffickers.[84]

In the recent past, law enforcement and other government agencies viewed the majority of these victims as teen minors who had independently made the choice to engage in the criminal act of prostitution. Correspondingly, the prevailing view of law enforcement, prosecutors, and other governmental personnel or agencies was that these minors were not victims of human trafficking. As a result, these adolescents were simply cited for solicitation of prostitution and provided with little or no services to address their exploitation and their trauma. The problem was further exacerbated by the lack of reporting to child welfare and by the agencies' limited resources and outdated training, limiting their provision of effective services to this population.

The task force, consistent with federal policy, recommends strongly that child victims of commercial sex trafficking be treated as victims and not as delinquents or criminals. They should not be locked up in juvenile detention facilities, placement programs, or jails but instead should be given safe harbor in facilities specifically designed to address their unique needs. States and localities need to develop new laws and procedures and imaginatively apply existing laws on victim protection to protect the rights of these child victims. State and local officials should coordinate efforts with federal officials and social service agencies to provide safe housing and other essential services. These children desperately need the benefit of trauma-informed assessments, care, and treatment to help them live meaningful lives in our society.

6.9 Whenever possible, prosecute young offenders in the juvenile justice system instead of transferring their cases to adult courts.

As noted earlier in this report, a majority of U.S. children, an estimated 46 million, are exposed to violence, crime, and abuse each year. Many of these children are at increased risk of being victimized and/or becoming violent themselves. Too often, these children are labeled as "bad," "delinquent," "troublemakers," or "lacking character and positive motivation." Many commit violent acts and enter the criminal justice system. However, enormous strides have been made in developing effective ways of interrupting the cycle of violence, responding to the consequences of the exposure of these youth to violence, and healing them from its effects. It is time to utilize effective coordinated approaches that address the needs of children traumatized by violence who commit violent acts.

We should stop treating juvenile offenders as if they were adults, prosecuting them as adults in adult courts, incarcerating them as adults, and sentencing them to harsh punishments that ignore their capacity to grow. When properly screened, assessed, and provided with trauma-informed care and evidence-based trauma-specific treatment, children who have been exposed to violence and are in trouble with the law have the capacity to grow, mature, and become productive citizens.

In the United States, over 200,000 children every year are tried as adults,[85,86] and on any given day an estimated 6,000 are incarcerated in an adult facility while they are still juveniles.[87] However, most adult jails or prisons are ill-equipped to meet the needs of children or keep them safe.[88] They are much more likely to commit suicide in an adult jail than in a juvenile facility.[89,90] They are also five times as likely to be sexually abused or raped as they would be in a juvenile facility.[91] Some of these youth are confined in facilities along with adults, where they may witness as well as be the target of violence.

While in adult jails and prisons, children are often housed in solitary confinement to protect them from adults. In a 2012 survey in Texas, for example, the majority of jails held juveniles in solitary confinement for an astounding 6 months to more than a year — with just 1 hour outside their cell per day.[92] Nowhere is the damaging impact of incarceration on vulnerable children more obvious than when it involves solitary confinement.[33] A 2002 investigation by the U.S. Department of Justice showed that juveniles experience symptoms of paranoia, anxiety, and depression even after very short periods of isolation.

In September 2009, three guards escorted a 16-year-old Troy to an interview with his lawyer in a New Jersey juvenile facility. He wore leg-irons and his body was covered only with a "Ferguson gown," a sleeveless-thigh-length robe that bound him with 242 Velcro strips. Self-mutilation scars too numerous to count covered his arms.[93] Troy had spent 24 hours a day in an isolation cell for approximately 180 of the 225 days he had been confined.[94] Citing dangers facing youth like Troy, the American Academy of Child and Adolescent Psychiatry recently issued a statement flatly opposing solitary confinement for juveniles.[95]

Treating young offenders like adults also puts society at greater risk. Children prosecuted as adults are 34 percent more likely to commit new crimes than are youth who remain in the juvenile justice system.[96]

In 2012, 32 members of the U.S. Congress cited these reasons and others in a letter to U.S. Attorney General Eric Holder urging him to strengthen federal regulations and essentially prohibit states and localities from incarcerating any person younger than 18 in an adult prison or jail as a condition of federal funding.[97] Current federal guidelines, including the Prison Rape Elimination Act standards, already require adult facilities to ensure that youth awaiting trial neither hear nor see adult inmates, but those restrictions have the unintended effect of promoting the use of solitary confinement.

On June 25, 2012, the Supreme Court reached a decision in *Miller v. Alabama* that it is unconstitutional for states to require a sentence of life without parole for anyone who is younger than 18 at the time of the crime. In writing for the majority, Justice Kagan affirmed that youth, and the hallmarks of youth, matter. "... a State's most severe penalties on juvenile offenders cannot proceed as though they were not children."[98]

Although the Court stopped short of an outright ban on life without parole for juveniles, Justice Kagan noted, "... we think appropriate occasions for sentencing juveniles to this harshest possible penalty will be uncommon. That is especially so because of the great difficulty we noted in *Roper* and *Graham* of distinguishing at this early age between the 'juvenile offender whose crime reflects unfortunate yet transient immaturity, and the rare juvenile offender whose crime reflects irreparable corruption.'"[99]

References

1. Abram, K. M., Teplin, L. A., Charles, D. R., Longworth, S. L., McClelland, G. M., & Dulcan, M. K. (2004). Posttraumatic stress disorder and trauma in youth in juvenile detention. *Archives of General Psychiatry, 61*(4), 403–410.

2. Ford, J. D., Chapman, J. C., Connor, D. F., & Cruise, K. C. (2012). Complex trauma and aggression in secure juvenile justice settings. *Criminal Justice & Behavior, 39*(5), 695–724.

3. Pope, K., Luna, B., & Thomas, C.R. (2012, April). Developmental neuroscience and the courts: How science is influencing the disposition of juvenile offenders. *Journal of the American Academy of Child and Adolescent Psychiatry. 51*(4), 341–342.

4. Giedd, J, Lalonde F. M., Celano, M. J., et al. (2009, May). Anatomical brain magnetic resonance imaging of typically developing children and adolescents. *Journal of the American Academy of Child and Adolescent Psychiatry. 48*(5), 465–470.

5. Obradovic, J., Burt, K. B., & Masten, A. S. (2006). Pathways of adaptation from adolescence to young adulthood: antecedents and correlates. *Annals of the New York Academy of Science, 1094,* 340–344.

6. Resnick, M. D., Bearman, P. S., Blum, R. W., Bauman, K. E., Harris, K. M., Jones, J., et al. (1997). Protecting adolescents from harm. Findings from the National Longitudinal Study on Adolescent Health. *JAMA: Journal of the American Medical Association, 278*(10), 823–832.

7. Roper v. Simmons 543 US 551; Graham v. Florida 130 S. Ct. 2011; Miller v. Alabama 132 S. Ct. 2455.

8. Rich, J. et al. (2009). *Healing the Hurt: Trauma-Informed Approaches to the Health of Boys and Young Men of Color.* (Center for Nonviolence and Social Justice, Drexel University School of Public Health and Department of Emergency Medicine.) p. 9. Retrieved from http://www1.calendow.org/uploadedFiles/Publications/BMOC/Drexel%20-%20Healing%20the%20Hurt%20-%20Full%20Report.pdf

9. Ford, J. D., & Cloitre, M. (2009). Best practices in psychotherapy for children and adolescents. In C. A. Courtois & J. D. Ford (Eds.), *Treating complex traumatic stress disorders: an evidence-based guide* (pp. 59–81). New York, NY: Guilford.

10. Saxe, G., MacDonald, H., & Ellis, H. (2007). Psychosocial approaches for children with PTSD. In E. B. Foa, M. J. Friedman, T. M. Keane, & P. Resick (Eds.), *Handbook of PTSD: Science and practice* (pp. 359–375). New York, NY: Guilford.

11. Anda, R. F., Butchart, A., Felitti, V. J., & Brown, D. W. (2010). Building a framework for global surveillance of the public health implications of adverse childhood experiences. *American Journal of Preventive Medicine, 39*(1), 93–98.

12. Finkelhor, D., Turner, H., Ormrod, R., & Hamby, S. L. (2010). Trends in childhood violence and abuse exposure: evidence from 2 national surveys. *Archives of Pediatric and Adolescent Medicine, 164*(3), 238–242.

13. Kerig, P. K. (2012). Trauma and juvenile delinquency: New directions in interventions. *Journal of Child & Adolescent Trauma, 5*(3), 187–190.

14. Glisson, C., & Green, P. (2006). The effects of organizational culture and climate on the access to mental health care in child welfare and juvenile justice systems. *Administration and Policy in Mental Health, 33*(4), 433–448.

15. Huey, S. J., Jr., & Polo, A. J. (2008). Evidence-based psychosocial treatments for ethnic minority youth. *Journal of Clinical Child and Adolescent Psychology, 37*(1), 262–301.

16. Crofoot Graham, T. L., & Corcoran, K. (2003). Mental health screening results for Native American and Euro-American youth in Oregon juvenile justice settings. *Psychological Reports, 92*(3 Pt 2), 1053–1060.

17. Estrada, R., & Marksamer, J. (2006). The legal rights of LGBT youth in state custody: what child welfare and juvenile justice professionals need to know. *Child Welfare, 85*(2), 171–194.

18. Finkelhor, D., Cross, T. P., & Cantor, E. N. (2005). The justice system for juvenile victims: a comprehensive model of case flow. *Trauma Violence & Abuse, 6*(2), 83–102.

19. Ko, S. J., Ford, J. D., Kassam-Adams, N., Berkowitz, S. J., Wilson, C., Wong, M., et al. (2008). Creating trauma-informed systems: Child welfare, education, first responders, health care, juvenile justice. *Professional Psychology: Research and Practice, 39*(4), 396–404.

20. Thomas, C. R., & Penn, J. V. (2002). Juvenile justice mental health services. *Child and Adolescent Psychiatric Clinics of North America, 11*(4), 731–748.

21. Committee on Adolescence. (2011). Health care for youth in the juvenile justice system. Pediatrics, 128(6), 1219–1235; Sukhodolsky, D. G., & Ruchkin, V. (2006). Evidence-based psychosocial treatments in the juvenile justice system. *Child and Adolescent Psychiatric Clinics of North America, 15*(2), 501–516.

22. Taxman, F. S., Henderson, C., Young, D., & Farrell, J. (2012). The Impact of training interventions on organizational readiness to support innovations in juvenile justice offices. *Administration and Policy in Mental Health.*

23. www.crimesolutions.gov; www.nrepp.samhsa.gov; www.ojjdp.gov/mpg

24. Grisso, T. (2007). Progress and perils in the juvenile justice and mental health movement. *Journal of the American Academy of Psychiatry and the Law, 35*(2), 158–167.

25. Henderson, C. E., Young, D. W., Jainchill, N., Hawke, J., Farkas, S., & Davis, R. M. (2007). Program use of effective drug abuse treatment practices for juvenile offenders. *Journal of Substance Abuse Treatment, 32*(3), 279–290.

26. Teplin L., et al. (2006, April). Psychiatric disorders of youth in detention. (Juvenile Justice Bulletin, Office of Juvenile Justice and Delinquency Prevention.) p. 9. Retrieved from http://www.ncjrs.gov/pdffiles1/ojjdp/210331.pdf; see also: Wasserman, G. A., et al. (2004, August). *Assessing the mental health status of youth in juvenile justice settings.* (Juvenile Justice Bulletin, Office of Juvenile Justice and Delinquency Prevention.) p. 3. Retrieved from https://www.ncjrs.gov/pdffiles1/ojjdp/202713.pdf

27. Sedlak, A.J. & McPherson, K. S. (2010, April). *Youth's needs and services: Findings from the survey of youth in residential placement online database.* (Office of Juvenile Justice and Delinquency Prevention, Office of Justice Programs, U.S. Department of Justice.) Retrieved from http://www.ncjrs.gov/pdffiles1/ojjdp/227728.pdf

28. Mendel, R. A. (2011). No place for kids: The case for reducing juvenile incarceration. Annie E. Casey Foundation, 24. Retrieved from http://www.aecf.org/OurWork/JuvenileJustice/~/media/Pubs/Topics/Juvenile%20Justice/Detention%20Reform/NoPlaceForKids/JJ_NoPlaceForKids_Full.pdf

29. Cooper, J. L. (2009, November). *Creating policies to support trauma-informed perspectives and practices.* Power point presentation at the Third Annual Symposium, Bridging the Gap. Fort Worth, TX. Retrieved from www.mentalhealthconnection.org/janice-cooper-ppt.ppt

30. Huckshorn, K. A. (2006, July). Re-designing state mental health policy to prevent the use of seclusion and restraint. *Administration and Policy in Mental Health and Mental Health Services Research, 33:*4, 1.

31. Caldwell, A. C. (2007). Attitudes of juvenile justice staff towards intellectual, psychiatric, and physical disabilities. *Intellectual and Developmental Disabilities, 45*(2), 77–89.

32. Mohr, H. (2008, March 2). 13K claims of abuse in juvenile detention since '04. *USA Today.* Retrieved from http://www.usatoday.com/news/nation/2008-03-02-juveniledetention_N.htm

33. Boyd, R. (2002, August). *Letter to Governor Parris N. Glendening from Assistant Attorney General Ralph F. Boyd, Jr.* United States Department of Justice, Civil Rights Division, Washington, D.C. Retrieved from http://www.justice.gov/crt/about/spl/documents/baltimore_findings_let.php

34. Hayes, L. M. (2004, February). *Juvenile suicide in confinement: A national survey.* National Center on Institutions and Alternatives, 24. Retrieved from http://www.ncjrs.gov/pdffiles1/ojjdp/grants/206354.pdf

35. Ford, J. D., Hartman, J. K., Hawke, J., & Chapman, J. C. (2008). Traumatic victimization, posttraumatic stress disorder, suicidal ideation, and substance abuse risk among juvenile justice-involved youths. *Journal of Child & Adolescent Trauma, 1,* 75–92.

36. Ford, J. D., Steinberg, K. L., Hawke, J., Levine, J., & Zhang, W. (2012). Randomized trial comparison of emotion regulation and relational psychotherapies for PTSD with girls involved in delinquency. *Journal of Clinical Child & Adolescent Psychology, 41*(1), 27–37.

37. Steinberg, A. M., Brymer, M. J., Decker, K. B., & Pynoos, R. S. (2004). The University of California at Los Angeles Post-traumatic Stress Disorder Reaction Index. *Current Psychiatry Reports, 6*(2), 96–100.

38. Essau, C. A., Sasagawa, S., & Frick, P. J. (2006). Callous-unemotional traits in a community sample of adolescents. *Assessment, 13*(4), 454–469.

39. Williams, J., Ford, J. D., Wolpaw, J., Pearson, G., & Chapman, J. (2005, July). *Not Just Child's Play: Mental Health Assessment in the Juvenile Justice System.* Farmington, CT: Connecticut Child Health and Development Institute.

40. Sickmund, M., et al. (2011). *Easy access to the census of juveniles in residential placement.* National Center for Juvenile Justice, Office of Juvenile Justice and Delinquency Prevention, Office of Justice Programs, U.S. Department of Justice. Retrieved from http://www.ojjdp.gov/ojstatbb/ezacjrp/asp/display.asp

41. U.S. Census Bureau. (2010). *State and county quickfacts.* Retrieved from http://quickfacts.census.gov/qfd/index.html

42. Teplin, L. A., Abram, K. M., McClelland, G. M., Dulcan, M. K., & Mericle, A. A. (2002). Psychiatric disorders in youth in juvenile detention. *Archives of General Psychiatry, 59*(12), 1133–1143.

43. Morrissey, J. P., Fagan, J. A., & Cocozza, J. J. (2009). New models of collaboration between criminal justice and mental health systems. *American Journal of Psychiatry, 166*(11), 1211–1214.

44. Steinberg, L. (2009). Adolescent development and juvenile justice. *Annual Review of Clinical Psychology, 5,* 459–485.

45. Wasserman, G. A., Jensen, P. S., Ko, S. J., et al. (2003). Mental health assessments in juvenile justice: report on the consensus conference. *Journal of the American Academy of Child & Adolescent Psychiatry, 42*(7), 752–761.

46. Gallagher, C. A., & Dobrin, A. (2006). Deaths in juvenile justice residential facilities. *Journal of Adolescent Health, 38*(6), 662–668.

47. Gallagher, C. A., & Dobrin, A. (2007). Can juvenile justice detention facilities meet the call of the American Academy of Pediatrics and National Commission on Correctional Health Care? A national analysis of current practices. *Pediatrics, 119*(4), e991–e1001.

48. Pottick, K. J., Bilder, S., Vander Stoep, A., Warner, L. A., & Alvarez, M. F. (2008). US patterns of mental health service utilization for transition-age youth and young adults. *Journal of Behavioral Health Services Research, 35*(4), 373–389.

49. Wasserman, G. A., McReynolds, L. S., Whited, A. L., Keating, J. M., Musabegovic, H., & Huo, Y. (2008). Juvenile probation officers' mental health decision making. *Administration and Policy in Mental Health, 35*(5), 410–422.

50. Abram, K. M., Teplin, L. A., McClelland, G. M., & Dulcan, M. K. (2003). Comorbid psychiatric disorders in youth in juvenile detention. *Archives of General Psychiatry, 60*(11), 1097–1108.

51. Lennings, C. J., Kenny, D. T., & Nelson, P. (2006). Substance use and treatment seeking in young offenders on community orders. *Journal of Substance Abuse Treatment, 31*(4), 425–432.

52. Teplin, L. A., Welty, L. J., Abram, K. M., Dulcan, M. K., & Washburn, J. J. (2012). Prevalence and persistence of psychiatric disorders in youth after detention: a prospective longitudinal study. *Archives of General Psychiatry, 69*(10), 1031–1043.

53. Mulvey, E. P. (2011, March). *Highlights from pathways to desistance: A longitudinal study of serious adolescent offenders.* Office of Juvenile Justice and Delinquency Prevention Fact Sheet, 2. Retrieved from http://ncjrs.gov/pdffiles1/ojjdp/230971.pdf

54. Baglivio, M. T. (2007). *The prediction of risk to recidivate among a juvenile offending population* (Doctoral Dissertation, 113–114. University of Florida). Retrieved from http://ufdcimages.uflib.ufl.edu/UF/E0/02/15/69/00001/baglivio_m.pdf.

55. Iguchi, M. Y., Bell, J., Ramchand, R. N., & Fain, T. (2005). How criminal system racial disparities may translate into health disparities. *Journal of Health Care for the Poor and Underserved, 16*(4 Suppl B), 48–56.

56. Teplin, L. A., Abram, K. M., McClelland, G. M., Washburn, J. J., & Pikus, A. K. (2005). Detecting mental disorder in juvenile detainees: who receives services. *American Journal of Public Health, 95*(10), 1773–1780.

57. Pole, N., Gone, J. P., & Kulkarni, M. (2008). Posttraumatic stress disorder among ethnoracial minorities in the United States. *Clinical Psychology: Science and Practice, 15*(1), 35–61.

58. Vazsonyi, A. T., & Chen, P. (2010). Entry risk into the juvenile justice system: African American, American Indian, Asian American, European American, and Hispanic children and adolescents. *Journal of Child Psychology, Psychiatry & Allied Disciplines, 51*(6), 668–678.

59. Maldonado-Molina, M. M., Reingle, J. M., Tobler, A. L., Jennings, W. G., & Komro, K. A. (2010). Trajectories of Physical Aggression Among Hispanic Urban Adolescents and Young Adults: An Application of Latent Trajectory Modeling from Ages 12 to 18. *American Journal of Criminal Justice, 35*(3), 121–133.

60. Vervoort, M. H., Scholte, R. H., & Overbeek, G. (2010). Bullying and victimization among adolescents: the role of ethnicity and ethnic composition of school class. *Journal of Youth and Adolescence, 39*(1), 1–11.

61. Ford, J. D., Chapman, J. F., Hawke, J., & Albert, D. (2007). *Trauma among youth in the juvenile justice system: Critical issues and new directions.* Delmar, NY: National Center for Mental Health and Juvenile Justice. www.ncmhjj.com

62. Jaycox, L. H., Stein, B. D., & Amaya-Jackson, L. (2009). School-based treatment for children and adolescents. In E. B. Foa, T. M. Keane, M. J. Friedman, & J. A. Cohen (Eds.), *Effective Treatments for PTSD* (2nd Ed) (pp. 327–345). New York, NY: Guilford.

63. Ford, J. D., & Hawke, J. (2012). Trauma affect regulation psychoeducation group and milieu intervention outcomes in juvenile detention facilities. *Journal of Aggression, Maltreatment & Trauma, 21*(4), 365–384.

64. Marrow, M., Knudsen, K., Olafson, E., & Bucher, S. (2012). The value of implementing TARGET within a trauma-informed juvenile justice setting. *Journal of Child & Adolescent Trauma, 5,* 257–270.

65. Ford, J. D., Steinberg, K. L., Hawke, J., Levine, J., & Zhang, W. (2012). Randomized trial comparison of emotion regulation and relational psychotherapies for PTSD with girls involved in delinquency. *Journal of Clinical Child Adolescent Psychology, 41*(1), 27–37.

66. Watson, L., & Edelman, P. (2012, October). Improving the juvenile justice system for girls: Lessons from the states. Washington, DC: Georgetown Center on Poverty, Inequality, and Public Policy (p. 1). Retrieved from http://www.law.georgetown.edu/academics/centers-institutes/poverty-inequality/upload/JDS_V1R4_Web_Singles.pdf

67. Acoca, L., & Dedel, K. (1998). *No place to hide: understanding and meeting the needs of girls in the California juvenile justice system.* (National Council on Crime and Delinquency.) Retrieved from http://www.nccdglobal.org/sites/default/files/publication_pdf/no-place-to-hide.pdf

68. Edwards, J. (2009). A lesson in unintended consequences: How juvenile justice and domestic violence reforms harm girls in violent family situations (and how to help them). *University of Pennsylvania Journal of Law and Social Change 13*(2), 219–241.

69. Patino, V., Ravoira, L., & Wolf, A. (2006). *A rallying cry for change: Charting a new directions in the state of Florida's response to girls in the juvenile justice system.* Oakland, CA: National Council on Crime and Delinquency.

70. Sherman, F. T. (2005). Detention Reform and Girls: Challenges and Solutions. Baltimore, MD: The Annie E. Casey Foundation. Retrieved from http://www.aecf.org/KnowledgeCenter/Publications.aspx?pubguid=%7BAA79FD34-42A5-4C5C-ADD4-C40BF1B34B5B%7D

71. Sedlak, A. J., & Bruce, C. (2010). Youth's characteristics and backgrounds. Juvenile Justice Bulletin. Washington, DC: Office of Juvenile Justice and Delinquency Prevention. Retrieved from https://www.ncjrs.gov/pdffiles1/ojjdp/227730.pdf

72. Datesman, S., & Scarpitti, F. (1977). Unequal protection for males and females in the juvenile court. In T. N. Ferdinand (Ed.), *Juvenile Delinquency: Little Brother Grows Up,* Newbury Park, CA: Sage; Goodkind, S. (2005). Gender-specific services in the juvenile justice system: A critical examination. *Affilia, 20*(1), 52–70.

73. Sherman, F. T., *Pathways to Juvenile Justice Reform: Detention Reform and Girls Challenges and Solutions,* 2005.

74. Stevens, J. (2012, June 27). Trauma-sensitive schools are better schools, part two. *Huffington Post.* Retrieved from http://www.huffingtonpost.com/jane-ellen-stevens/traumasensitive-schools-part-two_b_1632126.html

75. Davidson, R. J., et al. (2012). Contemplative Practices and Mental Training: Prospects for American Education. *Child Development Perspectives, 6*(2), 146–153.

76. Walker Sterling, R., Crawford, C., Harrison, S., & Henning, K. (2009). *Role of Juvenile Defense Counsel in Juvenile Court* (pp. 11–13), National Juvenile Defender Center.

77. *In re Gault, 387 U.S. 1* (1967).

78. Standards for the Administration of Assigned Counsel Systems. (1989). National Legal Aid and Defender Association.

79. *Raising the Standards for Indigent Defense, Models for Change systems Reform, Innovation Brief.* Available from www.modelsforchange.net/publications/312/Innovation_Brief_Raising_the_Standards_of_Juvenile_Indigent_Defense.pdf

80. National Juvenile Defender Center et. al. (2001). The Children Left Behind: An Assessment of Access to Counsel and Quality of Representation in Delinquency Proceedings in Louisiana. Available from http://www.njdc.info/pdf/LAreport.pdf; Jones, J. (2004), Access to counsel, *OJJDP Bulletin,* NCJ 204063; 2010 Pennsylvania Juvenile Court Dispositions, Juvenile Court Judges' Commission, Center for Juvenile Justice Training and Research.

81. http://www.polarisproject.org/human-trafficking/sex-trafficking-in-the-us

82. Murphy, P. (1993). *Making the Connections: Women, Work and Abuse.* Orlando, FL: Paul M. Deutsche Press. As cited in Girls Educational & Mentoring Services. (2011). Research and Resources. Retrieved from http://www.gems-girls.org/about/research-resources

83. Pennsylvania Interbranch Commission on Gender, Racial and Ethnic Fairness. *Justice in the Balance,* 2010–2011, Annual Report, p. 3.

84. International Association of Chiefs of Police. (2006). *The Crime of Human Trafficking: A Law Enforcement Guide to Identification and Investigation,* 8.

85. Wolfman, J. (2005). *Coalition for Juvenile Justice 2005 Annual Report: Childhood on trial: The failure of trying & sentencing youth in adult criminal court.* Retrieved from http://www.jillwolfson.com/journalism/trial.html

86. Griffin, P. (2010, June 18). National Center for Juvenile Justice, National Institute of Corrections Convening, as cited in Ziedenberg, J. (2011, December). *You're an adult now: Youth in adult criminal justice system.* (National Institute of Corrections, U.S. Department of Justice.) Retrieved from http://static.nicic.gov/Library/025555.pdf

87. Minton, T. (2011, April). *Jail inmates at midyear 2011: Statistical tables.* (Bureau of Justice Statistics, Office of Justice Programs, U.S. Department of Justice.) 6. Retrieved from http://www.bjs.gov/content/pub/pdf/jim11st.pdf

88. Campaign for Youth Justice. (2007, November). *Jailing juveniles: The dangers of incarcerating youth in adult jails in America.* p. 14. Retrieved from http://www.campaign4youthjustice.org/Downloads/NationalReportsArticles/CFYJ-Jailing_Juveniles_Report_2007-11-15.pdf

89. Memory, J. (1989). Juvenile suicides in secure detention facilities: correction of published rates. *Death Studies, 13*(5), 455–63. Retrieved from http://www.tandfonline.com/doi/abs/10.1080/07481188908252324; There is a dearth of research on juvenile suicide in adult jails, but newer figures show jail inmates under 18 had the highest suicide rate in local jails, 101 per 100,000. The suicide rate in local jails for all inmates was 47 per 100,000 inmates.

90. Mumola, C. J. (2005, August). *Special Report: Suicide and Homicide in State Prisons and Local Jails. (Bureau of Justice Statistics, U.S. Department of Justice,* 2–5). Retrieved from www.bjs.gov/content/pub/pdf/shsplj.pdf

91. Prison Rape Elimination Act of 2003. (2003, September 4). PL 108-79, 117 Stat. 972–973. Retrieved from http://www.gpo.gov/fdsys/pkg/PLAW-108publ79/pdf/PLAW-108publ79.pdf

92. Deitch, M., et al. (2012, May). *LBJ school releases report on conditions for certified juveniles in Texas county jails.* Lyndon B. Johnson School of Public Affairs, University of Texas at Austin, p. TK. Retrieved from http://www.utexas.edu/lbj/sites/default/files/file/news/Conditions%20for%20Certified%20Juveniles%20in%20Texas%20County%20Jails-FINAL4.pdf

93. Simkins, S., Beyer, M., & Geis, L. M. (2012). The harmful use of isolation in juvenile facilities: The need for post-disposition representation. *Washington University Journal of Law and Policy, 38*(241), 18.

94. Troy D. and O'Neill S. v. Mickens et al., No.10-2903, 3. (US District Court, State of New Jersey 2010). Retrieved from http://docs.justia.com/cases/federal/district-courts/new-jersey/njdce/1:2010cv02902/242291/50/0.pdf?1314451414; Simkins, S., Beyer, M., & Geis, L. M. (2012). The harmful use of isolation in juvenile facilities: The need for post-disposition representation. *Washington University Journal of Law and Policy, 38*(241), 1.

95. Solitary Confinement of Juvenile Offenders. (2012, April). *American Academy of Child & Adolescent Psychiatry: Policy Statements.* Retrieved from http://www.aacap.org/cs/root/policy_statements/solitary_confinement_of_juvenile_offenders

96. Task Force on Community Preventive Services. (2007, April 13). Recommendation against policies facilitating the transfer of juveniles from juvenile to adult justice systems for the purpose of reducing violence. *American Journal of Preventive Medicine, Vol. 32, No.4S, S5–S6.* Retrieved from www.thecommunityguide.org/violence/taskforcearticle3.pdf

97. Rush, B. L., et al. (2012, April 3). *House members to Holder: Remove children from adult jails and prisons.* U.S. House of Representatives. Retrieved from http://www.njjn.org/uploads/digital-library/HRLetter-to-AG_PREA_032012-Remove-Youth-from-Adult-Prisons-Jails.pdf

98. *Miller v. Alabama,* No. 10-9646. (2012, June 25). pp. 11–12. Retrieved from http://www.supremecourt.gov/opinions/11pdf/10-9646.pdf

99. *Miller v. Alabama.* No. 10-9646. (2012, June 25), p. 17. Retrieved from http://www.supremecourt.gov/opinions/11pdf/10-9646.pdf

CONCLUSION

CONCLUSION

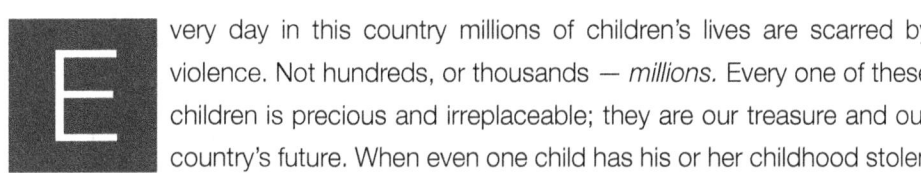very day in this country millions of children's lives are scarred by violence. Not hundreds, or thousands — *millions.* Every one of these children is precious and irreplaceable; they are our treasure and our country's future. When even one child has his or her childhood stolen by violence, the loss is incalculable. The wounds our children endure from exposure to violence must be healed. There is no more time to waste — we can no longer wait. Decisive action is required, now.

This report guides the way forward. The actions we must take are clearly stated in each of our recommendations. Change can — and must — begin immediately, at every level of government and in every community.

Ultimately, every family must be empowered to join this effort, and every community must rise up to protect and heal children who are exposed to violence and ensuing psychological trauma. We all know that children should be protected and kept safe from violence. Yet we have not, as a nation, firmly repudiated all forms of violence that harm our children. We must now commit, unreservedly, to sustained efforts at protecting our children from violence.

We can protect and heal our children from exposure to violence by mobilizing resources that currently exist but are not sufficiently organized and accessible. Steps must be taken nationally, regionally, and locally to inform and support every teacher, healthcare professional, police officer, judge, attorney, social worker, clergyperson, therapist, advocate, and paraprofessional who serves and guides children and their families to implement effective policies, practices, and procedures to protect and heal children exposed to violence.

Children and families in tribal communities, and others in rural or urban settings who live with poverty or discrimination because of their race, culture or language, sexual orientation, or mental or physical disabilities, have experienced decades and generations of exposure to violence and extreme psychological trauma. They require special attention, and they must receive it. We must take steps politically, economically, and socially to restore these communities and their children and families from the chronic and debilitating exposure to violence they face every day.

Although this is a hard time for countless families in our country who are struggling financially, and for all parts of government facing immense economic challenges, we must not let these realities diminish our resolve to face and address the ongoing epidemic of children exposed to violence. We must continue to identify opportunities for the federal, state, tribal, and local governments to redirect the funds currently available and to achieve new efficiencies with this funding. We can and must use our resources more wisely to produce better outcomes and to defend children against exposure to violence.

We must actively engage youth, their families, and local leaders in urban, suburban, rural, and tribal communities to drastically reduce children's exposure to violence.

This report is a call to action for every person in America to rise up to defend our children! We must dedicate ourselves to creating safe places and healthy relationships in which every one of our children can grow, succeed, and carry forward the blessings of liberty, fraternity, and equality.

When we dedicate ourselves as a country to defending our children from violence, we will provide hope and a way forward for every person in America to thrive, because we will have made our country safe for all.

GLOSSARY OF
KEY TERMS

GLOSSARY OF KEY TERMS

American Indian/Alaska Native: As a general principle, an Indian is a person who is of some degree Indian blood and is recognized as an Indian by a Tribe and/or the United States. No single federal or tribal criterion establishes a person's identity as an Indian. Government agencies use differing criteria to determine eligibility for programs and services. Tribes also have varying eligibility criteria for membership.

It is important to distinguish between the ethnological term "Indian" and the political/legal term "Indian." The protections and services provided by the United States for tribal members flow not from an individual's status as an American Indian in an ethnological sense, but because the person is a member of a Tribe recognized by the United States and with which the United States has a special trust relationship. (Please see http://www.justice.gov/otj/nafaqs.htm).

Assessment: Determining the specific nature of an individual's needs or problems using professional interviews, tests, questionnaires, or observations.

Child- and family-serving organizations: Agencies, facilities, and programs that provide children or families with services that may include education, assistance, rehabilitation, or treatment for medical or mental health, learning, social, financial, child protection, or legal needs.

Child exposed to violence: Any individual who is not yet an adult (threshold age varies across jurisdictions, typically birth to either 18 or 21 years old) who is directly or indirectly exposed to violence that poses a real threat or a perceived threat to the individual's or an affiliated person's life or bodily integrity. Children exposed to violence are at much greater risk of developing lethal medical illnesses in their early adult years; to utilize disproportionately costly medical, psychological, and public health services; and to die prematurely.

Ethnocultural: Characteristics of individuals or their communities that are related to race, ethnicity, or cultural beliefs and practices.

Evidence-based treatment: Interventions and services provided by a credentialed professional or paraprofessional to serve as a therapy or community-based service to promote recovery from psychosocial, psychological, or medical problems or to prevent these problems altogether. These interventions and services: (a) have been scientifically tested and demonstrated to be effective, (b) have clearly defined procedures that can be taught and implemented consistently with fidelity, (c) are feasible and useful for clinical practitioners and programs, and (d) are credible and acceptable to the recipients.

Screening: Asking brief questions or gathering existing information to determine if an individual should be identified as having a specific need or problem.

Trauma-informed care: This is a new form of evidence-based interventions and service delivery, implemented by multiple service providers, that identifies, assesses, and heals people injured by, or exposed to, violence and other traumatic events.

Trauma-focused services: Services are considered trauma-focused when caregivers (such as biological, foster, or adoptive parents, mentors, spiritual advisors, coaches, or line staff in child-serving programs) or professionals providing services (a) *realize* (understand) the impact that exposure to violence and trauma have on victims' physical, psychological, and psychosocial development and well-being, (b) *recognize* when a specific person who has been exposed to violence and trauma is in need of help to recover from trauma's adverse impacts, and (c) *respond* by helping in ways that reflect awareness of trauma's adverse impacts and consistently support the person's recovery from them (adapted from the 2012 SAMHSA [Substance Abuse and Mental Health Services Administration] "Working Definition of Trauma and Guidance for a Trauma-Informed Approach").

Trauma-specific treatment: Medical, physiological, psychological, and psychosocial therapies that are (a) free from the use of coercion, restraints, seclusion, and isolation, (b) provided by a trained professional to an individual, a family, or a group adversely affected by violence exposure and trauma, and (c) designed specifically to promote recovery from the adverse impacts of violence exposure and trauma on physical, psychological, and psychosocial development, health, and well-being.

Violence: The World Report on Violence and Health (WRVH) (http://www.who.int/ violenceprevention/approach/definition/en/) defines violence as "the intentional use of physical force or power, threatened or actual, against oneself, another person, or against a group or community that either results in or has a high likelihood of resulting in injury, death, psychological harm, maldevelopment, or deprivation."

Violence exposure: Violence exposure can be *direct,* where the victim or community of victims is the direct target of the intentional use of force or power, but it can also be *indirect,* where the victim or community of victims is witness to the intentional use of force or power or has lost a loved one to violence. In both cases, over 20 years of scientific literature on the impact of violence demonstrates that violence exposure results in significant short- and long-term debilitating and costly impacts on the victim's physical, emotional, cognitive, and social health and well-being.

Violence exposure variables (magnitude of impact): Scientists and health professionals unanimously agree that specific violence exposure variables, whether direct or indirect, drastically increase negative health outcomes. Primary exposure variables include *duration of exposure* (being repeatedly victimized over months and years), *proximity to exposure* (remaining physically close to the perpetrator during the violence), *type of violence or perpetration* (combat, kidnapping, sexual assault and rape, assault and battery, torture, being buried alive, human trafficking, genocide, homeland displacement, and mass political violence), and *relationship to the perpetrator* (the perpetrator is a known figure of trust and protection like a parent, spouse, partner, or trusted authority figure).

A further critical aspect of violence exposure is the intentional selection of a victim or victims to do harm to that victim, that victim's property, that victim's family, or that victim's tribe. When the intentional selection to do harm is based on a victim's age, gender, race, ethnicity, tribal affiliation, or beliefs and orientations, the negative health outcomes may be even more significant.

Workforce protections: Adaptations to a workplace's environment or its policies and procedures or to the education, supervision, and supportive services provided to the personnel that are designed to foster *workplace wellness* and provide protection from psychological or physical harm. A fundamental adaptation to promote wellness and protect workers is a workplace that is free from the use of coercion, restraints, seclusion, and isolation.

ACTIVITIES OF THE TASK FORCE AND LIST OF WITNESSES

ACTIVITIES OF THE TASK FORCE AND LIST OF WITNESSES

Lists and quotations from witnesses in the report reflect organizational affiliation at the time of participation and may not represent participants' current positions.

Hearing 1: Understanding the Scope of Children's Exposure to Violence

University of Maryland Francis King Carey School of Law
Baltimore, Maryland

November 29, 2011

The task force's first hearing focused on the scope of children's exposure to violence from the perspectives of law, medicine, law enforcement, and research. The task force heard from experts about the prevalence of children's exposure to violence; the burden on care providers to recognize and record children's experience with violence; the challenge of tracking the intergenerational impact of violence; and the lasting effects exposure to violence can have on children, from brain development to juvenile justice system contact. Several leaders in the field spoke about innovative and collaborative approaches to addressing these problems and protecting and healing children exposed to violence.

Witnesses: Lauren Abramson, PhD, Founder and Executive Director, Community Conferencing Center; **Rosa Almond**, parent of children exposed to violence; **Sheila Bedi, Esq.**, Deputy Legal Director, Southern Poverty Law Center; **Steven Berkowitz, MD**, Associate Professor of Clinical Psychiatry, University of Pennsylvania, Department of Psychiatry; **Mitru Ciarlante**, Director of Youth Initiative at National Center for Victims of Crime; **Michaele Cohen**, Executive Director, Maryland Network Against Domestic Violence; **Theodore Corbin, MD, MPP**, Medical Director, Healing Hurt People violence intervention program, Co-Director of the Center for Nonviolence and Social Justice; **Nigel Cox**, Chair, Students Against Violence Everywhere National Youth Advisory Board; **Howard Dubowitz, MB, ChB**, Head of the Division of Child Protection, Director of the Center for Families, University of Maryland Medical Center; **Jeffrey Edleson, PhD**, Professor and Director of Research, University of Minnesota School of Social Work, Director, Minnesota Center Against Violence and Abuse; **Earl El-Amin**, Resident Imam, Muslim Community Cultural Center of Baltimore; **David Finkelhor, PhD**, Professor of Sociology, Director of the Crimes Against Children Research Center, Co-Director of the Family Research Laboratory at the University of New Hampshire; **Josh Giunta**, member of the public; **Marshall T. Goodwin**, Chief of Police, Baltimore City Schools; **Jabriera Handy**, youth advocate, Community Law in Action; **Geraldine Hawkins, PhD**, survivor of childhood exposure to violence; **Ellsworth Johnson-Bey**, Founder of Fraternal Order of Ex-Offenders; **Jacquelynn Kuhn**, survivor of childhood exposure to violence; **Phil Leaf, PhD**, Professor and Director, Johns Hopkins Center for the Prevention of Youth Violence; **Ellyn Loy**, Clinical Director, House of Ruth; **Hon. Patricia M. Martin**, President, National Council of Juvenile and Family Court Judges; **Patrick McCarthy, PhD**, President and Chief Executive Officer, Annie E. Casey Foundation; **Adam Rosenberg, Esq.**, Executive Director, Baltimore Child Abuse Center; **Liz Ryan**, President and Chief Executive Officer, Campaign for Youth Justice; **Sonja Sohn**, actor and founder of ReWired for Change; **Elizabeth Thompson, PhD**, Director, Kennedy Krieger Institute Family Center, Project Director for the Integrated Trauma Approaches Program; **Deborah Young**, advocate, Justice for Families

Hearing 2: Children's Exposure to Violence in Rural and Tribal Communities

Vincent E. Griego Council Chambers & U.S. Attorney's Office, District of New Mexico Albuquerque, New Mexico

January 31, 2012

The task force's second hearing focused on the unique issues that children, families, and service providers in rural and tribal communities face when experiencing or addressing exposure to violence. The task force heard from several young people about their own experiences, from experts on the relationship between the juvenile justice system and tribal courts, and from organization heads about their approaches to serving youth in rural and tribal communities. Witnesses also discussed how to use the strengths of these communities to address children's exposure to violence.

Witnesses: Rochelle A., Vice President, Leaders Uniting Voices Youth Advocates, New Mexico; **Victoria Amado**, New Mexico Victims' Rights Project; **Sharon**

Basinti, member of the public; **Dolores Subia BigFoot, PhD**, Director, Indian Country Child Trauma Center and Project Making Medicine, University of Oklahoma Health Sciences Center (OUHSC); **Evelyn Blanchard, PhD**, Tribal Court Advocate for families and children; **Maria Brock, LISW**, Tribal Home Visiting Project Director, Native American Professional Parent Resources, Inc.; **Elsie Boudreau, LMSW**, Alaska Native Justice Center; **Shelly Chimoni**, Executive Director, All Indian Pueblo Council; **Lyle Claw**, President, Changing Lives Around the World (CLAW) Inc.; **Kim Garcia**, member of the public; **Carole Justice**, Coordinator, Indian Country Methamphetamine Program; **Annie Pelletier Kerrick**, Idaho Teen Violence Awareness & Prevention Project; **Walter Lamar**, President, Lamar and Associates; **Coloradas Mangas**, Youth Board Member, Center for Native American Youth; **Nate Monson**, Executive Director, Iowa Safe Schools; **Anna Nelson**, Executive Director, New Mexico Forum for Youth, Professor, New Mexico State University; **Elaine Nolan**, Director of Tribal Programs, Big Brothers, Big Sisters of Central New Mexico; **Janell Regimbal**, Senior Vice President, Children and Family Lutheran Social Services of North Dakota; **Barbara Romo**, Assistant District Attorney, Thirteenth Judicial District, New Mexico; **Kathleen Sanchez**, TEWA Women United; **Paul Smokowski, MSW, PhD, CP**, Director, North Carolina Academic Center for Excellence in Youth Violence Prevention; **Esta Soler**, President, Futures Without Violence; **Mato Standing High**, Attorney General, Rosebud Sioux Tribe; **Gil Vigil**, National Indian Child Welfare Association Board Member, Tribal/Governmental Liaison, Santa Fe Indian School; **Ivy Wright-Bryan**, National Director, Native American Mentoring, Big Brothers Big Sisters of America

Hearing 3: Children's Exposure to Violence in the Community

University of Miami Newman Alumni Center
Coral Gables, FL

March 19–21, 2012

On the first day of its third hearing, the task force heard testimony from experts in addressing community violence. Witnesses spoke about addressing the effects of gang violence and of violence in immigrant communities and about coordinating first responses to incidents of violence. On the second day, the task force participated in an interactive discussion facilitated by Professor Charles J. Ogletree, Jr., of Harvard Law School. Professor Ogletree guided the task force and two witnesses through a series of hypothetical situations involving children exposed to violence, calling on the expertise of the participants to explain their responses.

Witnesses: Michael Aptman, MD, Vice President, Melissa Institute; **Alexis Brimberry, MD**, A Child Is Missing, Inc.; **Dawn L. Brown**, former Executive Director, Girls and Gangs; **Helene Buster**, Director of Family Services, Seminole Tribe of Florida; **Hon. Donald Cannava**, Judge, Miami-Dade County Domestic Violence Court; **Michael de Arellano, PhD**, National Crime Victims Research and Treatment Center, Department of Psychiatry and Behavioral Sciences, Medical University of South Carolina; **Sarah Greene, ACSW, LCSW**, Program Administrator of Criminal Justice Partnerships, Mecklenburg County, North Carolina; **Renita "Biggie Mama" Holmes**, Executive Director and Founder, Women's Association and Alliance Against Justice and Violence for Empowerment; **Keante Humphries**, Advocate, Southern Poverty Law Center; **Charles Hurley**, Chief of Police, Miami-Dade County Schools Police Department; **Hon. Dwight C. Jones**, Mayor of Richmond, Virginia; **Laura Kallus**, Executive Director, PanZOu Project, Inc.; **Walter Lambert, MD**, University of Miami School of Medicine; **Lisa Lampkin**, parent of child exposed to violence; **Maj. Eddie Levins**, Charlotte-Mecklenburg Police Department, North Carolina; Hon. **Mark Luttrell, Jr.**, Mayor of Shelby County, Tennessee; **Roy Martin**, Program Manager, Partnership Advancing Communities Together, Boston Health Commission; **Carlos Martinez**, Public Defender, Miami-Dade County; **Ed Mashek**, survivor of childhood exposure to violence; **Charles J. Ogletree, Jr.**, Director, Charles Hamilton Houston Institute for Race and Justice, Harvard Law School Jesse Climenko Professor of Law; **Carolyn Reyes, JD, MSW**, Senior Staff Attorney of Legal Services for Children (LSC); **Hon. Michael J. Ryan**, Cleveland Municipal Court Judge; **Bryan Samuels**, Commissioner, Administration on Children, Youth, and Families, Department of Health and Human Services; **Isis Snow**, parent of child exposed to violence; **Shellie Solomon**, Project Director, Service Network of Children of Inmates; **Vicki Spriggs**, CEO, Texas Court Appointed Special Advocates (CASA); **Lyn Tan**, Program Director, Youth Gang Prevention, at Immigrant and Refugee Community Organization

Hearing 4: Protect, Heal, Thrive

David Adamany Undergraduate Library, Wayne State University
Detroit, Michigan

April 23–24, 2012

At its final hearing, the task force heard from experts in research and programming and from organization and foundation heads whose work is successfully addressing exposure to violence. The task force also heard from young leaders who have taken an active role in encouraging their peers and communities to stand against violence.

Witnesses: **William Bell, PhD**, President and Chief Executive Officer, Casey Family Programs; **Sandra Bloom, MD**, Associate Professor, Health Management and Policy Co-Director, Center for Nonviolence and Social Justice, Drexel University School of Public Health; Distinguished Fellow, Andrus Children's Center; **Joron Burnett**, Founder and CEO, Green Light Movement; **Larry Cohen, MSW**, Founder and Executive Director of Prevention Institute; **Phil Coke**, Detroit Tigers; **Lois DeMott**, Co-Founder of Citizens for Prison Reform, Association for Children's Mental Health, parent of child exposed to violence; **David Esquith**, Acting Director, Office of Safe and Healthy Students; **Vincent Felitti, MD**, President and CEO of California Institutes of Preventive Medicine, Clinical Professor of Medicine at University of California, San Diego, and Fellow of The American College of Physicians; **Jordan Field**, Director, Detroit Tigers Foundation; **Ralph L. Godbee, Jr.**, Chief of the Police Department, City of Detroit; **Carol Goss**, President and Chief Executive Officer, The Skillman Foundation; **Frank Grijalva**, Co-Director of Midwest Trauma Services Network; **Neil Guterman, PhD**, Mose and Sylvia Firestone Professor, Director of the Beatrice Cummings Mayer Program in Violence Prevention, and Dean of the School of Social Service Administration, University of Chicago; **Kathy Hagenian**, Michigan Coalition Against Domestic and Sexual Violence; **Jim Henderson**, Battered Women's Justice Project, Office on Violence Against Women; **Gary Ivory**, Youth Advocate Programs, Inc.; **Cory Jackson**, Senior Pastor, Detroit Burns Seventh Day Adventist Church; **Hon. Darnell Jackson**, Circuit Court Judge, Saginaw County Circuit Court; **Doncella Floyd Jones**, Program Administrator, Children's Aid Society; **Candice Kane**, CEO, CeaseFire Chicago, University of Illinois at Chicago, School of Public Health; **Debbie Kane**, Executive Director, Michigan Domestic Violence and Sexual Assault Prevention and Treatment Board; **Mary Lee**, Deputy Director, PolicyLink; **James McCurtis**, Director of Crime Victim Services, Michigan Department of Community Health; **Rodney Nelson**, Team Captain and Assistant Instructor, South Shore Drill Team; **Leslie O'Reilly**, Program Specialist, Crime Victim Services, Michigan Department of Community Health; **Alex Piquero, PhD**, Ashbel Smith Professor in the Program in Criminology in the School of Economic, Political, and Policy Sciences at the University of Texas at Dallas; **Karen Rivera**, Veteran, US Navy; **Héctor Sánchez-Flores**, Executive Director, National Compadres Network; **Vincent Schiraldi**, Commissioner, New York City Department of Probation; **Lawnya Sherrod**, youth representative, National Forum on Youth Violence Prevention, Founder of Glimpse of Hope and Youth Voice; **Pamela Shifman**, Director, Initiatives for Girls and Women, NoVo Foundation; **Aisha Stubbs**, Struggling Youth Into Successful Adults; **Tadarial Sturdivant**, Director, Wayne County Child and Family Services; **Michelle Weemhoff**, Senior Policy Associate, Michigan Council on Crime and Delinquency

Listening Sessions

The task force held three listening sessions to learn about children's exposure to violence as it is experienced and addressed at a local level. Fifteen to twenty local experts were invited to each session to discuss the issues that affect them and tell the task force what would help them tackle these issues more effectively. At least one task force member attended each listening session.

Listening Session 1: National Council on Crime & Delinquency

Oakland, California

January 12, 2012

Local social workers, child psychiatrists, school administrators, law enforcement officials, and doctors shared their experiences and approaches to addressing children's exposure to violence in an urban area with high rates of many forms of violence. Topics included the need to incorporate trauma-informed responses to children's behavior into schools, the juvenile justice system, and other institutions that interact with children. Participants also discussed the need for inter-agency community partnerships to address children's exposure to violence and develop a holistic approach to the issue.

Witnesses: Cherri Allison, Esq., Alameda County Family Justice Center; **Tatiana Colon**, Dating Matters; **Tony Crear**, Alameda County Probation Department; **Steve Eckert, LCSW**, East Bay Agency for Children; **Lt. Jason Fox**, San Francisco Police Department; **George Galvez**, Communities United for Restorative Youth Justice; **Carlos Guerrero, MSW**, Children's Hospital and Research Center, Oakland; **Joe Jackson**, advocate for foster youth; **Priya Jaggannathan**, Measure Y, Oakland; **Vassilisa Johri**, Ashland Youth Center Project; **Lori Jones**, Alameda County Social Service Agency; **Janet King**, Native American Health Center; **Chen Kong-Wick**, Oakland Unified School District; **Barbara Loza-Muriera**, Alameda County Interagency Children's Policy Council; **Bert Lubin, MD**, Children's Hospital and Research Center, Oakland; **Annie Lyles**, Prevention Institute; **Anne Marks**, YouthALIVE! – Caught in the Crossfire; **Barbara McClung**, Oakland Unified School District; **Sokhom Mao**, Commissioner on Juvenile Justice Delinquency Prevention for Alameda County; **Chief David Muhammad**, Alameda County Probation Department; **Alisha Murdock**, Project WHAT!; **Amy Price**, Zellerbach Family Foundation; **Shanta Ramdeholl, RN, BSN**, Juvenile Justice Center Medical Services; **Ginni Ring**, CASA of Alameda County; **Barbara Staggers, MD**, Children's Hospital and Research Center, Oakland; **Gary V. Thompson**, Alameda Social Services; **Tina Wadhwa**, Seneca Center; **Mailee Wang**, Project WHAT!

Listening Session 2: Joint Base Lewis-McChord Family Resource Center

Tacoma, Washington

March 13, 2012

At the second listening session, task force members heard about the issues facing children and families on U.S. military bases, including high rates of domestic and family violence. The participants, including professionals working on base and in the surrounding community, shared their experiences in drawing on the unique resources offered by military bases to address children's exposure to violence. Participants spoke about creating a larger network of care for children on and off base and working with military employees and community advocates to coordinate care for traumatized children.

Witnesses: Col. Thomas Brittain, Joint Base Lewis-McChord; **Ginny Clausen**, Office of the Staff Judge Advocate; **Diane Debiec, OIC, MHS, FAP**, Joint Base Lewis-McChord; **Yolanda Duralde, MD**, Mary Bridge Children's Hospital; **Tamara Grigsby, CAPT, MC, USN**, General and Child Abuse Pediatrics; **Billy Harvey**, DFMWR, Joint Base Lewis-McChord; **Beth Holmes**, Pierce County Juvenile Court; **William Huges**, PMO; **Emma Jones**, Department of Social and Health Services; **Eleuthera Lisch**, Alive & Free Street Outreach Network; **Mariko Lockhart**, Seattle Youth Violence Prevention Initiative; **Patty Jo McGill**, Family Advocacy Victim Advocacy Program; **Larry Nelson**, Children's Administration, Department of Social and Health Services; **Tanya Nowak**, Focus Program; **Lindsay Paden, MD**, Child and Family Assistance Center; **David Raines**, Department of Social and Health Services, Pierce County South Child Protective Services; **Barb Richards**, New Parent Support Program; **Nolita Reynolds**, Catholic Community Services; **Jennifer Schott**, Young Women's Christian Association; **Holly Shaffer**, Clover Park School District; **Elaine Valentine**, Army Community Services, Joint Base Lewis-McChord; **Tina Wright**, IMCOM G-9 FAP Specialist, Joint Base Lewis-McChord

Listening Session 3: U.S. Attorney's Office, District of Alaska

Anchorage, Alaska

May 7–8, 2012

The third listening session provided further insight into rural communities' and Alaska Native villages' experiences with children's exposure to violence. Participants discussed the legacies of historical trauma experienced in Alaska Native villages and the challenges Alaska and the large number of tribes there face. They also discussed cultural strengths and grassroots efforts to address children's exposure to violence.

Witnesses: Elsie Boudreau, LMSW, Alaska Native Justice Center; **Corinne Bryant**, Alaska CARES; **Barbara Cooper, MD**, Providence Hospital; **Mary Elam**, Alaska Native Justice Center; **Elizabeth Sunnyboy Elder**, Speaking on Grief Issues; **Dr. Gary Ferguson**, Alaska Native Tribal Health Consortium; **Yvonne Wu Goldsmith**, Alaska Department of Health and Social Services; **Kim Guay**, Alaska Department of Health and Social Services; **Pam Karalunas**, Alaska Children's Alliance; **Alison Kear**, Covenant House; **Kathy Mayo**, Tanana Chiefs Conference; **Linda McLaughlin**, Alaska Native Justice Center; **Walt Monegan**, Alaska Native Justice Center; **Shirley Moses**, Alaska Native Women's Coalition on Domestic and Sexual Assault; **Diane Payne**, Alaska Summit Enterprise Inc.; **Ann Rausch**, Council on Domestic Violence and Sexual Assault; **Lisa Rieger**, Cook Inlet Tribal Council; **Margaret Volz**, Alaska CARES; **Emily Wright**, Alaska Network on Domestic Violence and Sexual Assault

INDIVIDUALS AND ORGANIZATIONS THAT SUBMITTED WRITTEN TESTIMONY

INDIVIDUALS AND ORGANIZATIONS THAT SUBMITTED WRITTEN TESTIMONY

T o ensure that its information-gathering efforts included as many people and perspectives as possible, the National Task Force on Children Exposed to Violence accepted written testimony from any individual or organization. Submissions were accepted through April 24, 2012. Through this written testimony, the task force was able to see a wide range of perspectives and gain valuable knowledge. The task force thanks the individuals and organizations who submitted written testimony for their time and expertise.

This list and quotations from written testimony in the report reflect organizational affiliation at the time of participation and may not represent submitters' current positions.

Ruth Abeyta

Nilofer Ahsan, Center for the Study of Social Policy

M. Victoria Amada, New Mexico Victims' Rights Project

Dawn Ammesmaki

Dr. Michael Aptman, Melissa Institute for Violence Prevention and Treatment

Zahra Arbelo

Dora Arey, Native Village of Barrow Tribal Court

Phil Arkow, National Link Coalition

Dr. Marilyn Armour, University of Texas at Austin

Elizabeth Baker

Melissa Barnett

William Bedrossian, Olive Crest

U.S. Senator Mark Begich

J. Benjamin, Sr.

Dr. Ronald Beverly

Thomas Birch, Founding Director of National Child Abuse Coalition

Dr. Evelyn Lance Blanchard

Dr. Ioakim Boutakidis, California State University, Fullerton

Ann Brickson, Wisconsin Coalition Against Domestic Violence

Dr. Alexis Brimberry, A Child Is Missing, Inc.

Tina Bryant, Trauma Counseling Services

Dr. Erica Buhrmann, Children's Hospital and Research Center

Paul Castillo

Dr. Michael Chen, Children's Center

Capt. D. C. Clayton, Winston-Salem Police Department

Tom Cochran, United States Conference of Mayors

Susan Cole, Trauma and Learning Policy Initiative, Massachusetts Advocates for Children and Harvard Law School

Morris Copeland, Miami-Dade Juvenile Services Department

Rosemary Creeden, Mental Health Services, Inc.

Sgt. B. E. Creswell, Newport News Police Department

Kimberly Dalferes, Child Sexual Abuse Prevention Alliance

Dr. Betty Lee Davis

Dr. Frank G. DeLaurier, Melissa Institute for Violence Prevention and Treatment

Lois DeMott, Association for Children's Mental Health and Citizens for Prison Reform

Elaine Diserio, Massachusetts Department of Children and Families

The Hon. Byron Dorgan, Center for Native American Youth

Stephanie Doyle, Boston Defending Childhood Initiative

Erin Fairchild, Multnomah County Domestic Violence Coordination Office

Elaine Flowers

Brian Foster

Andrew Gammicchia, L.E.A.N. On Us

K. Garcia

Jerry Gardner, Tribal Law and Policy Institute

Adrienne Gasperoni, Turning Point, Inc.

Dr. Ellen Gerrity, National Center for Child Traumatic Stress

Kelley Gilbert, Big Brothers Big Sisters of America

Amy Gilvary

Det. John Gomez, Fresno Police Department

Josh Gonze

Jakolya Gordon, Cuyahoga County Defending Childhood Initiative

Christine Gradert, Family Resources, Inc.

Georgia Green, Police Action Counseling Team

Cheryl Greene

Paul Griego

Dr. Frank Grijalva, Midwest Trauma Services Network

Dr. John Grych, Marquette University

Kathy Hagenian, Michigan Coalition Against Domestic and Sexual Violence

Patricia Duncan Hall

Dr. Sherry Hamby, Sewanee, the University of the South

Jabriera Handy, Community Law in Action

David J. Hearndon, Sr.

Dr. Judith Herrman, University of Delaware

Dr. Arthur Horton, Lewis University

Laura Huot, the Guidance Center

Gary Ivory, Youth Advocate Programs, Inc.

The Hon. Darnell Jackson, Saginaw County (Michigan) Circuit Court

Sue Ellen Jackson, Aware Central Texas

Edward G. Jacoubs, Plymouth County (Massachusetts) District Attorney's Office

Sarah Jakiel, Polaris Project

Cathi Kelley, Washtenaw Child Advocacy Center

B. Kennedy Kent, Justice for Kids Now

Faye Kihne, Community Violence Intervention Center

Suzanne Koepplinger, Minnesota Indian Women's Resource Center

Kristina Konnath, Metrowest Behavioral Health Center

Janet Kronenberg, Cuyahoga County Defending Childhood Initiative

Barbara Laman

Walter Lamar, Lamar Associates

Maria Larrison, Sheltering Wings

Jessica Lawmaster, Alaska Children's Alliance

Dr. Phil Leaf, Johns Hopkins Bloomberg School of Public Health (addendum to written testimony provided for Baltimore hearing)

Sara Leathers, Sheltering Wings

Devorah Levine, Contra Costa County Zero Tolerance for Domestic Violence Initiative

David Llewellyn, Conscious Care Counseling

Greg Loughlin, Georgia Commission on Family Violence

Dr. Jane Isaacs Lowe, Robert Wood Johnson Foundation

Annie Lyles, Prevention Institute

Helen Lynn, Safe Child Coalition

Lawrence Lynott

Sgt. Daniel Macias, Fresno Police Department

Doris Maya

Cathy McClain, Safe Streets Cherry Hill

James McCurtis, Crime Victims Services Commission, Michigan Department of Community Health

Matthew Melmed, Zero to Three

Crystal Miller

Betsy Morrison, Portland Maine Defending Childhood Initiative

Diane Moyer, Pennsylvania Coalition Against Rape

Dara Munson, Big Brothers Big Sisters of Metropolitan Detroit

National Sexual Violence Resource Center

Chuck Noerenberg, National Alliance for Drug Endangered Children

Terry Nowakowski, Connecticut Department of Children and Families

Cheryl O'Neill

Maureen O'Neill-Davis

Leslie O'Reilly, Michigan Crime Victims Services Commission, Michigan Department of Community Health

Tony Ostos, Gang Resistance Is Paramount

Jeannette Pai-Espinosa, the National Crittenton Foundation

Donna Pendergast, Michigan Department of the Attorney General

Pennsylvania Coalition Against Rape

Dr. Frank Putnam, University of North Carolina

Efrain Ramirez

Wayne Rawlins, Miami-Dade Anti-Gang Strategy

Barbara Raymond, The California Endowment

Earl Richards

Cassandra Richerson

Wendy Running Crane, Bureau of Indian Affairs Victim Assistance Program

Khalilah Sabra, Muslim American Society Immigrant Justice Center

Debra Scelsi

Cynthia Schneider, Multnomah Teen Parents Branch

Joni Silverstein, Delaware Girls Initiative

Jill Smialek, Cuyahoga County Defending Childhood Initiative

TuLynn Smylie, WomenShelter of Long Beach

Beth Snedeker, Sheltering Wings

Mark Soler, Center for Children's Law and Policy

Shellie Solomon, Service Network for Children of Inmates

Christina Stallings

Thomas Susman, American Bar Association

The Hon. John Suthers

Amita Swadhin

Lawrence Swalley, Oglala Lakota Court Appointed Special Advocates

Joyce Thomas, Center for Child Protection and Family Support, Inc.

Linda M. Thomas, Sheltering Wings

Dr. Cynthia Thompson-Randle, Children's Institute, Inc.

Cora Tomalinas

Beverly Tran

Steve Trubow, Olympic Behavior Labs

Gregory Volz, Stoneleigh Foundation Fellow

Becky Webber, Big Brothers Big Sisters of Yellowstone County (Montana)

James A. Whitaker, Justice for Kids Now

Hallie Bongar White, Southwest Center for Law and Social Policy

Bao Yang, Marjaree Mason Center

Deborah Young, Justice for Families and Children

TASK FORCE MEMBER BIOGRAPHIES

TASK FORCE MEMBER BIOGRAPHIES

Task Force Co-Chair: Robert L. Listenbee, Jr., JD

Robert Listenbee, Jr., JD, has been a trial lawyer at the Defender Association of Philadelphia since 1986 and Chief of the Juvenile Unit since 1997. He is a member of the Juvenile Justice and Delinquency Prevention Committee (JJDPC) of the Pennsylvania Commission on Crime and Delinquency, which advises Pennsylvania's governor on juvenile justice policy. He also is a member of the Disproportionate Minority Contact Subcommittee of the JJDPC. In this role, he has worked collaboratively to develop the Youth/Law Enforcement Curriculum that is used throughout Pennsylvania to reduce negative contact between youth and law enforcement. He served on the Interbranch Commission on Juvenile Justice, which examined the "kids for cash" scandal in the juvenile courts of Luzerne County, Pennsylvania, and recommended major reforms to the statewide system.

Mr. Listenbee serves on policy committees of the National Legal Aid and Defender Association and the National Center for Juvenile Justice and on the advisory board of the National Juvenile Defender Center (NJDC). He has participated in NJDC-sponsored statewide assessments of the juvenile justice systems in Indiana and Louisiana. He is actively involved in the MacArthur Foundation's Models for Change initiative and is a board member and former president of the Juvenile Defenders Association of Pennsylvania, a statewide nonprofit professional organization that advocates for the rights and interests of children and speaks on behalf of juvenile defenders throughout Pennsylvania. Finally, he is a consultant for the International Association of Chiefs of Police on juvenile training programs, and in 2011, he was appointed to the Federal Advisory Committee on Juvenile Justice, which advises the president and Congress on juvenile justice policy.

Mr. Listenbee received his BA degree from Harvard University and his juris doctor from the Boalt Hall School of Law at the University of California, Berkeley.

Task Force Co-Chair: Joe Torre

Joe Torre is Chairman of the Joe Torre Safe At Home® Foundation, whose mission is "educating to end the cycle of domestic violence and save lives." In the 10 years since its inception, the Foundation has educated thousands of students, parents, teachers, and school faculty about the devastating effects of domestic violence. Margaret's Place, a tribute to Mr. Torre's mother, Margaret, provides middle and high school students with a "safe room" to talk about violence-related issues with each other and a professional counselor trained in domestic violence intervention and prevention. The program currently reaches kids in 10 schools and two family justice centers in the New York City metropolitan area and Los Angeles.

Mr. Torre also serves as Major League Baseball's Executive Vice President for Baseball Operations. Previously, he was a Major League manager for 29 seasons, 12 of them with the New York Yankees, whom he led to 12 playoff appearances, six World Series appearances, and four World Series Championships. During his 17-year playing career, Mr. Torre compiled a .297 batting average, 2,342 hits, 252 home runs, and 1,185 RBIs. He hit over .300 five times in his career, was a nine-time All-Star, and was named the 1971 National League MVP.

Mr. Torre is the coauthor of three books: *The Yankee Years* (Doubleday, 2009), *Chasing the Dream: My Lifelong Journey to the World Series* (Bantam, 1997, 1998), and *Joe Torre's Ground Rules for Winners: 12 Keys to Managing Team Players, Tough Bosses, Setbacks, and Success* (Hyperion, 1999).

The Rev. Gregory Boyle, SJ

The Rev. Gregory Boyle, SJ, has been an advocate for at-risk and gang-involved youth in Los Angeles and around the world for more than 25 years. In 1988, Father Boyle launched Jobs for a Future (which later became Homeboy Industries) to create an environment that provided training, work experience, and, above all, the opportunity for rival gang members to work side by side. Today, Homeboy Industries' nonprofit economic development enterprises include Homeboy Bakery, Homeboy Diner at Los Angeles City Hall, Homeboy Silkscreen & Embroidery, Homeboy/Homegirl Merchandise, and Homegirl Café & Catering.

Father Boyle is also a consultant to youth service and governmental agencies, policymakers, and employers. He serves on the advisory board of the National Gang Center, a program of the U.S. Department of Justice (DOJ) Office of Juvenile Justice and Delinquency Prevention. He also is a member of the advisory board for the Loyola Law School Center for Juvenile Law and Policy in Los Angeles.

Father Boyle entered the order of the Society of Jesus (Jesuits) and was ordained a priest in 1984. He received his BA degree from Gonzaga University and MA degrees from Loyola Marymount University, the Weston School of Theology, and the Jesuit School of Theology at Berkeley. His first book, *Tattoos on the Heart: The Power of Boundless Compassion,* was released March 2010 and received the 2010 SCIBA (Southern California Independent Booksellers Association) Non-Fiction Book Award and the 2011 PEN Center USA Literary Award for Creative Nonfiction. *Publishers Weekly* named it one of the Best Books of 2010. Among numerous accolades on behalf of Homeboy Industries and for his work with former gang members, Father Boyle received the 2000 California Peace Prize from The California Wellness Foundation and was inducted into the California Hall of Fame in December 2011.

Sharon Cooper, MD

Sharon Cooper, MD, is the CEO of Developmental & Forensic Pediatrics, P.A., a consulting firm providing medical care to victims of child maltreatment and children with developmental disabilities, research and training, and expert witness experience in child maltreatment cases. She holds faculty positions at the University of North Carolina at Chapel Hill School of Medicine and the Uniformed Services University of the Health Sciences in Bethesda, Maryland. Dr. Cooper serves as a consultant and board member for the National Center for Missing and Exploited Children.

Dr. Cooper spent 21 years in the U.S. Army, retiring as a colonel, and for the past several years has worked in both the civilian and military arenas to help identify and prevent child abuse. She also has served as a lecturer and board member for the American Professional Society on the Abuse of Children and is a member of the International Society for the Prevention of Child Abuse and Neglect. She is on the national advisory board for safety and protection for the Boy Scouts of America and has served for 5 years as the appointed chairperson for the Cumberland County Child Homicide Identification and Prevention Council. She has testified as an expert witness in several hundred child maltreatment cases in numerous courts of law. She also has provided testimony on child sexual exploitation before the U.S. Congress, the Russian Duma (parliament), the European Commission, and the Italian Senate.

Dr. Cooper is the lead author of one of the most comprehensive texts on the medical, legal, and social science aspects of child sexual exploitation and has contributed many chapters to other texts on this subject.

Sarah Deer, JD

Sarah Deer, JD, is a citizen of the Muscogee (Creek) Nation of Oklahoma, and her scholarship focuses on the intersection of tribal law and victims' rights. She is an associate professor at William Mitchell College of Law in St. Paul, Minnesota, and has taught at the University of California, Los Angeles, School of Law; the University of Minnesota; and Lewis & Clark Law School.

From 1999 to 2002, Ms. Deer was employed by DOJ in the Office on Violence Against Women. In 2002, she began working with the Tribal Law and Policy Institute, a Native-owned and -operated nonprofit organization, to strengthen tribal responses to violent crime. Ms. Deer has served on advisory boards for several anti-violence organizations and projects, including the American Bar Association Commission on Domestic & Sexual Violence and the National Alliance to End Sexual Violence. From 2005 to 2007, she worked with Amnesty International USA to develop research strategies and outreach for the "Maze of Injustice" report.

Ms. Deer received her BA degree in women's studies and philosophy from the University of Kansas. She received her juris doctor with a Tribal Lawyer Certificate from the University of Kansas School of Law. In addition to authoring several articles on the issues facing Native women in the United States, Ms. Deer is a coauthor of two textbooks on tribal law, *Introduction to Tribal Legal Studies* and *Tribal Criminal Law and Procedure*, and a co-editor of *Sharing Our Stories of Survival: Native Women Surviving Violence.* She received the 2010 Sheila Wellstone Award and was named one of 12 Emerging Scholars class of 2011 by *Diverse: Issues In Higher Education.* In April 2011, Ms. Deer received the Allied Professional Award from DOJ for her work on victims' issues.

Deanne Tilton Durfee

Deanne Tilton Durfee is the executive director of the Los Angeles County Inter-Agency Council on Child Abuse and Neglect (ICAN). ICAN is the largest county-based child abuse council in the nation and includes heads of 32 city, county, and state departments and professional experts in all human services fields. ICAN's work has had national impact in many areas, including child death review, child abduction, multidisciplinary child abuse evaluations, and legislation. In addition to directing ICAN, Ms. Tilton Durfee serves as the chairperson of the National Center on Child Fatality Review and is a member of the Board of Commissioners for First 5 LA, the Los Angeles County Commission on Children and Families.

Ms. Tilton Durfee, a former child welfare administrator, is past chairperson of the U.S. Advisory Board on Child Abuse and Neglect. This board declared child abuse to be a "national emergency" in 1990 and subsequently issued comprehensive reports recommending a major local and federal focus on child abuse prevention. In 1995, Ms. Tilton Durfee presided over the release of the board's report "A Nation's Shame: Fatal Child Abuse and Neglect in the United States." This report was the culmination of 2½ years of study and public hearings throughout the nation.

Ms. Tilton Durfee is past president of Prevent Child Abuse–California and was a member of the board of directors of the National Committee to Prevent Child Abuse. She also served on the California Attorney General's Commission on the Enforcement of Child Abuse Laws and was appointed by California's governor to the Child Abuse Prevention Committee of the State Social Services Advisory Board and to the California Child Victim Witness Judicial Advisory Committee.

Ms. Tilton Durfee served on the U.S. Attorney General's Commission on Pornography, chairing the committee on child pornography. She has received commendations for her work from the President's Child Safety Partnership; the Commissioner of the Administration on Children, Youth and Families; the Disability, Abuse and Personal Rights Project; and the Los Angeles Latino community. She was recognized in 1992 as an honorary member of the National Association of African American Grandmothers. In 1999, she received the Humanitarian Award from the Child and Family Guidance Center, and in 2007, she was honored as a "Woman of Distinction" by Soroptimist International of Los Angeles.

Thea James, MD

Thea James, MD, is an associate professor of emergency medicine at Boston Medical Center and Boston University School of Medicine and immediate past president of the Medical-Dental Staff at Boston Medical Center. She has served on the Board of Trustees and the Quality and Patient Safety Committee of Boston Medical Center. She also is the director of the Boston Medical Center Massachusetts Violence Intervention Advocacy Program. Dr. James is a founding member of the National Network of Hospital-Based Violence Intervention Programs (NNHVIP). She serves on the steering committee and the research group of NNHVIP.

Dr. James is an assistant dean for the Office of Diversity and Multicultural Affairs and a member of the Admissions Committee at Boston University School of Medicine. In 2009, Dr. James was appointed to the Massachusetts Board of Registration in Medicine, where she now serves as chair of the board's Licensing Committee. Dr. James has chaired and served on national committees within the Society for Academic Emergency Medicine (SAEM), was appointed to the SAEM Women in Academic Emergency Medicine Task Force, and chaired the Diversity Interest Group for 3 years.

A graduate of Georgetown University School of Medicine, Dr. James trained in emergency medicine at Boston City Hospital, where she was a chief resident. Dr. James is a supervising medical officer on the Metro-Boston Disaster Medical Assistance Team (MA-1 DMAT), under the Department of Health and Human Services, which has responded to disasters in the United States and across the globe. For many years, Dr. James has traveled to Haiti with teams of emergency medicine residents. In 2006, she and a colleague co-founded a nonprofit organization called Unified for Global Healing, and for the past 3 years this multidisciplinary team has worked in Ghana, West Africa, India, and Haiti. Dr. James received the David H. Mulligan Award for Leadership and Public Service from the Boston Public Health Commission in 2008 and the Boston District Attorney's Role Model Award in 2012. *The Boston Business Journal* honored her as one of its 2012 Champions in Health Care.

Alicia Lieberman, PhD

Alicia Lieberman, PhD, is the Irving B. Harris Endowed Chair of Infant Mental Health, professor and vice chair for academic affairs, and director of the Child Trauma Research Program at the University of California, San Francisco, Department of Psychiatry.

Dr. Lieberman directs the Early Trauma Treatment Network, part of the Substance Abuse and Mental Health Services Administration (SAMHSA)–funded National Child Traumatic Stress Network, which aims to increase access and raise the standard of care for traumatized children, families, and communities across the United States. She serves on the board of the Irving Harris Foundation and is a member of the board of directors and past president of Zero to Three: The National Center for Infants, Toddlers and Families. She developed Child-Parent Psychotherapy, an evidence-based treatment for children ages 5 and under exposed to trauma or multiple adversities. She served on the National Research Council and Institute of Medicine Committee on Integrating the Science of Early Childhood Development, whose work resulted in the publication of the influential *From Neurons to Neighborhoods: The Science of Early Childhood Development,* and has been a member of National Institute of Mental Health grant review committees. Her areas of special interest are the impact of traumatic exposure and adversity on infants and young children and cultural issues in child and family well-being.

Dr. Lieberman received her BA degree from the Hebrew University of Jerusalem and her PhD from Johns Hopkins University. She is the author or senior author of several books for parents and clinicians, including *The Emotional Life of the Toddler; Psychotherapy With Infants and Young Children: Repairing the Effect of Stress and Trauma on Early Attachment; Losing a Parent to Death in the Early Years: Guidelines for the Treatment of Traumatic Bereavement in Infancy and Early Childhood;* and *Don't Hit My Mommy: A Manual for Child-Parent Psychotherapy with Young Witnesses of Domestic Violence,* as well as numerous articles and chapters. She is senior editor of *DC: 0–3 Casebook: A Guide to ZERO TO THREE's Diagnostic Classification of Mental Health and Developmental Disorders of Infancy and Early Childhood in Assessment* and other books on early trauma.

Robert Macy, PhD

Robert Macy, PhD, is a trained martial artist, dance movement therapist, clinical psychologist, traumatologist, and neuroscience researcher with more than 30 years' experience in the field of psychological trauma response and in violence prevention, intervention development, and trauma-informed care development and dissemination. Dr. Macy is a founder and director and the president of the International Center for Disaster Resilience and the founder and executive director of The Boston Children's Foundation. He also is the founder and director of the Midwest Trauma Services Network. As a member of the SAMHSA Disaster Technical Assistance Center, Dr. Macy works nationally to assist SAMHSA in disaster response and recovery.

Dr. Macy is a pioneer in the field of psychological trauma, psychosocial recovery and resiliency research, and interventions and violence prevention initiatives for children and youth, their families, and adults and communities exposed to traumatic events, including large-scale disasters; terrorist events; and political, school-based, community, and armed conflict violence. Dr. Macy has devoted a significant portion of his career to working with local, state, and federal court systems and law enforcement agencies to develop customized protocols for reducing posttraumatic stress disorder and vicarious trauma among field officers and in the SpecOps community.

Dr. Macy co-directs the Division of Disaster Resilience at the Beth Israel Deaconess Medical Center, a Harvard Medical School teaching hospital, and is an instructor in the Division of Emergency Medicine at Harvard Medical School. Dr. Macy designs, implements, and evaluates trauma-focused psychosocial resiliency initiatives, violence prevention programs, and trauma-informed care initiatives in the United States, Europe, the Middle East, Eurasia, and Africa.

Steven Marans, PhD

Steven Marans, PhD, is the Harris Professor of Child Psychiatry at the Yale Child Study Center and a professor in the Department of Psychiatry at Yale University's School of Medicine. He directs the National Center for Children Exposed to

Violence, established by the White House and DOJ in 1999, and the SAMHSA-funded Childhood Violent Trauma Clinic at Yale. Dr. Marans is the founder of the Child Development Community Policing Program, a pioneering collaboration between mental health and law enforcement professionals that provides collaborative responses to children and families exposed to violence that occurs in homes, neighborhoods, and schools.

Dr. Marans co-developed the Child and Family Traumatic Stress Intervention, a brief model of treatment for children and families that has demonstrated effectiveness in reducing long-term posttraumatic disorders. Over the past 20 years, Dr. Marans has worked closely with the White House, DOJ, the U.S. Department of Health and Human Services (HHS), the U.S. Department of Education, the state of Connecticut, and the city of New Haven to shape policy and response plans around issues of violence exposure, terrorism, and disasters. He has served as part of a national advisory group regarding children and violence and was a member of an HHS commission on children, terrorism, and disasters.

Dr. Marans received his MA degree in clinical social work from Smith College and his PhD in psychology from University College at London University. He trained in child and adolescent psychoanalysis at the Anna Freud Centre in London and received his adult psychoanalytic training at the Western New England Institute for Psychoanalysis, where he is on the faculty. In addition to numerous academic publications in the areas of trauma, mental health–law enforcement partnerships, child development, and clinical treatment, Dr. Marans authored a book titled *Listening to Fear: Helping Kids Cope, From Nightmares to the Nightly News,* published by Holt in 2005.

Jim McDonnell

Jim McDonnell is the chief of the Long Beach Police Department. He has held the position for almost 3 years, and he previously served with the Los Angeles Police Department (LAPD) for 29 years. He worked a wide variety of assignments at LAPD and served as second in command for his last 7 years.

Chief McDonnell serves on numerous boards of directors that focus on furthering the interests of local youth and leadership in the policing profession on local, statewide, and national levels. He is an active member of several organizations, including the International Association of Chiefs of Police, Major Cities Chiefs, California Peace Officers' Association, California Police Chiefs Association, Los Angeles County Chiefs of Police, the Peace Officers' Association of Los Angeles County, and the Southern California Leadership Network. He was recently appointed by the California governor to the state's Commission on Peace Officer Standards and Training.

Chief McDonnell holds a BS degree in criminal justice from Saint Anselm College and an MPA degree from the University of Southern California. He also is a graduate of the FBI's prestigious National Executive Institute and the Senior Management Institute for Police, and he has completed executive education programs at Harvard's Kennedy School of Government.

Georgina B. Mendoza, JD

Georgina B. Mendoza, JD, currently serves as Community Safety Director for the city of Salinas, California. In this role, Ms. Mendoza is leading an effort to develop and implement a comprehensive strategic work plan that incorporates evidence-based strategies for gang prevention, intervention, suppression, and reentry. She represents the city in multi-jurisdictional efforts to coordinate funding and leverage community resources.

Ms. Mendoza has been involved in the California Cities Gang Prevention Network as a city point member for the past 5 years and serves as the Salinas lead in the National Forum on Youth Violence Prevention, a new pilot initiative launched by the White House. She received her BA degree in history and political science from Santa Clara University and her juris doctor from Loyola Law School Los Angeles.

Major General Antonio M. Taguba

Major General Antonio M. Taguba, U.S. Army (Retired), has served in numerous command and staff positions from platoon to General Officer level. His service tours included assignments in the continental United States, South Korea, Germany, and Kuwait. He retired on January 1, 2007, after serving on active duty for 34 years. He is president of TDLS Consulting, LLC, and chairman of Pan-Pacific American Leaders and Mentors, a national, volunteer, nonprofit, tax-exempt organization committed to mentoring and leadership development of military and civilian leaders.

During Operation Iraqi Freedom, Major General Taguba served as Deputy Commanding General for Support, Coalition Forces Land Component Command Third Army/ARCENT, forward deployed to Kuwait and Iraq. He oversaw the logistical and support services to U.S. and coalition forces, totaling more than 150,000 troops conducting combat operations. His duty included the coordination of host-nation support from the government of Kuwait and security cooperation and training requirements with Saudi Arabia, Jordan, Egypt, and Qatar. Upon his redeployment, Major General Taguba served as Deputy Assistant Secretary of Defense for Reserve Affairs in the Office of the Secretary of Defense. In his final assignment on active duty, he served as Deputy Commanding General for Transformation in the U.S. Army Reserve Command.

Major General Taguba is a graduate of Idaho State University with a BA degree in history, Webster University with an MA degree in public administration, Salve Regina University with an MA degree in international relations, and the U.S. College of Naval Command and Staff with an MA degree in national security and strategic studies. He also is a graduate of the U.S. Army Command and General Staff College and the U.S. Army War College. He was conferred the degree of doctor of humane letters from the University of San Francisco on May 17, 2008.

www.ingramcontent.com/pod-product-compliance
Lightning Source LLC
Chambersburg PA
CBHW080244290526
45790CB00005B/1694